**Israel Lessons**
Industrial Arcadia

PARK BOOKS

> Comment veut-on que des idées nouvelles puissent se développer? A peine peuvent-elles se faire jour sur le papier; comment pourraient-elles se traduire en pierre? C'est à développer l'indépendance de l'artiste et à lui assurer cette indépendance qu'il faut tendre si l'on veut avoir un art de notre temps.[1]
> — Eugène Viollet-Le-Duc

## Teaching and Research in Architecture

From classical antiquity to the fifteenth century, architects were both planners and builders. As "master builders," architects were responsible for both the design and overseeing of construction. The master builder was a highly skilled and highly experienced leader of the construction team. He was apprenticed in all the main construction crafts, such as masonry, carpentry, plumbing, and roofing. He possessed a range of skills that were immediately related to the design, the engineering, the materials, and the overall concept for construction.

From the fifteenth century onwards, the unity of art and technology, of designer and craftsman, began to disintegrate. This was due primarily to the emergence of a less regulated, expanded concept of art. In the quest for a new complexity in art, the loss of the unity of the conceptual and the practical was less of a preoccupation. In consequence the concept of the master builder disappeared and the process of designing and constructing a building became fragmented. This division was further underlined by the foundation of the École National des Ponts et Chaussées in 1747, when training in engineering became independent of architecture.

The architect's influence on the shape of our built environment has declined ever since. There has been a dramatic reduction in both the variety and range of the architect's activities. Whereas architects once designed a building by themselves, they now share the task with many consultants. In addition, the range of the architect's involvement in the process of planning and construction has diminished over time. As such, the architect's traditional role of integrating and coordinating the entire planning and building process is undermined.

Today, architecture finds itself in the paradoxical situation of being more popular than ever before, but at the same time being exposed to total decline. Never before has architecture had such a high profile. Yet never before have architects had so little influence on the actual construction of buildings. What does this mean for teaching and research in architecture?

laba's primary goal is to ensure the architect's continued role in the planning and building process and to reinforce the architect's position as a central, integrating, and coordinating force. Architecture is understood as a technical, scientific, and yet an artistic and creative discipline. Architecture is an instrument of perception and as such a tool for understanding the world and society.

The working methodology proposed by laba merges analytical research methodologies with creative design, developing investigative processes for urban design and architecture. This procedural approach promotes the interdisciplinary process of planning production. The teaching objective is to show that the role of the architect is not limited to the planning and design of the individual building but that it encompasses the construction and operation of the built and natural environment in its integrity. Students are asked to develop a frame of mind that engages in critical dialogue, and they come to the realization that design is not a mathematical process of solving problems, but a creative process of consciously confronting them.

Each academic year laba chooses a specific territory as the focus of its teaching and research project. Sites are selected based on their relevance for the investigation of the manifold phenomena of urbanization with the mission to question the age-old opposition between architecture and nature—the object-sculpture and the landscape-background—in light of today's ecological crisis. At present the idea of Nature (as something nurturing, autonomous, and in continuous renewal) is put into question by both the natural and the social sciences.

How can architecture contribute to this larger ontological debate? The Anthropocene has proven and doubled down on William Morris's eminent statement that "everything except the desert is architecture."[2] It demands that architecture no longer stops at the threshold of the window sill or the edge of the building plot. It asks us to question the fundamental opposition between architecture and nature and to disrupt the relation of privilege between the meaningful object-sculpture in the foreground and the unconscious landscape background. Amidst wider struggles for environmental justice and nature-rights, we need ways of integrating ecology into architecture as more than just a collection of techno-engineering fixes (green roofs, solar appliances, energy efficiency plans) but moreover through the promotion of an environmental architecture as a collection of aesthetic principles and values.

Each research and teaching project brings together specialists and project partners to expand the field of research in order to ensure the inclusion of contextual factors and relevant issues that affect the overall methodological approach and the design results. The approach to teaching in architecture at laba is informed by the procedures and project experience of international practice and the desire to establish a comprehensive and transdisciplinary culture of analysis and design in architecture.

— *Harry Gugger*

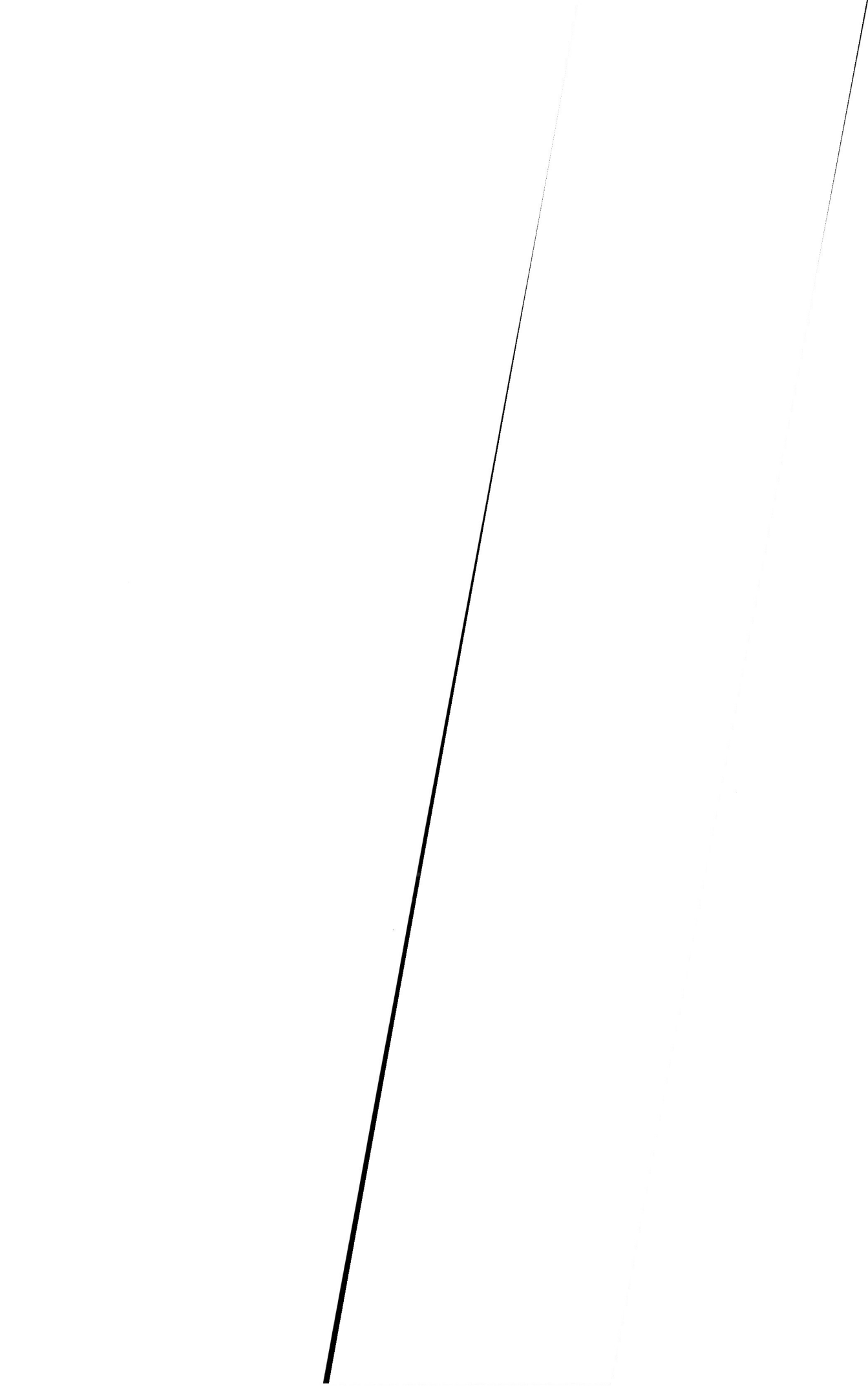

# Introduction

Arcadian Dreams and Agricultural Myths: Israel's Promised Land

1. The Garden of Eden and the Promised Land   9
2. Drain the Swamps and Make the Desert Bloom   10
3. Lines in the Sand and Walls in the Garden   11
4. Lessons from Israel: Imagining Hospitable Environments   12

# 1. The Garden of Eden and the Promised Land

> Now the Lord God had planted a garden in the east, in Eden; and there he put the man he had formed. The Lord God made all kinds of trees grow out of the ground—trees that were pleasing to the eye and good for food.
> — Genesis 2:8

The Middle East and its ancient territory of the Fertile Crescent are historically considered to be the cradle of Western civilization, home to a myriad of human inventions, such as agriculture, writing, and the city. It is the place where "humans"—from the Latin *humus*, meaning "land, soil, country"—defined themselves as "land creatures." It is also the region where religions were manufactured, and where, in the beginning, God planted a garden and promised the land.

Human land appropriation has always been layered with cultural and metaphysical meanings. Migration, agriculture, religion, and industrialization have all contributed levels of symbolic attachment to nature. In Western culture, environmental imagination is rooted in a myriad of landscape tropes, such as the Garden, the Wilderness, the Virgin Land, the Desert, and the Swamp.[1] These metaphors have become universal rhetorical figures, ideological filters that capture our dreams of environmental harmony with nature and inform our worldviews, our positions within the world.

Adam, the name of the Bible's first man, is the Hebrew word for "human," "man," and "mankind." It is also the masculine form of the word *adamah*, which means "ground" or "earth." *Hava*, the original Hebrew name for Eve, also means "farm." God created Adam "of the dust from the ground"[2] and told him to "Remember, O man, that dust thou art, and to dust thou shalt return."[3] The Bible tells us that God "planted a garden in the east, in Eden,"[4] and the Quran describes heaven as a garden. The Persians planted oases in the desert and called them *pairidaeza* (*pairi* means "behind," and *daeza* means "wall"), a term that was later adopted by Christianity as "paradise garden," or the *hortus conclusus* (enclosed garden).

The word *garden* derives from the Indo-European root *gher*, which appears in many Latin, Greek, Slavic, and Germanic words for things such as farmyard, pasture, field, hedge, house, fence, enclosure, stable, girder, fortified place, and garden. All of these words imply enclosure.[5] In his 1755 book *Discourse on Inequality*, Jean-Jacques Rousseau writes that "the first man who, having enclosed a piece of land, said 'This is mine,' and found people simple enough to believe him, was the true founder of civil society."[6] Gardens are the result of this primordial act of land appropriation that separates a familiar inside from a strange outside. The act of framing an inner space of residence, storage, and defense, makes the garden an agent of social cohesion and segregation, identity and difference, thereby establishing a physical link between clan and land, "blood and soil." Through collective solidarity in domestic labor, gardening acquires a mythical dimension that has been echoed in literature since ancient times, from the Bible to Homer and Virgil: the act of cultivating a homeland.[7] Gardening shapes the land and the people.

Gardens are a symbol of the human urge to cultivate and civilize. Within enclosures, nature is ordered rationally according to ecological and aesthetic considerations, and every aspect of plant reproduction is carefully and constantly regulated. Its outer correlate is the wasteland (the *terra nullius* awaiting *occupacio*[8]) and incidentally, to colonize means "to farm" (from Latin *colonia*, "settled land, farm" and *colere*, "to cultivate, to inhabit, to guard"). The very concept of Western progress indicates this idea of advancement from wilderness toward agri-culture (*agros* means field), whereby nature must be fought and sanctified.

The secular parallel of the Judeo-Christian garden is the neo-classical Arcadia. The term is derived from the Greek province of Arkadia, a remote and mountainous region located at the heart of the Peloponnese. As may be expected, the mythical Arcadia is as far removed from its geographical eponym as the Garden of Eden is from the Levant. Virgil's Eclogues described it is a pastoral scene where young shepherds and shepherdesses (*pastor* is Latin for "shepherd") roam with their flocks in an everlasting and blissful spring.[9] Like Eden, Arcadia is a fantasy realm of freedom and plenty located somewhere between the restrictions of society and the violence of nature. Its secular idealism struck a chord in Western Enlightenment, during which time divine authority gradually gave way to scientific interpretations of natural law as the mirror of social order. Romantic nationalism and its plethora of nature representations found a new political power in landscape: When site turns into sight and soil into country (from the Latin *terra contrata*, meaning "land lying opposite"), land becomes the *locus* of the nation, and nationalist claims over the territory become naturalized, ahistorical.

Nevertheless, despite its secular associations, the pastoral Arcadia still harkens back to a quasi-religious nostalgia for a Golden Age and to various mythologies about ancient creation. In a lecture delivered in 1966 titled "The Historical Roots of Our Ecological Crisis," American historian Lynn White Jr. claimed that Western concepts of nature can, to this day, be traced back to Judeo-Christian theology: "... modern science is an extrapolation of natural theology and ... modern technology is at least partly to be explained as an Occidental, voluntarist realization of the Christian dogma of man's transcendence of, and rightful mastery over, nature."[10] White claims that modern secularism has not broken with the creationist dogma completely and has in fact sustained the idea of human ownership over our planet, still seen as if it were rightfully promised to us: "Despite Copernicus, all the cosmos rotates around our little globe. Despite Darwin, we are *not*, in our hearts, part of the natural process. We are superior to nature, contemptuous of it, willing to use it for our slightest whim."[11]

All forms of life affect and modify their contexts, but humans have achieved the unthinkable feat of changing the planet's biosphere. It began 9000 years ago, when humans started domesticating plants and animals in order to mitigate seasonal variations. Today, domestic animals far outnumber the nondomesticated ones,[12] and 83 percent of the earth's land surface has been directly influenced by human activities.[13] Atmospheric concentrations of "greenhouse gases" are rapidly warming the Earth's climate, and thin layers of carbon residue have permanently deposited in the Earth's crust.[14] Pollution, mass extinction, global warming, and population explosion are today's haunting fallouts of civilization, summed up in the poignant name given to the dawn of this new era: the Anthropocene.

In a lecture delivered in 2015 at Barnard College, American anthropologist Anna Tsing described the global phenomenon of the Anthropocene as an assembly of landscape patches with different local impacts on livability and place, enacted and operated through the landscape metaphor of the "plantation": "By plantation I mean those ecological simplifications in which living things are transformed into resources, future assets, by removing them from their life-worlds. Plantations are machines of replication, ecologies devoted to purification and the production of the same."[15] Plantations are the agricultural acts of ecological acculturation that are at the root of our environmental dilemmas and at the origin of the nature-culture split. *[Fig. 1–2]*

## 2. Drain the Swamps and Make the Desert Bloom

> God blessed them and said to them, "Be fruitful and increase in number; fill the earth and subdue it. Rule over the fish in the sea and the birds in the sky and over every living creature that moves on the ground."
> — Genesis 1:28

The word *homeland* appears in the Bible 19 times, mostly in the Genesis. Its meaning has to do with birthplace and familial heritage, and there is no mention of the political, civil, or public dimensions of the national homeland as encountered, for example, in the cultures of the Greek *polis* or the ancient Roman Republic. The word *land*, however, shows up more than a thousand times.[16] The land that God gave Abraham, "from the river of Egypt to the Euphrates,"[17] is described as a place of compensation, inheritance, and bounty: "a land of wheat and barley, of vines and fig trees and pomegranates,"[18] a land "flowing with milk and honey."[19] But the people that God chose for the Holy Land were actually not the land's natives. Immediately after delivering the Ten Commandments on Mount Sinai, God promised Moses to expel the autochthonous inhabitants of Canaan in order to make room for the Israelites. The land of the chosen people was not their homeland, it was their destiny.

There is a paradoxical, double temporality in this idea of a predestined homeland. It holds both the traces of ancient origins as well as the prospects of utopian futures, while remaining always beyond the present. In other words, it is heir to a noble and idealized past, but its full potential can be fulfilled only in the form of a redeemed, and improved version of itself. Consequently, the present becomes the in-between predicament that must be wandered, in the hopeful promise of something ever about to be.[20] In 1902, Zionist forefather Theodor Herzl identified the Holy Land as the *Altneuland*, the "Old New Land," in his literary account of a utopian *Judenstaat* named the "New Society" established in Palestine by European Jews. The *Altneuland* is a literal testimony to the double temporality of the Holy Land: It is both the old home of the primordial Israelites and the new home of the future Jewish state, while the present is stalled in the diaspora. The Holy Land has a messianic impulse marked by idealism and a crusading spirit. Jews do not immigrate to the land, they "ascend" to it, through *aliyah*. In settling the territory, they do not merely occupy it, they fulfil their destiny to cultivate and "redeem" it.

Traditionally, the idea of redemption has the meaning of "salvation, rebirth, and liberation from enemy hands." In a literal sense, it can also mean "to buy, or take something back." In the context of Zionist self-determination, these meanings came together in a new heroic slogan whereby the purchase, reclamation, and settlement of land in Eretz Israel became equated with the moral redemption of the Jewish nation. Integral to this process was an overarching image of Palestine as a desolate land, a boundless, virginal environment eagerly waiting to be fertilized. A wasteland needed to exist in order to justify the need for a garden and in order to portray, as is usually required, the national project as a natural process. According to this conception, Palestine was a desolate combination of desert and swamp, and only the true love of the land's true people could ever restore it back to "milk and honey." The land is hence conceived as being metaphorically empty—"a land without a people for a people without a land"²¹—until the long-awaited arrival of its predestined pioneers, conquerors and saviors. [Fig. 3–5]

> From the nation's valley of death rose a new generation. This generation finds life's meaning in toiling our ancestors' land and reviving our ancient tongue. The draining of the Harod swamps, which only covered the land after our people were forced to go into exile, is a true wonder. But this wonder also symbolizes the draining of the swamp our nation was bogged down in during two millennia of exile. You, the pioneers of Harod, are the heroes of the new generation. What you are doing is healing the land and healing the nation. You are taking us back to the source.²²

> The trees were our proxy immigrants, the forests our implantation. And while we assumed that a pinewood was more beautiful than a hill denuded by grazing flocks of goats and sheep, we were never exactly sure what all the trees were *for*. What we did know was that a rooted forest was the opposite landscape to a place of drifting sand, of exposed rock and red dirt blown by the winds. The diaspora was sand. So what should Israel be, if not a forest, fixed and tall?²³

## 3. Lines in the Sand and Walls in the Garden

> On that day the Lord made a covenant with Abram and said, "To your descendants I give this land, from the Wadi of Egypt to the great river, the Euphrates—the land of the Kenites, Kenizzites, Kadmonites, Hittites, Perizzites, Rephaites, Amorites, Canaanites, Girgashites, and Jebusites."
> — Genesis 15:18–21

All nationalisms are a retroactive combination of historical and literary constructions. Zionism emerges in the context of European nationalist outbreak, with its inherent racism and Judeophobia, that swept across the continent in the nineteenth century. This new shared identity was achieved in the combination of ideas of cultural background, such as linguistic past and religion, and a notion of biological origin, or blood ties, then understood as a category of natural fact. In its many variations, the idea of nationhood oscillated between three complimentary principles: the softer idea of "people" as a dynamic cultural aggregate; the more rigid concept of *"ethnos"* as a cultural unit; and the utterly problematic concept of "race" as a group that shares a common descent.²⁴ In any of these circumstances, however, human rights became tied with national citizenship, and contrary to the concept of "humanity," "nationality" is an idea that includes some but excludes others, so that the non-citizen (the foreigner, the refugee, the illegal alien) can be placed in a condition of sub-humanity.²⁵

It was in this context that the Jewish Question came into existence, originating for the first time in Great Britain in 1750, and further evolving into a 200-year-long debate dealing with the civil, legal, national, and political status of Jews as a minority within modern European society. It was especially fervent in Central and Eastern Europe, where conceptions of citizenship were linked more to parental descent than to place of birth (*jus sanguinis*, the right of blood, rather than *jus soli*, the right of soil). In this context, Zionism set out to guarantee the stateless Jews of the diaspora a place where they could claim national citizenship and emancipation. It was a colonialist movement born out of precariousness, violence and oppression, fuelled by romantic idealism and a sense of religious predestination.

> Under the political conditions that prevailed in the late 19th and early 20th centuries, the notion of settlement in "desolate" areas was still credited with considerable logic. It was the high point of the age of imperialism, and the project was enabled by the fact that its land of destination was populated by an anonymous local population, devoid of national identity. Had the vision and the movement appeared earlier … the process of colonization, and the displacement of the local population, as had been taking place in other colonial areas, could perhaps have been achieved with greater ease and fewer misgivings. … The Second World War and the Jewish destruction it wreaked created circumstances that enabled the West to impose a settler state on the local population. The establishment of the State of Israel as a place of refuge for persecuted Jews took place during the last hours, or, to be more precise, the final moments, of the dying colonial era.²⁶

The year 2017 marks the the fiftieth anniversary of the Six Day War and the Israeli occupation of the Palestinian territories. 1967 was the year when the Holy Land became sacralized from a nationalist perspective and was elevated to the status of an idol, a magic object that compels human sacrifices and conjures feelings of mass hysteria.²⁷ Today, large blocks of ethnocentric, religious nationalists have a solid presence amongst Israeli society. Hard-right Israeli Education Minister Naftali Bennett said recently in an interview with Al Jazeera that Israel has a right to occupy the West Bank because it says so in the Bible.²⁸ In 2016, Minister of Agriculture and Rural Development Uri Ariel declared that the world should forget about a Palestinian state, and that Israel has to aspire to the annexation of Area C,²⁹ a region that covers 60 percent of the West Bank and is home to 300,000 Palestinians. Over the course of the past five decades, Israel has succeeded in settling over half a million people inside the occupied territories, keeping the Arab population fenced off in complicated ways that deny them basic human rights and encourage a desperate and brutal feedback loop of terrorism and counterterrorism.

The occupation is carried out through a complex land entanglement designed to generate structural chaos and misunderstanding. Settlement spots grow into enclave alignments that swell up into corridors and eventually form a network thread of controlled space. Almost three million Palestinians are confined to 40 percent of the West Bank, Areas A and B. Their daily movements are restricted by Israeli checkpoints and travel permits. A multilayered separation barrier, measuring 708 kilometers in length and reaching as high as 8 meters, runs roughly along the Green Line,[30] sometimes cutting as far as 18 kilometers deep into Palestinian land. In the Gaza Strip, the West Bank and East Jerusalem, Palestinians are registered in a Population Registry controlled by Israel. About a quarter of Gazans have family in the West Bank, in occupied East Jerusalem, and in Israel itself. The main currency traded throughout the whole territory is the Israeli shekel. Inside Israel's recognized borders, there live 1.5 million Palestinians (20 percent of the Israeli population) who are Israeli Arab citizens.[31] Most, if not all the residents of Palestine, especially the refugees, have a historical, familial, real-estate, and emotional connection to the area inside Israel. Therefore, as the likelihood of a double-state solution appears ever more implausible, it is useful to underline the fact that, for 50 years, Israel-Palestine has existed as single state. In the dream of creating a worldwide Jewish nation, Zionism created an Israeli nation—bilingual, bicultural, and binational—albeit one with massive inequalities.

Jewish-French philosopher Emmanuel Levinas wrote a text in 1961 titled "Heidegger, Gagarin and Us." In it he opposes Russian Cosmonaut Yuri Gagarin's "absolute homogeneous space" to German philosopher Martin Heidegger's mysticism of place, memory, and landscape: "One's implementation in a landscape, one's attachment to Place, without which the universe would become insignificant and would scarcely exist, is the very splitting of humanity into natives and strangers. ... [Hence, w]hat is admirable about Gagarin's feat is [that] for one hour, man existed beyond any horizon—everything around him was sky or, more exactly, everything was geometrical space." He claims that, contrary to Christianity and its nurturing of local cults, saints, and household gods, Judaism has always been detached from place and idols. Like Gagarin, Judaism aspires to dwell in the abstract spaces of humanist values rather than in the landscapes of superstition and mysticism. For Levinas, home is not a correlate of autochthony. Rather, home realizes its potential for being a place of dignity only when it becomes open to the Other, the stranger. Home, and one might extrapolate homeland, is a place of hospitality and welcome. Ecology, we might add, is the same thing.[32] *[Fig. 6–8]*

# 4. Lessons from Israel: Imagining Hospitable Environments

> For the Lord shall comfort Zion: He will comfort all her waste places; and he will make her wilderness like Eden, and her desert like the garden of the Lord; joy and gladness shall be found therein, thanksgiving, and the voice of melody.
> — Isaiah 51:3

The present book presents the results of the studio course offered in the 2016–17 academic year by laba (Laboratoire Bâle), the architecture and urban design studio of the École Polytechnique Fédérale de Lausanne (EPFL). As a European institution of education, we wanted to look at Israel in order to examine Western conceptions of social space rooted in land domestication and landscape idolatry, demonstrating the ways in which facts and narratives related to agriculture and the climate crisis are intertwined with geopolitics and sectarian ideals of earthly paradises. We wanted to critically examine our collective responsibility as inheritors of the European colonial project, the many waves of Jewish persecution across our continent, and our ongoing military and political meddling in the region. It is our obligation to help turn the European gaze back on itself and to learn from the experiences of those who have been historically excluded and dehumanized, especially when faced with the ecological challenges to come. As Barry Commoner said in his 1971 book *The Closing Circle*, a human economy based on ecological principles should be aware that "everything is connected to everything else" and "everything must go somewhere." In our global age of pollution and contamination, thresholds have become blurry, and what affects some affects us all. Our landscape tropes need to be updated beyond identitary ideals of ethnical purity and moral redemption. They must include borderlands, toxic waste, the home, the body, landscapes of resistance, and other strange trans-corporealities.[33] This shift needs to happen with the collaboration of those excluded from the garden trope so far, if we wish to construct a progressive ethics of environmental hospitality that might mend the damage inflicted by supremacist ideologies of nationalism and imperialism upon our landscapes and geographies.[34]

As editors of this book and educators in this studio, we wish to clarify that this work does not, at any moment, aspire to question the right to self-determination of modern-day Judeo-Israelis or the legitimacy of the State of Israel. Nor does it wish to conflate criticism of Israel and its policies with anti-Semitism or to promulgate any kind of gross generalization about the Jewish people as a whole. The studio and its faculty stand with the international consensus that opposes the Israeli occupation of Palestine since 1967.[35] We support any solution to the conflict that is consistent with the full rights of both Palestinians and Israeli Jews, be it in the form of two nation-states, one binational state, or some other configuration that they might agree upon. In accordance with the Universal Declaration of Human Rights, we defend the right of return for all refugees. We do not oppose the Boycott Divest Sanction (BDS) movement, as long as it does not discriminate against individuals on the basis of their national citizenship and is instead directed exclusively at Israeli state agencies and corporations that are complicit with the occupation. Consequently, we do not support the Academic Boycott of Israel or any kind of collective punishment of Israeli academia. We believe that the principle of academic freedom is designed to provide platforms in which we might be able to reflect together on difficult problems, generating safe spaces for the kind of democratic debate that the academy is morally obliged to uphold. This especially applies to our academic field of architecture, urbanism, and landscape design, for which the politics of territorial occupation through architecture must be critically addressed as the central core of our discipline. We have tried to provide our students with the chance to listen to multiple points of view and the right to concur or dissent from those points of view individually. Therefore, while this introduction exposes a political and ethical consensus shared by laba's faculty, it does not in any willful way reflect the views of our mother institution, the EPFL, nor those of our Israeli partners at the Technion.[36]

"Israel Lessons: Industrial Arcadia" is third of a series of studio courses offered by laba titled "Industrial Earth" that addresses issues of environmental aesthetics in our advanced industrial society. In the present volume, our focus was directed to the role played by agriculture in contributing to climate change, structuring urban development, and supporting homeland narratives. The book's three-part structure reflects the academic method employed in the studio. Part 1, "Territory," presents a territorial reading based on cartography. Part 2, titled "Field," shows photographs of a trip to Israel-Palestine that took place in December 2016. And part 3, "Architecture," presents 18 architecture designs produced by our students as critical syntheses and proof of concept of the analysis and commentary generated in the territorial reading.

— *Bárbara M. Costa*
— *Harry Gugger*

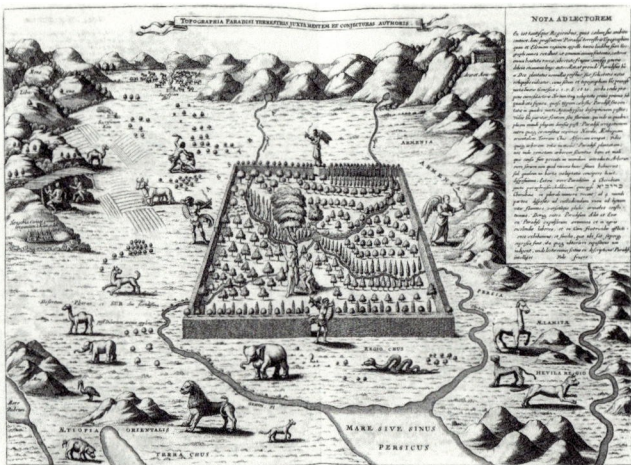

[Fig. 1] *Topographia Paradisi Terrestris*, illustration from *Arca Nöe* by Athanasius Kircher, 1675.

[Fig. 2] *The Golden Age*, by Lucas Cranach the Elder, ca. 1530. Oil on Panel, 75×103.5 cm. National Gallery, London.

[Fig. 3] *May our eyes behold your return in mercy to Zion*, illustration by Ephraim Moses Lilien for the Fifth Zionist Congress, Basel, 1901.

[Fig. 4] *Cotton fields of Kibbutz Shamir*, ca. 1958. Photograph from the Shamir archive.

[Fig. 5] *Inmates in the uniform of Holocaust survivors holding the flag of Israel on the deck of an illegal immigration ship prior to their arrest by British soldiers.* Photograph by Uri Dan, 1945.

[Fig. 6] *Israeli settlement in Jordan Valley.* Ma'ale Adumim, Occupied West Bank. Photograph by Alan Whelan, 2012.

[Fig. 7] *Shoaffat refugee camp near Jerusalem*, 2007. Photograph by Tamarah.

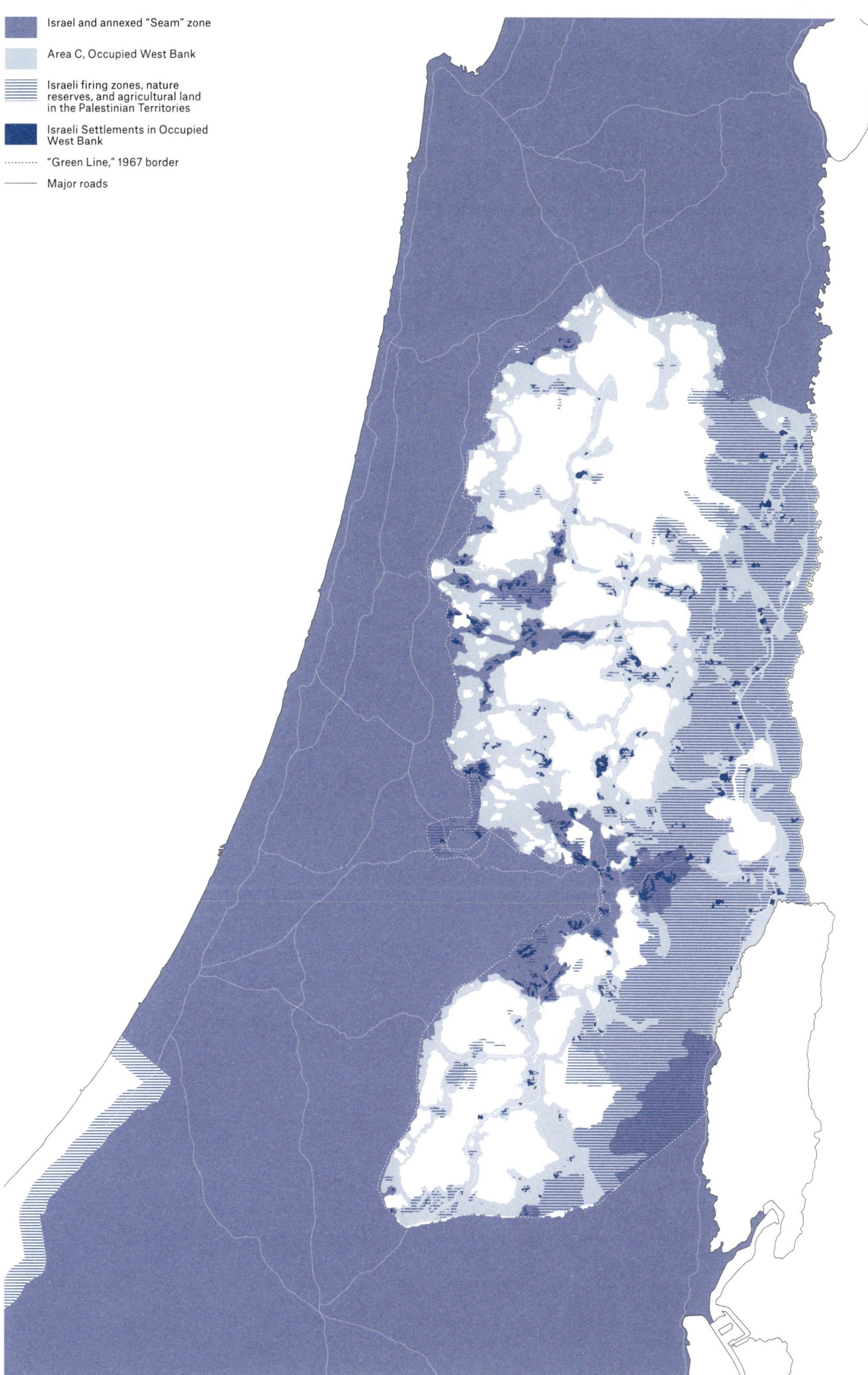

[Fig. 8] Map of Israel-Palestine

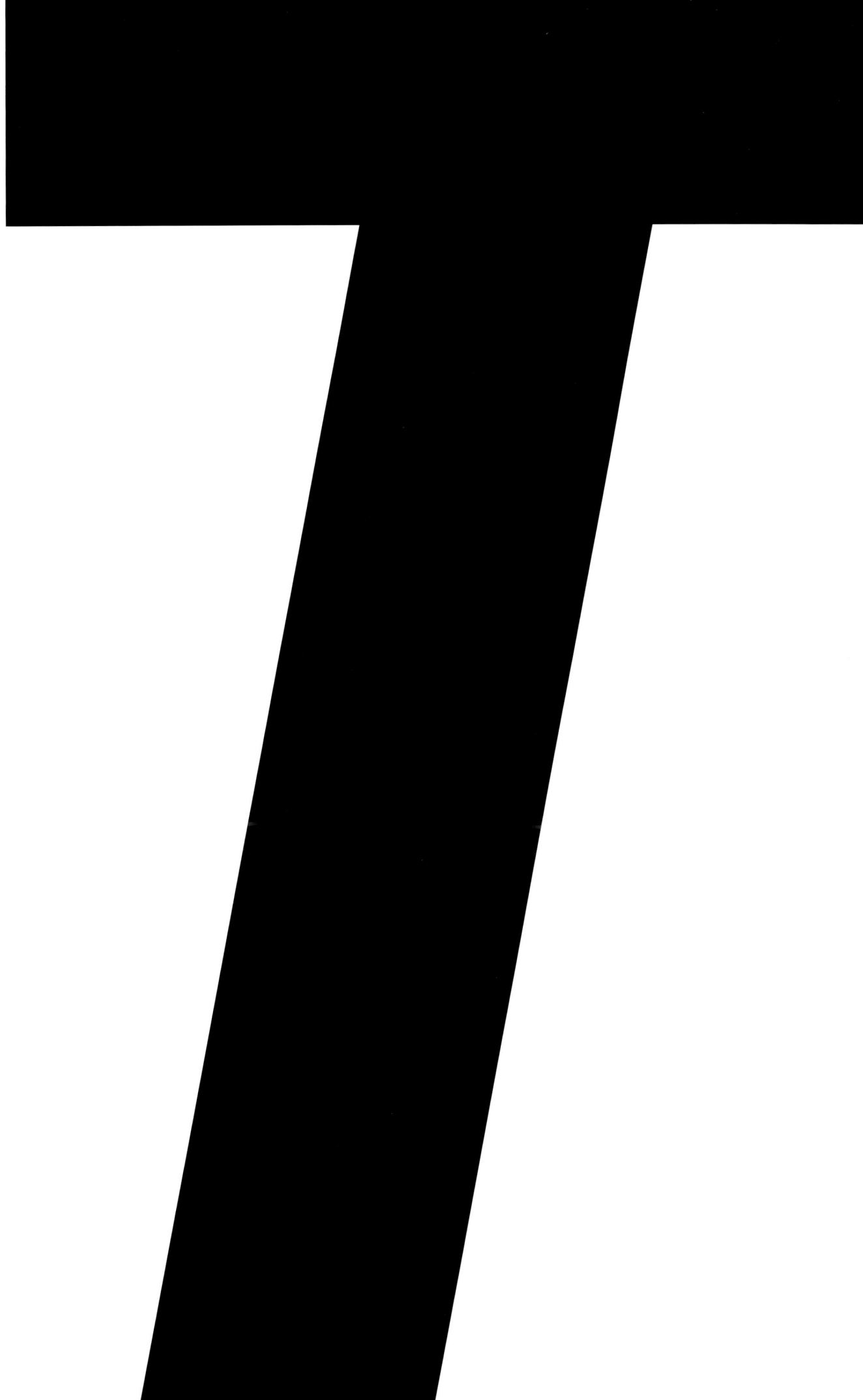

# Territory

Agriculture as Settlement: Territorial Agriculture in Israel
1. History of Agriculture 19
2. Agriculture as Settlement 22
3. Settlement without Agriculture, Agriculture without Settlement 24

— *by Matanya Sack*

Israel is a fascinating, and extreme, laboratory for the notion of "industrial arcadia." On a rather small scale and within a short time frame, Israel went through all the stages of a typical Modernist project.

The cultivated space of agriculture forms the foundation of Israeli territory. In order to address the spatial issues we deal with today, we must first examine the origins and effects of this territorial agriculture. It defines not only the landscape, but also the economies, politics, laws, beliefs, and cultures that shape the land.

Israel exhibits densely populated "regional-urban" entities intertwined with intensive agricultural rural regions that cover the entire land. Diverse populations, economies, and cultures interact across a multitude of landscape units and ecologies.

Since the beginning of Zionism, agriculture and settlement have gone hand in hand. It is customary to view agriculture in terms of the idea of the "new Jew" who works the land (work that was forbidden in the diaspora) and even in the context of labor supply and food production. All this is true of course, but the territorial aspect is the most important and is most revolutionary. Territorial agriculture was in fact the only option for settling a relatively small number of people across relatively large areas.

# 1. History of Agriculture

Iaba's work on Israel as an industrial arcadia highlights the undercurrents that shape Israeli territory. In order to understand how these are brought to the surface as possible readings for future actions, we must look at the history of agriculture in the region.

## 1.1. An agricultural society
(Jewish settlement in Palestine from tenth century BCE to first century CE)

Judaism was originally an agricultural religion based on the needs of an agrarian society. This is exemplified in the three pilgrimage festivals: Sukkot, Passover, and Shavuot, which are all related to agrarian calendar activities like spring reaping and summer and autumn harvests. During these holidays, 10 percent of the crops were brought to the Temple in Jerusalem.

## 1.2. A society without agriculture
(*Yishuv Yashan*, first century CE to nineteenth century CE)

After the expulsion of Jews from Jerusalem under the Romans, Judaism changed from an agricultural religion centered on the Temple to a knowledge religion centered on prayer. Throughout the Middle Ages there was a continuous trickle of Jewish immigration from the diaspora back to the Land of Israel. This immigration had primarily religious purposes, and the immigrants settled mostly in one of the four sacred cities of the "Old Settlement" (*Yishuv Yashan*): Hebron, Jerusalem, Tiberias, Safed. Other Jewish immigrants, mainly from Arab countries, mingled in local Arab villages and practiced agriculture.

## 1.3. New agriculture

(Nineteenth century CE)

Mikveh Israel—An open field in the midst of the Tel Aviv metropolitan area.[1]

The first modern manifestation of the "New Settlement" (*Yishuv Khadash*) was the agricultural school of Mikve Israel. It was funded in 1870 by the French-Jewish Alliance Israélite Universelle, to support Jews from the *Yishuv Yashan*. At that time, there were fewer than 15,000 Jews in the Ottoman region, which is now the State of Israel.

In 1878 a group of Orthodox Jews from Jerusalem bought land in the *shfela* (lowlands) area and established Petah Tikva as a *moshava* (village). A new type of settlement arose: agricultural and based on private ownership.

## 1.4. New territory

("Auto-Emancipation," nineteenth century CE)

With the rise of national identities, and the formulation of nation-states, Jews began to suffer from increasing limitations by governments, accompanied by vast pogroms, mostly in Eastern Europe. One of the defining moments of this period came in 1881 with the passing of the May Laws in Russia, which, among other limitations, prohibited Jews from working in agriculture.

These events led to the publication of a pamphlet titled *Auto-Emancipation*, by Leon Pinsker, calling for a national independent territory for Jews, one that must include fertile land for agriculture.

# 2. Agriculture as Settlement

In 1884 a group of immigrants from Russia established Rishon LeZion as a *moshava* on the central Mediterranean coastal plain. Together with Petah Tikva, it was the precursor to similar typological settlements in the next twenty-five years. Thus the *Yishuv Khadash* began to take shape. The farms in the *moshavot* were based on two types of agriculture: citrus orchards and vineyards, and dry farming grain. This type of agriculture was not driven by subsistence, but rather the export of produce (predominantly citrus).

## 2.1. New settlement

The *moshavot* were built in the coastal plain and the valleys of the Galilee. This fact directly influenced the evolution of the Zionist settlement of the territory and later the establishment of the first borders of Israel.

We should therefore detail the reasons for this new geography:
— Ottoman land ownership: Landlords, mostly living abroad, owned large land units (purchased from the Sultanate). They did not work the land but leased it to tenants. They were willing to sell land at market prices.
— Swamp areas: After 3,000 years of farming, the land in the plains and valleys had to be constantly irrigated and maintained. In the eighteenth century, these areas were neglected and turned into swamps. They were readily sold to Jewish immigrants.
— Access to international trade routes: The *moshavot* placed emphasis on exports, and transportation to the ports of Jaffa and Tantura was crucial.
— Conceptual and geographical distancing from the *Yishuv Yashan* in the mountain ridge.
— East European agricultural education brought training and experience of cultivating plains and their typical crops.

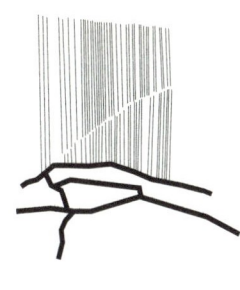
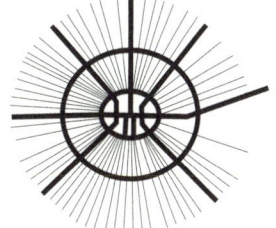

The first *moshavot* were supported by private funding. However, in 1908 these efforts began to be co-organized under Arthur Rupin of The Zionist Organization (founded by Theodore Herzl in 1897). This had a clear effect on the new type of settlements that were developed. The *kibbutz* (Hebrew for "grouping") combined social ideals with Zionist aspirations. The *moshav ovdim* ("workers village") was a hybrid between the private and the communal in terms of ownership and as an adopted way of life. The group ethos was not only born of the idealism of the young pioneers from Europe but was also in the interest of the settlement organizations, who did not want to hand over large tracts of land to individuals who lacked agricultural training.

Village Typologies **2**
— Arab: Nujeidat
— Labor Village: Nahalal
— Cluster of Olim Villages: Pduyim, Ranen, Maslul

What should be emphasized here is that these rural settlements were all architecturally planned. This gave birth to a somewhat new profession—the rural planner—practiced by architects such as Richard Kauffman, Arieh Sharon, and Zeev Rechter.

## 2.2. Settling for a border

> Where the Jewish plow will plow the last furrow, where our border will pass.
> — Attributed to Joseph Trumpeldor (1880–1920), Tel Hai, year unknown.

After the First World War, the Sykes-Picot Agreement between France and Britain divided the Ottoman Empire, defining the area with geopolitical borders for the first time. The agreement was famous for its schematic lines on the map. The northern border for example, was drawn as a straight line between Acre on the Mediterranean and the Sea of Galilee. *[Fig. 1]*

Kibbutz Shoval at the first year after its foundation, 1947.**3**

In the following years, small amendments had to be made due to local considerations. While becoming quite articulated, the border was moved further north to include Jewish-owned rural land. It is interesting to note that these large land units were cultivated by only 4 very small Jewish agricultural settlements (of 15 to 17 pioneers each).

The initial commitment of Britain under the Mandate—to achieve a future division of the land between Jews and Arabs—changed the Zionist mode of operation. This was a crucial moment, as the Zionist

Kibbutz Shoval—a view from the field.**4**

organizations understood that the future division would be based on land ownership and cultivation. From this moment on, agricultural settlement became directed toward a future map of Israel. It also raised the importance of planning.

As a result, a plan to create a continuous agricultural territory between the coastal plain and the Galilee was developed. Nicknamed the "N-Plan," it required the purchase of the fertile lands of the Yizre'el Valley, regardless of their high market price. Another direction of the plan was southward, to the Negev Desert.

These efforts culminated in the U.N. Division Plan of 1947. As can be seen on the map, it was a result of cultivated land ownership and land continuity. We can therefore conclude by discussing the direct effect territorial agriculture had on the character of Israel today and the present geopolitical situation. [Fig. 2-4]

## 2.3. Settling the territory, within the borders

The Histadrut calls: *From City to Village*. Campaign poster, 1955.[5]

With the establishment of the Israeli nation state, mass migration to Israel started and the Jewish population doubled from 650,000 to 1.3 million in 18 months. The immigrants being from the surviving remnant of Eastern Europe after the Holocaust and the Jewish exodus from Arab countries following new hardships such as the Farhud (pogrom) in Iraq. Already during the Independence War the need to build new settlements arose and was discussed and pushed forward. In 1951 the First National Plan, "Physical Planning in Israel," led by Architect Arieh Sharon, was ready to be implemented. Its main emphasis was on rural villages and towns as means of settling immigrants. In the chapter titled "Five Branches of Planning," "Directed Agriculture" is the first.

In the early 1950s, the young government, led by Prime Minister David Ben-Gurion, launched a campaign dubbed "From City to Village" that aimed toward a different distribution of population within the new borders. Under this campaign new villages were established, settling the territory within the borders of the new state.

The campaign was supported by large-scale infrastructure projects, most famously the National Water Carrier of Israel, which brought fresh water from the Sea of Galilee to the Negev. Furthermore, Israel quickly became a leader in agricultural research and development. At that time, Norman Borlaug initiated the Green Revolution, which Israel ardently adopted and improved with inventions such as drip irrigation and plant varieties for arid climates that were soon exported globally.

# 3. Settlement without Agriculture, Agriculture without Settlement

The population distribution in small towns and villages by the first national plan was perhaps inadvertently the foundation of Israeli suburbs and urban sprawl. The Committee for Conservation of Agricultural Land (VALKAH) was established in 1968. This committee operates on a national level, meaning all regional and local plans are subject to it.

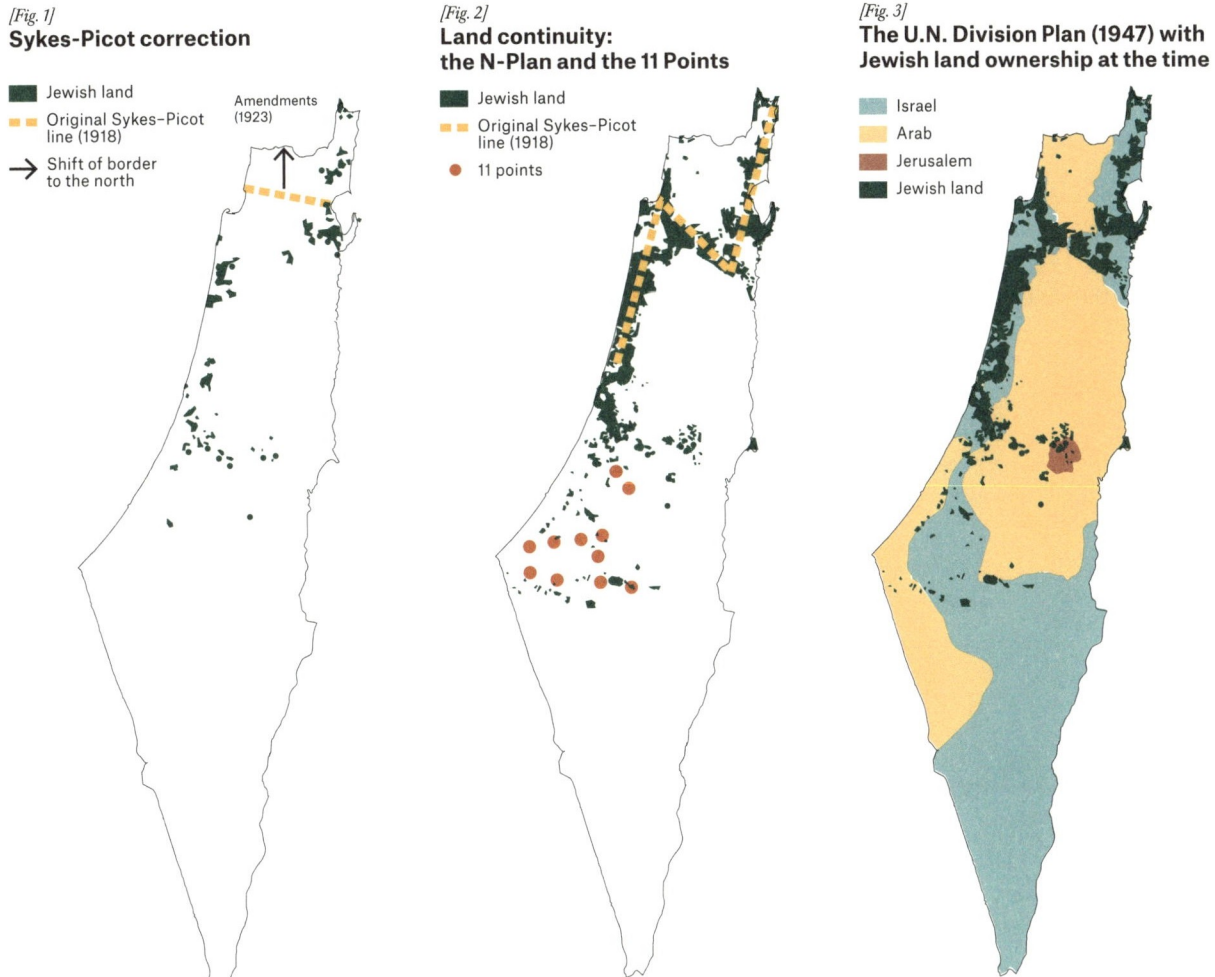

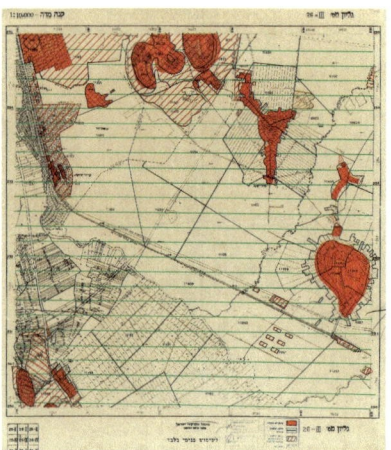
Declared agricultural land—VALKAH, 1968. **6**

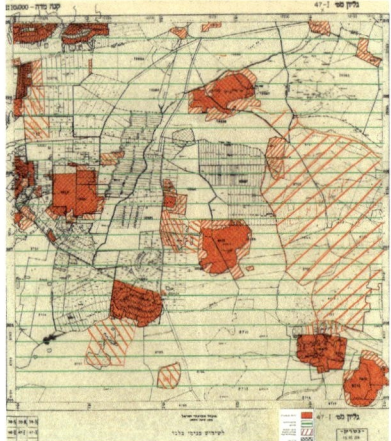
VALKAH **7**

## 3.1. Agriculture as land use

In the VALKAH plan, built and planned spaces were marked in red, while the rest of the land, declared as agricultural, was marked with green stripes. Agriculture thereby turned into a statutory layer. The ethos of agriculture had come a long way, even turned on its head. From an idealistic, pragmatic, and productive tool of settlement, building, and development it turned into a public policy for conservation, aimed at limiting urban development.

At first impression it seems that agriculture, now as a protected statutory layer, is at the highest level of conservation. But actually this reading triggers the inverse. When all space is given the status of agriculture one can have the impression that there is enough, if not too much. Since agriculture designates one unified layer, it can be negotiated, and it becomes in effect a tool of private and public real estate. With the right arguments, each plan can convince the committee that the designated area is not appropriate for agricultural use, or that it is needed more for development purposes.

## 3.2. Settlement without agriculture

From the changing role and ethos of agriculture, exemplified by the VALKAH, several trends evolved:

From *moshavot* to regional urbanism:
From the 1970s to the present, massive urbanization took place, mainly in the center and northern part of Israel. The population grew from 3 million citizens to 8.7 million today (including the Arab population). Cities became regional entities, encompassing urban, rural, agricultural, natural, and infrastructural spaces. Today agricultural areas are the last large open land units in central Israel. In recent decades, we have seen speculation on agricultural land especially in the central part of Israel where land prices are high. Some of the former *moshavot* became highly developed urban centers. There are still some cultivated fields in their municipal territory, but they are expected to be the first vacant lots for future development. The bulk of this expansion covers the most fertile land in Israel.

Suburbanization of the rural:
Due to the highly increased productivity of the industrial agriculture of the Green Revolution, fewer and fewer workers are required in the fields. As in rural areas all over the world, the number of farmers in Israel has reduced from 80 percent to only 2 percent of the workforce. While agriculture is thriving, the farmers in the villages are disappearing. Since Israel is a small country, most villages are within commuting distances to central employment areas and so serve as an "urban hinterland." Villages that were once communities of farmers continue to grow but with no one employed in agriculture.

New settlements—spiritual agriculture:
After 1967, Israel kept building new settlements, primarily in the Galilee, the Negev, and the West Bank. Now situated in the mountains rather

than valleys, most new settlements are urban or suburban. The tiny fraction of settlements that work the land do not follow the ethos of the productive, industrial agriculture of modern Zionism. The new settlements do not feel responsible for feeding the population that supports them. The small farms practice "post-modern" agriculture, which is boutique, organic, traditional, and often combined with tourism. In an outpost in the West Bank we find a sign "God is the King" over an organic dairy: a signal of aspiring to go back to Judaism as an agricultural religion. In the Negev, new settlements named "Solitary Farms" indicate the stark departure from the idea of the *kibbutz* ("grouping").

## 3.3. Agriculture without settlement

What lies in the future? Recent evolutions in agricultural technologies go along with socio-spatial trends. The laboratory becomes the new field. Agri-tech can be described as a post-industrial agriculture, a precision agriculture using GPS and self-driving tractors, an agriculture detached from the ground, not dependent on fertile soil, rainwater, or working hands. New crops such as algae, hohova for cosmetics, marijuana for medicine, genetically modified tobacco, collagen for 3-D printing of human tissues, and even solar panels, replace crops for food, due to their economic yields per hectare. Agriculture is more and more detached from the land and from the rural. A new relationship between a rural way of living and cultivating, between agriculture and settlement, gets established.

## 3.4. New readings, new typologies

The agricultural revolution of eighteenth-century England brought mass immigration from rural to urban areas, promoting the Industrial Revolution and the industrial city, which in turn brought about the rise of the Garden City. Next, the Green Revolution of the twentieth century prompted even more farmers to lay down their tools and move to cities, which have since transformed into regional entities.

What will be the next urban typology, as a reaction to the evolution of regional cities? Perhaps a clue can be found in the ongoing agri-tech revolution of today, along with socio-political aspirations for the future.

# Territory

Israel: A Land of Scarcity

1. Growing Population 27
2. Land of Limited Resources 27
3. Water Scarcity 27
4. Desertification 27

# 1. Growing Population

Since the foundation of the State of Israel in 1948, the country's population has grown tenfold from 800,000 in 1948 to 8,585,500 in 2017. The Law of Return, granting all people of Jewish descent the right to citizenship, led to the rapid population influx. Migration combined with a high fertility rate (3.1 children per woman) makes Israel one of the fastest-growing countries in the OECD. The population of Israel is predicted to grow by 4 million by 2050. *[Fig. 1–2]* Israel has a deeply divided society, separating the Jewish and the Arab populations. The ethnic/religious disconnection has been at the heart of repeated conflicts in the region for more than a century.

**Facts about Israel (2015)[1]**

| | |
|---|---|
| Population | 8,585,500 |
| Density | 377/sq. km |
| Growth rate | 2.0 % |
| Birth rate | 21.5 births/1,000 population |
| Death rate | 5.2 deaths/1,000 population |
| Life expectancy | 82.01 years |
| Fertility rate | 3.08 children born/woman |
| Infant mortality | 4.03 deaths/1,000 live births |
| Age structure | 0–14 years: 27.3 % |
| | 15–64 years: 62.2 % |
| | 65 and over: 10.5 % |

# 2. Land of Limited Resources

Israel's fertile land resources are limited. Two-thirds of its territory are classified as hyper-arid and arid areas, with 57 percent of the territory covered by the Negev Desert. Israel has taken a number of countermeasures to address the desertification processes, such as planning, environmental, and development strategies for the sustainable use of natural resources. But the rapidly growing population demands new constructions to cover valuable arable land and reduce the already largely disrupted open landscape. *[Fig. 3–5]*

**Demographic composition of Israel (2012)[2]**

| | | |
|---|---|---|
| Jews | 6,119,000 | 75.0 % |
| — Non-Haredi | 5,499 000 | 65.1 % |
| — Haredi | 750,000 | 9.9 % |
| Arabs | 1,688,600 | 20.7 % |
| Other | 349,700 | 4.3 % |

# 3. Water Scarcity

Situated in one of the world's most arid regions, Israel and its neighboring countries face an enormous challenge with regard to water supply. Israel, Palestine, Jordan, Syria, and Lebanon are all part of the Dead Sea catchment basin. Constant water scarcity, caused by desertification, pollution, and a growing demand for water, plays a fundamental part in many conflicts arising in the area. The main challenges of water management in Israel include: building desalination plants; improving reuse of recycled water and sewage treatment; promoting urban water conservation; and maintaining the natural environment of the riverbeds. *[Fig. 6–8]*

# 4. Desertification

Israel's territory, being exposed to the threat of desertification, is counteracting the phenomenon through sustainable agricultural development e.g., centralized national water management. The country, thanks to advanced research and new technologies, became a leader in desert farming. Nevertheless, rapid urbanization, intensive agriculture, polluting industries and extensive afforestations accelerate the phenomena of desertification, and threaten the desert ecosystems, as well as the Bedouin culture. *[Fig. 9–10]*

[Fig. 1]
**Projected population growth**
in millions

[Fig. 2]
**Fertility rate in OECD countries (2015)**
in children per woman

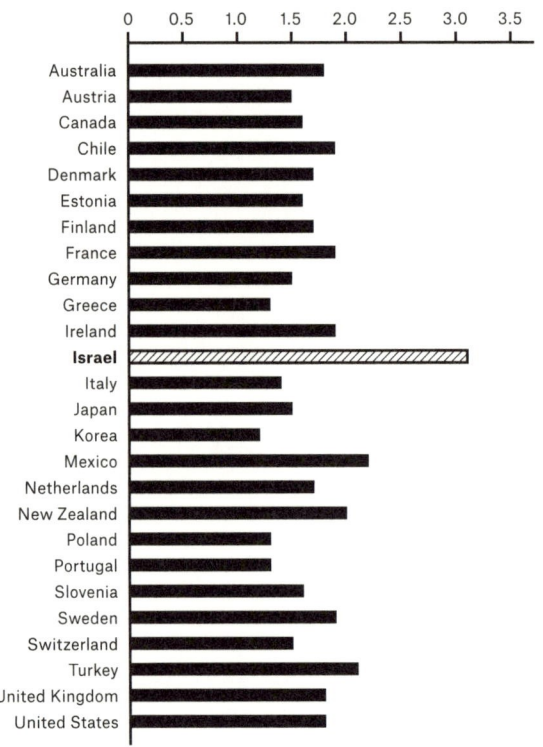

[Fig. 3]
**Land use**
Total area: 22,000 sq. km (with Golan heights but without Gaza Strip and Occupied West Bank)

- Various purpose
- Agricultural use
- Forest and nature reserves
- Urban areas

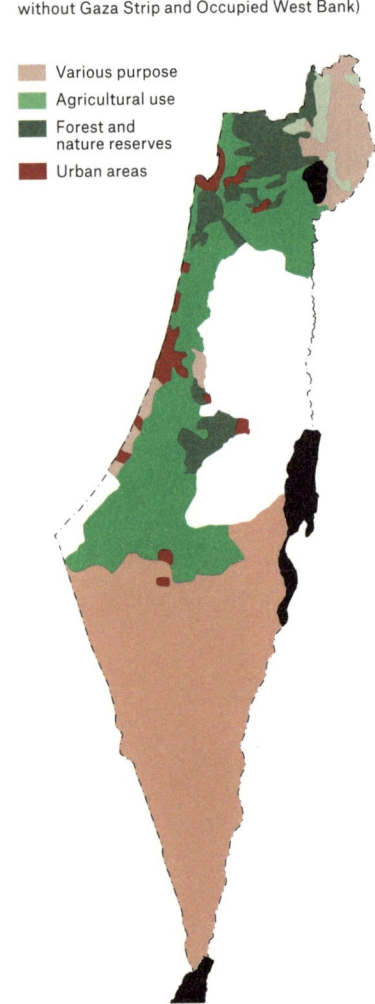

[Fig. 4]
**Agriculture**

**Irrigated land**
2,200 sq. km

**Pasture**
1,300 sq. km

**Non-irrigated field crops**
2,100 sq. km

Part of agriculture in exports

Israel
3.5 %

Palestine
16.3 %

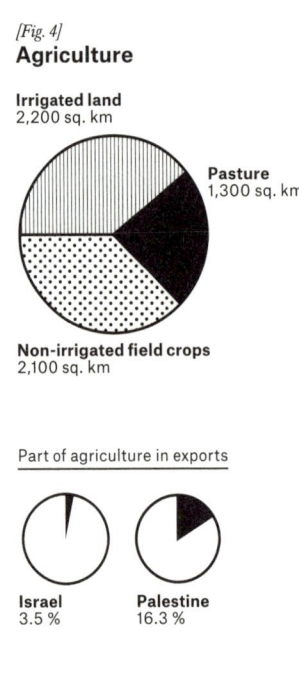

[Fig. 5]
**Ecosystem map**

- Extreme desert
- Negev and Arava sand
- Arid steppe
- Loessial plain
- Mediterranean plain
- Coastal plain sand
- Light, sandy soil
- Dead Sea
- Intermediate steppe
- Mediterranean mountain
- Alluvial valley
- Mediterranean forest
- Sea of Galilee

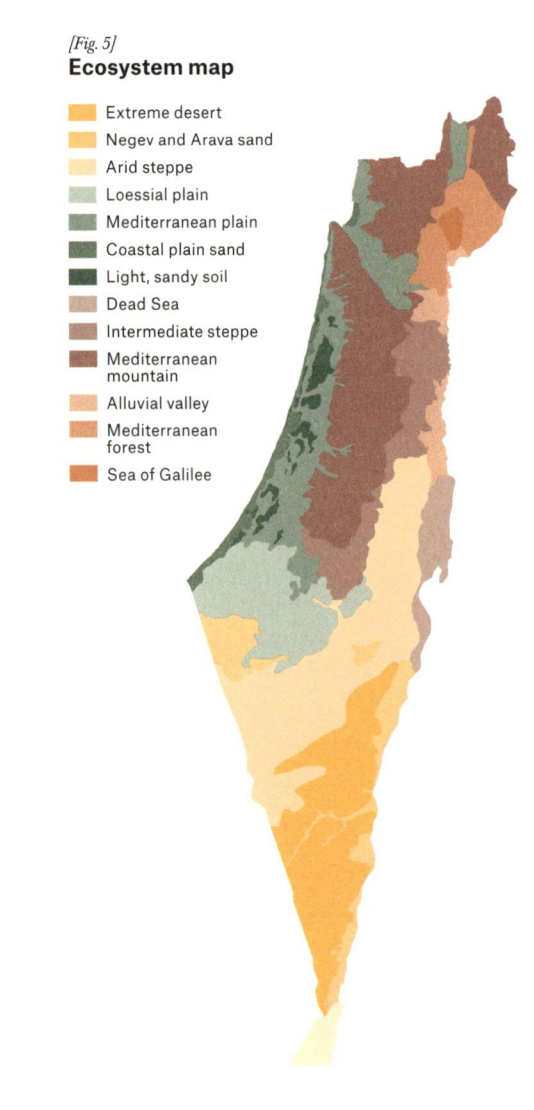

*[Fig. 6]*
**Watersheds**

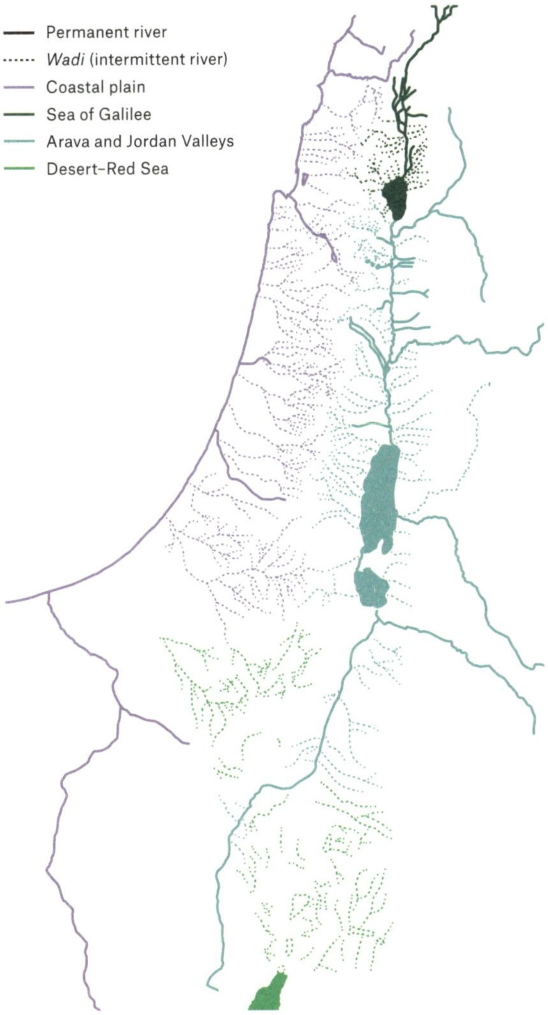

— Permanent river
····· *Wadi* (intermittent river)
— Coastal plain
— Sea of Galilee
— Arava and Jordan Valleys
— Desert–Red Sea

*[Fig. 7]*
**Annual rainfall**
in millimeters

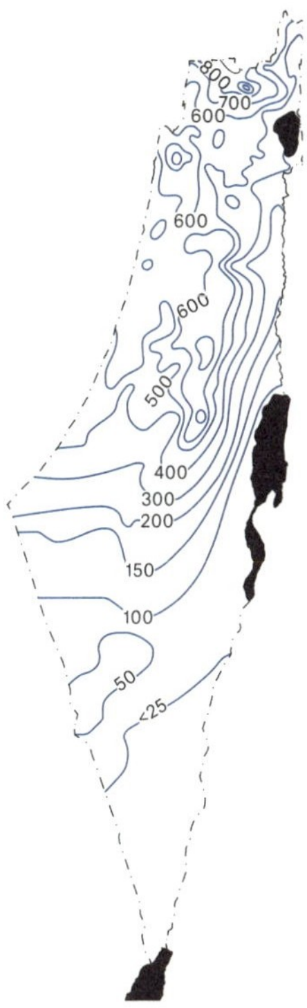

Rainwater status

**30%** Underground infiltration
**5%** Surface flow
**65%** Immediate evaporation

*[Fig. 8]*
**Climatic regions**
According to Köppen climate classification

- Csa (Hot-summer Mediterranean)
- BSh (Hot semi-arid)
- BWk (Cold desert)
- BWh (Hot desert)

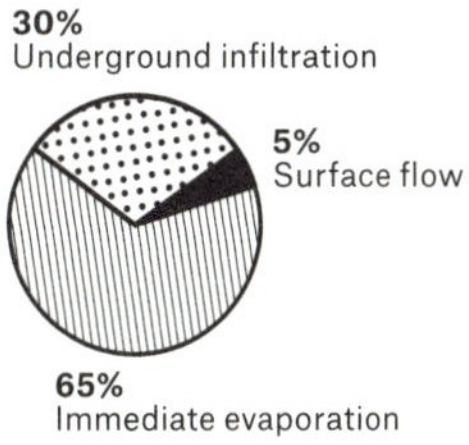

*[Fig. 9]*
**Desertification world map**

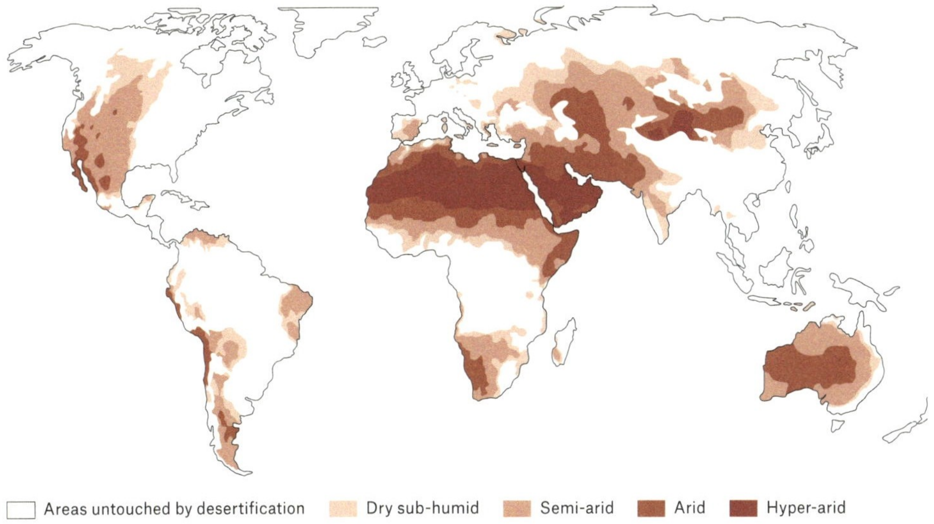

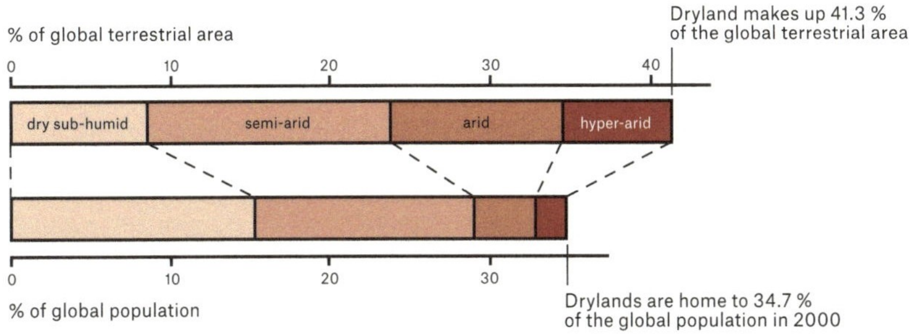

☐ Areas untouched by desertification   Dry sub-humid   Semi-arid   Arid   Hyper-arid

% of global terrestrial area

| dry sub-humid | semi-arid | arid | hyper-arid |

Dryland makes up 41.3 % of the global terrestrial area

% of global population

Drylands are home to 34.7 % of the global population in 2000

*[Fig. 10]*
**Aridity in Israel and the region**

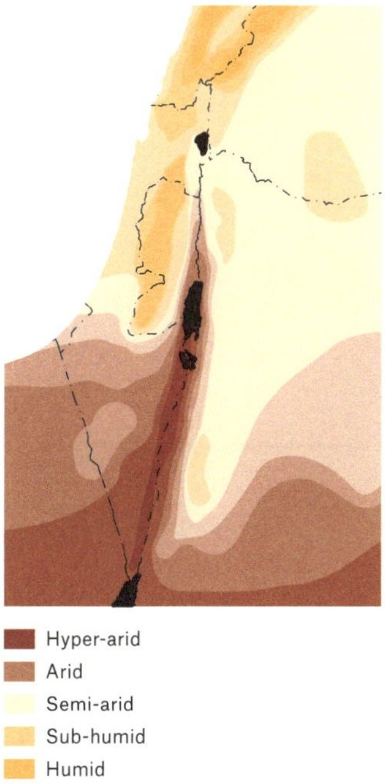

- Hyper-arid
- Arid
- Semi-arid
- Sub-humid
- Humid

Territory: Land of Scarcity   29

# Territory

The Jordan Rift Valley: A Water Management System

1. The Conflict on Water Resources    31
2. The Idle Valley    34
3. Constitution: A Water Management System    36

*The constitutions in the 3 following subchapters represent a conceptual strategy comprising a spatial plan and a series of proposals that describe a scenario for long-term territorial development.*

# 1. The Conflict on Water Resources

The Jordan Rift Valley showcases a great diversity of geographic and climatic zones within a rather small area. It ranges from desert landscapes in the south to fertile valleys in the north, with natural and historic tourist attractions throughout. Human interventions in the natural water system of the Jordan Rift Valley, driven by water scarcity in the bordering countries, have destabilized the region on ecological and political levels.

## 1.1. Diverse geography and climate

The history of water-bodies in the Dead Sea commenced with the intrusion of the Sedom Lagoon during the Neogene. The Sedom Lagoon extended from the Mediterranean Sea to the Dead Sea Rift valley. [Fig. 1] Approximately 2 million years ago the land between the Rift Valley and the Mediterranean Sea rose to such an extent that the ocean could no longer flood the area. The lagoon became a landlocked lake. [Fig. 2]

The Dead Sea catchment basin is topographically defined by the Jordan Rift Valley, also called the Syro-African Depression. It is an elongated depression, created by the Arabian tectonic plate moving north-eastward, away from the African tectonic plate. [Fig. 3] This geographic region includes the entire Jordan River—from its sources, through the Hula Valley, the Korazim block, the Sea of Galilee, the Jordan Valley, all the way to the Dead Sea, the lowest land elevation on Earth—and then continues through the Arava Valley to the Red Sea.

Located in the north, the Jordan Valley is several degrees warmer than adjacent areas and exhibits a temperate climate. The Arava Valley south of the Dead Sea is characterized by extremely strong insolation, prominent dryness, high temperatures, and low annual rainfalls. [Fig. 4–5]

## 1.2 Transboundary river basin

The Jordan River is 251 kilometers long, flowing roughly north to south through the Sea of Galilee and on into the Dead Sea. The river and its tributaries, the Banias, Hasbani, Dan, Yarmouk, and Zarqa Rivers, are shared between five riparian nations. [Fig. 6–7]

The water-scarce Middle East region is known for the fact that a considerable amount of its freshwater resources cross national boundaries. Thus, increasing pressures on water resources in the area requires adequate planning and management to promote cooperation between all riparian countries to achieve an equitable distribution of water.

This planning process also involves conflict resolution in international territories such as the Jordan River Basin. Major hydropolitical and geopolitical events have impacted this basin since the Ottoman Empire in 1299, and water allocation has been an element of tension among riparian countries for more than the past 50 years. Many water allocation plans were proposed, such as the Johnston Water Allocation Plan of 1955, but all failed to be ratified. Moreover, the historical and political instability in the region has hindered the possibility for any basin-wide agreement on water.[1]

Abandonned touristic infrastructures on the Dead Sea

[Fig. 1]
**Sedom Lagoon and Mediterranean Sea**
Pliocene—geologic timescale that extends from 5.333 million to 2.58 million years BCE

[Fig. 2]
**Historical Lake Lisan**
Pleistocene to Holocene—geological timescale that extends from 2.58 million years to 11,700 years BCE

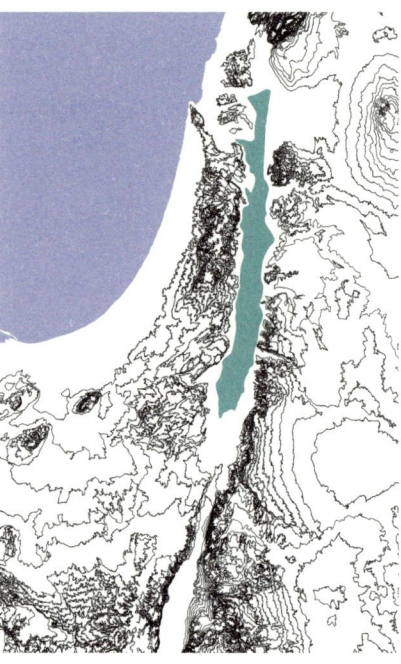

[Fig. 3]
**Main east Mediterranean tectonic features**

Mediterranean Sea
Sinai-Palestine Subplate
Arabian Plate
African Plate

⇔ Strike-Split / Transform fault
— Unspecified fault

[Fig. 4]
**Combined profiles of Jordanian Highlands and Jordan Rift Valley**

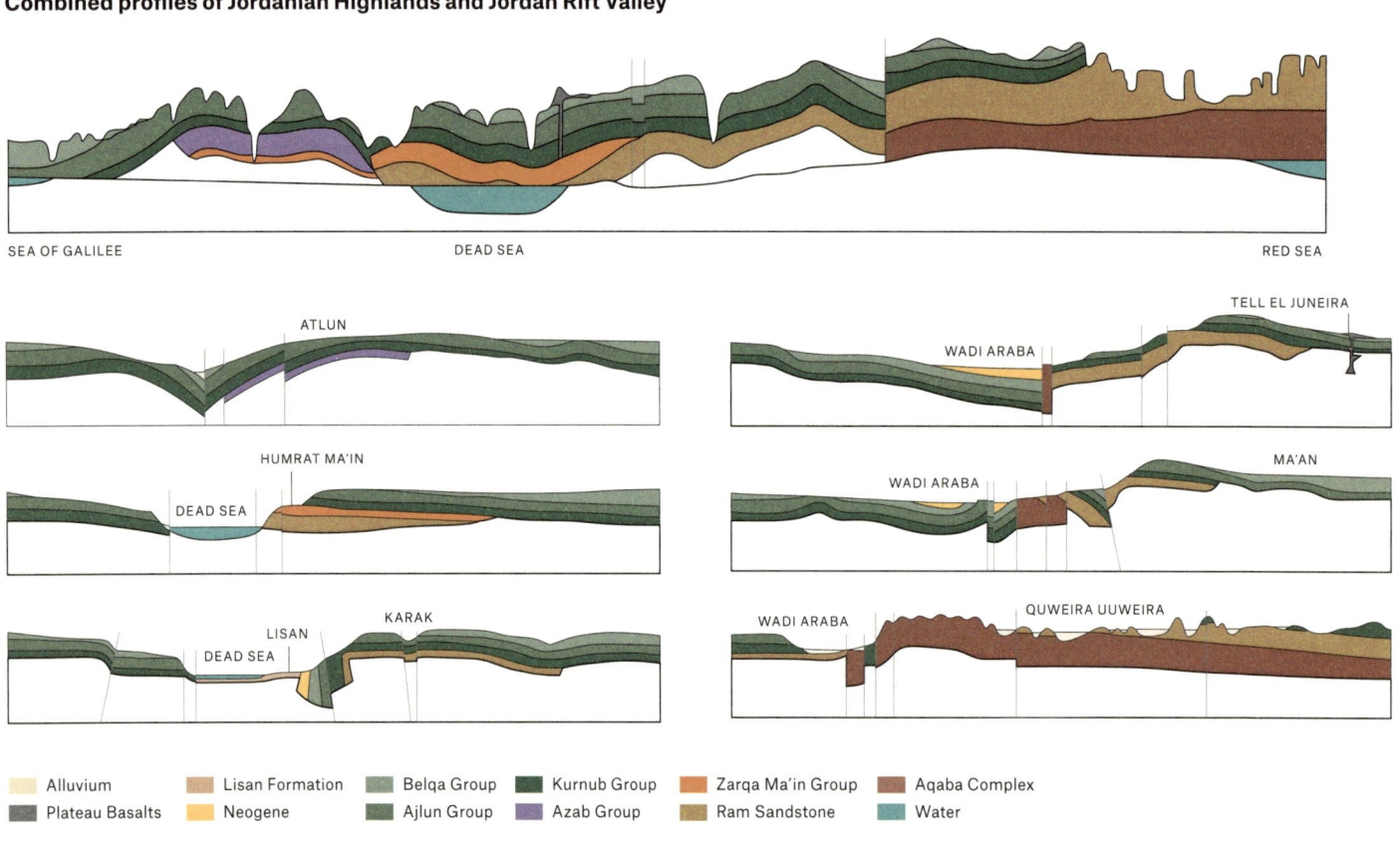

SEA OF GALILEE — DEAD SEA — RED SEA

ATLUN
HUMRAT MA'IN — DEAD SEA
LISAN — DEAD SEA — KARAK

TELL EL JUNEIRA — WADI ARABA
WADI ARABA — MA'AN
WADI ARABA — QUWEIRA UUWEIRA

- Alluvium
- Plateau Basalts
- Lisan Formation
- Neogene
- Belqa Group
- Ajlun Group
- Kurnub Group
- Azab Group
- Zarqa Ma'in Group
- Ram Sandstone
- Aqaba Complex
- Water

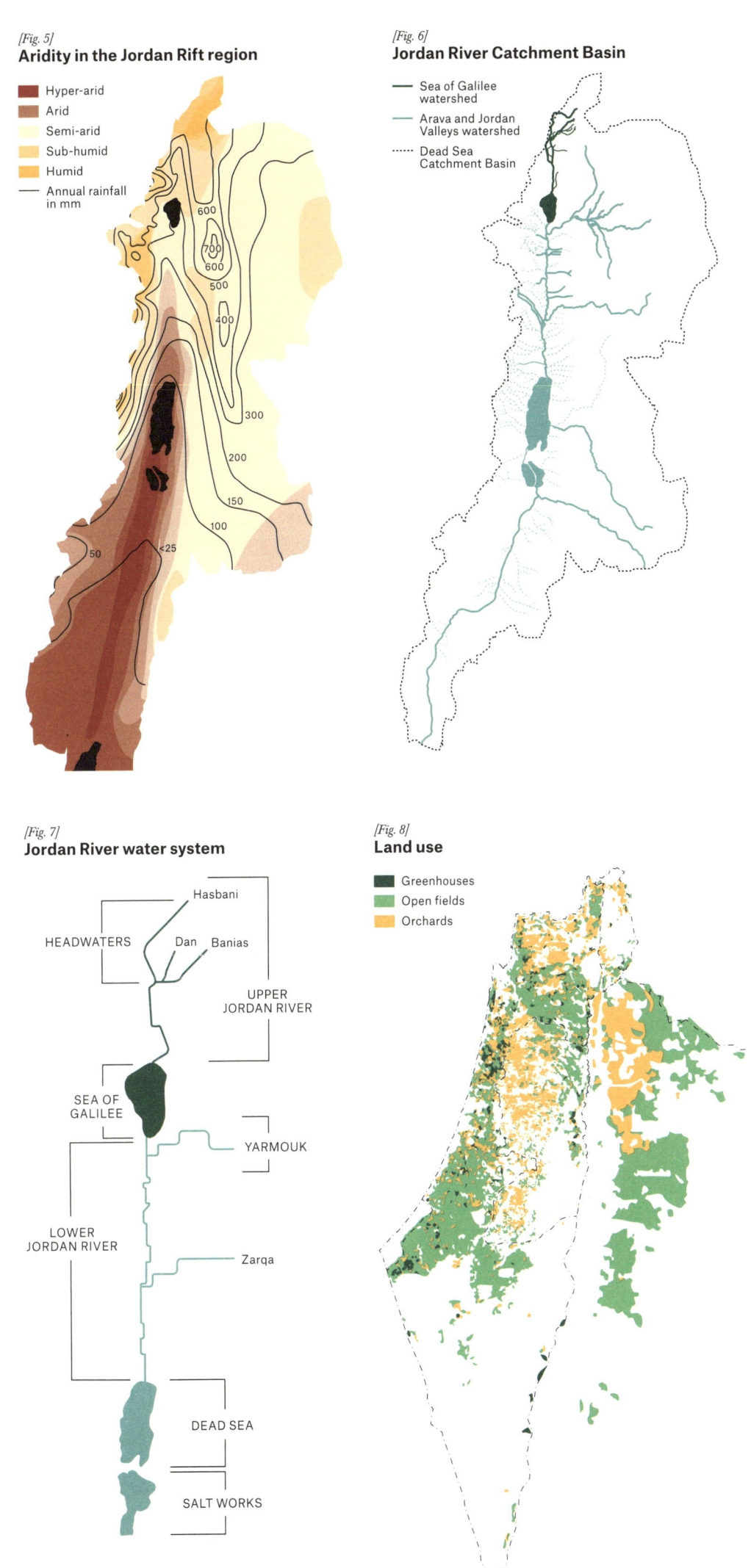

## 1.3. Continuous land use

The Jordan Valley, with its year-round temperate climate, fertile soils, and water supply, made it a propitious site for agriculture as far back as 10,000 years ago. By about 3000 BCE, produce from the valley was being exported to neighboring regions. Today agriculture is still the predominant land use along the Jordan River with *kibbutzim* in Israel and family farms in the Palestinian Territories and Jordan. [Fig. 8]

The Dead Sea has attracted visitors from around the Mediterranean basin for thousands of years. With around 5,500 hotels and more than 11,000 employees, the tourist sector is a major economic source for the region today. [Fig. 9-12]

Since the 1930s a wide variety of raw materials have been extracted locally on an industrial scale, ranging from potash for fertilizers to salt and minerals used in cosmetics.

Aerial view of the Dead Sea coastline damaged by sinkholes

Sinkhole 3

## 1.4. Man-made interventions

The region is under a great hydric stress. All five nations located in the catchment basin of the Jordan River (Lebanon, Syria, Jordan, Palestine, and Israel) have made efforts to utilize the natural resource water for their own benefit. [Fig. 13-14] Military conflicts with the goal of controlling the water sources triggered the militarization of the entire Jordan River Valley today. Vast areas of fertile land are now mined zones inaccessible for civilians.

Since the 1950s a growing population and the intensification of agriculture have led to large water infrastructure projects, such as canals and dams, channeling water away from the original stream. As a result, the Jordan River discharge into the Dead Sea has reduced massively, from 1,360 metric cubic meters in 1950 to 200 metric cubic meters today.

The large quantity of water evaporating from the surface of the Dead Sea is no longer balanced by the reduced water inflow from the Jordan River, causing the sea level to sink by 1.1 meter annually. Potash industries in Israeli and Jordan also play a significant role in depleting the Dead Sea, since the extraction process relies heavily on evaporation ponds. [Fig. 15-16]

Sinkhole incident

A side effect of the decreasing sea level are sinkholes appearing around the entire sea, making large areas of the seashore inaccessible. This phenomena appears when salted water recedes and fresh groundwater flows and dissolves layers of salt. It creates large underground cavities which can open up suddenly. As a consequence, some large areas of the seashore are today inaccessible.[2] [Fig. 17-19]

## 2. The Idle Valley

A valley that used to be the center of a fertile region has today turned into the militarized periphery of its bordering nations. The ecological effects of draining of the Jordan River and the Dead Sea have major economic implications for the region.

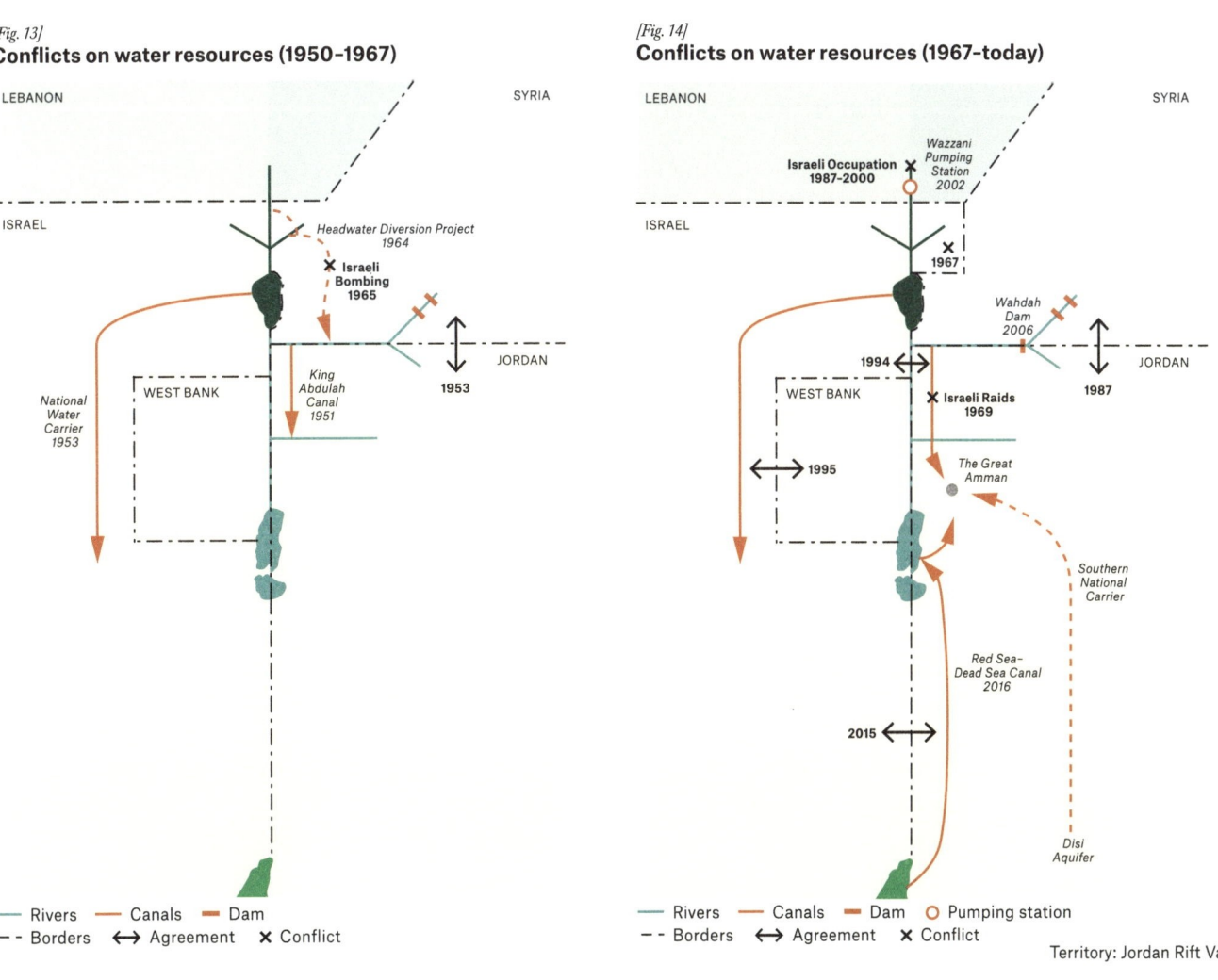

Territory: Jordan Rift Valley   35

## 2.1. Stagnant agriculture

The lack of trans-border agreements on sharing and managing water resources could potentially stagnate the peace process. With large portions of the fertile land in the Jordan Valley cut off from access to water and located in a militarized zone, agriculture, the economic basis for most of the basins population, will have little to no chance of prospering.

## 2.2. Endangered tourist industry

At the current rate of the sinking sea level, the Dead Sea shoreline will have dropped by another 35 meters in altitude by 2050. [Fig. 19] Thousands of new sinkholes will have made it impossible or too hazardous to access the sea in most places, threatening its tourist industry, a major contributor to the local economy.

# 3. Constitution: A Water Management System

This constitution attempts to implement a new and fair water management system for all riparian nations. Cooperation on water issues could accelerate the peace process in the region. By demilitarizing the Jordan and Arava Valleys and a stabilizing the Dead Sea the now idle valley could again be a revitalized.

## 3.1. Multinational water agreement

The establishment of a multinational water agreement among all bordering countries guaranteeing an equitable distribution of water is the foundation of a durable peace process in the region and the precondition to bring use of the existing landscape to its full potential. After the fair distribution of water, sustainable and technological aspects, the setting of national borders, and the creation of an agricultural trade union are key elements.

Fair division of water resources in the Jordan and Arava Valleys [Fig. 20]
— Sustainability
    — Control water quality passing to riparian countries and Dead Sea
    — Define minimum water volume to Dead Sea, stabilizing sea level
    — Establish waste water plants (recycling 20 percent of waste water)
    — Limit human water consumption to 50 liters per capita per day
— Technology
    — Israel to share technology with region
      (establishment of the Dead Sea Transfer Unit)
    — Produce development plan on water efficiency
— Flexibility
    — All countries must be able to reallocate water to neighboring
      countries in case of water shortage (climate impact)

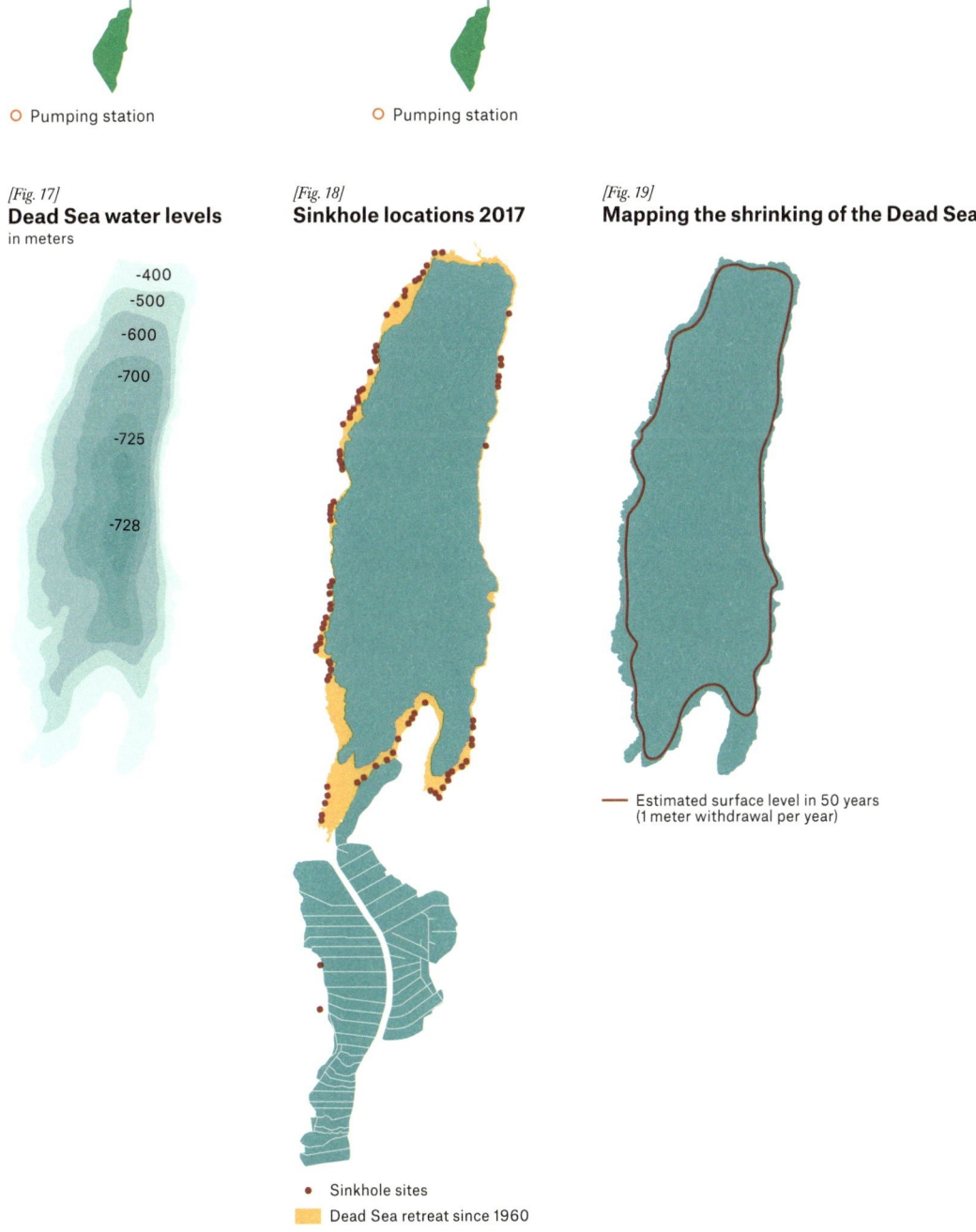

[Fig. 15]
**Jordan River water flow (1950)**
Water inflow along the Jordan Valley

463 MCM
890 MCM
1095 MCM
1300 MCM

○ Pumping station

[Fig. 16]
**Jordan River water flow (2016)**
Growing population, agriculture intensification, and infrastructure causing reduction of water inflow to the Dead Sea

453 MCM
760 MCM
120 MCM
275 MCM

○ Pumping station

[Fig. 17]
**Dead Sea water levels**
in meters

-400
-500
-600
-700
-725
-728

[Fig. 18]
**Sinkhole locations 2017**

• Sinkhole sites
▨ Dead Sea retreat since 1960

[Fig. 19]
**Mapping the shrinking of the Dead Sea**

— Estimated surface level in 50 years (1 meter withdrawal per year)

Territory: Jordan Rift Valley

- Joint Water Commission
    - Re-adjust water re-division in case needed
    - Monitor withdrawals and pollution
    - Establish database
    - Develop Dead Sea Transfer Unit
- Agriculture
    - Feasibility study of the potential establishment of free trade union for agricultural produce (U.N.-controlled study)
- Borders
    - Accept Israeli/Palestinian border according to Geneva Accord (2003)
    - Accept Israeli/Lebanese border according to blue line (U.N. resolution 2000)
    - All borders according to U.N. resolutions
    - Borders along rivers to be demilitarized

## 3.2. Water infrastructure

A fundamental part of the agreement is the creation of a new multinational water infrastructure for the entire basin. Erecting additional desalination plants along the Israeli Mediterranean shoreline will obviate any further need to feed the National Water Carrier with water from the Sea of Galilee. Through knowledge transfer in the field of waste water recycling and efficient irrigation systems from Israel to Palestine, Syria, and Jordan, the fresh water consumption could be reduced by 20 percent. [Fig. 21–23]

Additionally, a common effort to limit human fresh water consumption in the entire region will be necessary. The construction of a Red Sea–Dead Sea pipeline will help irrigate the extremely arid zone of the Arava Valley and support the potash industry with brine from desalination plants. All interventions combined will help re-establish the water flow of the Jordan River to the levels of 1950 and stabilize the water level of the Dead Sea. [Fig. 24–25]

## 3.3. Water network

The multinational water agreement can accelerate the peace process in the Middle East and in consequence lead to the demilitarization of all borders along the Jordan Rift Valley. [Fig. 26] This will allow for full exploration of a continuous linear zone, reaching from the Hula Valley in the north to the Red Sea in the south. Here a combined ancient and new water network will create a cultural landscape that visibly connects agriculture, research, and tourism with the element of water across borders.

## 3.4. Revitalized Jordan Rift Valley

New fertile land along the revived Jordan River will be made accessible for agricultural use. In this linear zone water treatment centers and hydropower stations will be built. From the Hula Valley past the Sea of Galilee to the Dead Sea, a newly created public spine along the Jordan

*[Fig. 20]*
## Jordan River Basin population 2016 and 2050
2050 projection by laba

Jordan River Basin
- ■ Total basin area: 18,285 sq. km
- 👤 Population: 7,810,000 inhabitants (2050: 14,178,614 inh.)
- 🌾 Agricultural land: 150,000 hectare (2050: 181,000 ha)

By country in percentages of total basin numbers 2016 (2050)

LEBANON
- ■ 4 %
- 👤 1 % (2050: 0.9 %)
- 🌾 10 % (2050: 25 %)

SYRIA
- ■ 37 %
- 👤 18 % (2050: 13.5 %)
- 🌾 30 % (2050: 25 %)

ISRAEL
- ■ 10 %
- 👤 4 % (2050: 3.4 %)
- 🌾 30 % (2050: 25 %)

WEST BANK
- ■ 9 %
- 👤 6 % (2050: 13.8 %)
- 🌾 n/a (2050: 8.5 %)

JORDAN
- ■ 40 %
- 👤 71 % (2050: 68.4 %)
- 🌾 30 % (2050: 25 %)

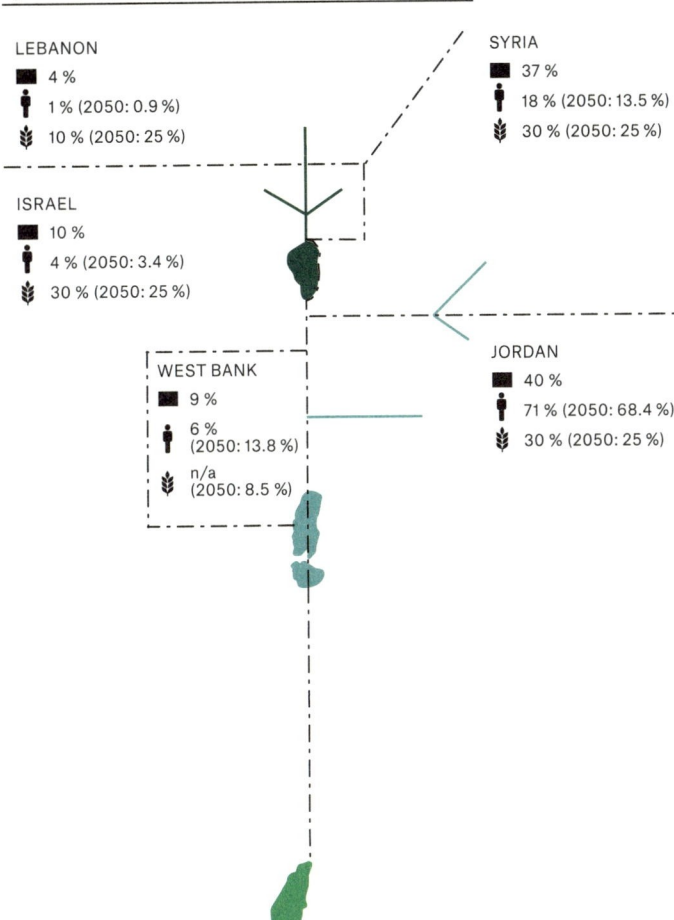

*[Fig. 21]*
## Water consumption: population
in liters/capita/day

☐ 2016    ■ 2050, projection by laba

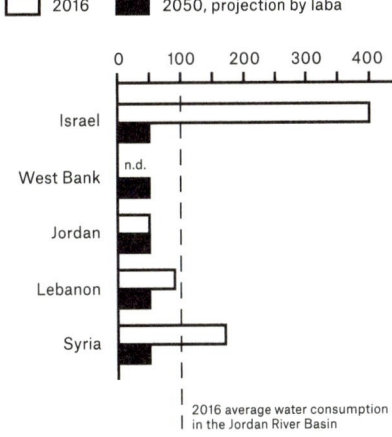

*[Fig. 22]*
## Water consumption: agriculture
in cubic meters/hectare/year

☐ 2016    ■ 2050, projection by laba

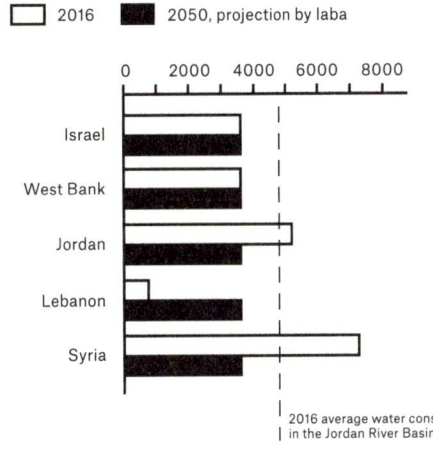

*[Fig. 23]*
## Distribution of water in the Jordan River Basin

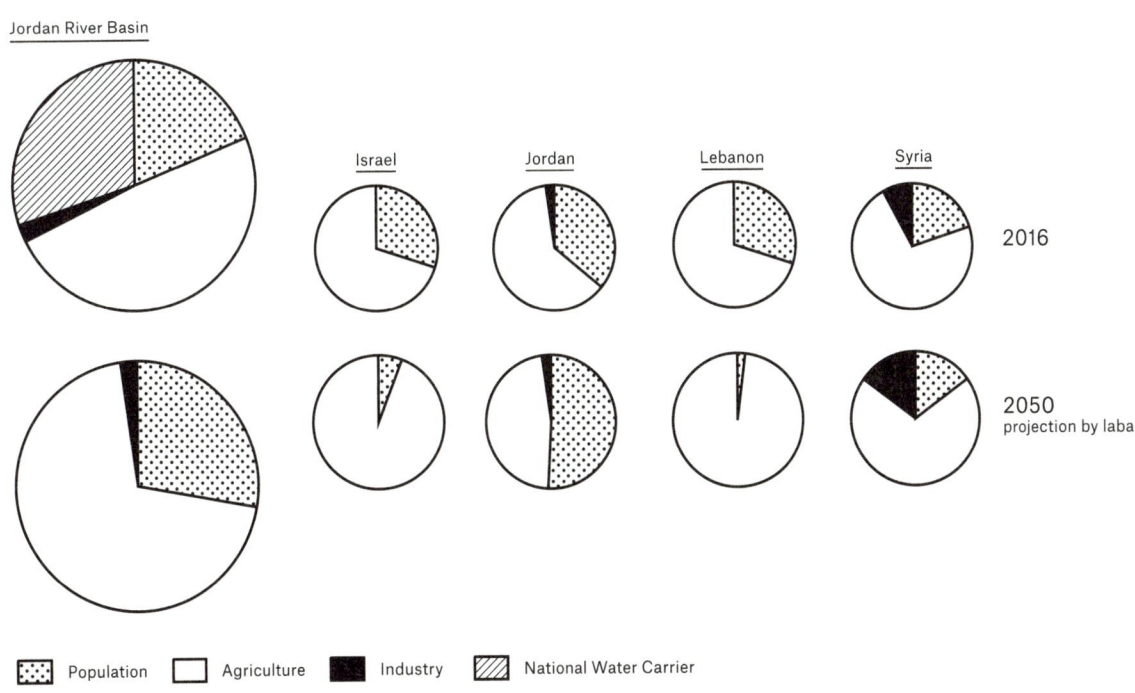

Population · Agriculture · Industry · National Water Carrier

West Bank: n/a

Territory: Jordan Rift Valley

riverbanks will connect recreational, historical, and religious sites with the agrarian/industrial landscape. *[Fig. 27]*

## 3.5. Saving the Dead Sea

Stabilizing the Dead Sea water level will stop further occurrences of sinkholes. Part of the land surrounding the Dead Sea that has been gained by this process will be turned into a nature reserve, preserving the existing sinkholes as a memorial for future generations. Areas close to existing resorts will be utilized for recreational use, reviving the local tourist industry. The excess brine from the desalination plants along the new Red Sea–Dead Sea pipeline will be pumped into the southern evaporation ponds, minimizing the need to use Dead Sea water for the local potash industries.

## 3.6. Research lab Arava Valley

Additional fresh water from the desalination plants along the Red Sea–Dead Sea pipeline allows for the development of new areas for intensive agriculture in the extremely arid climate of the Arava Valley. As a result, the valley's existing research poles will be strengthened, furthering the knowledge of agriculture in arid zones worldwide.

The Jordan Rift Valley: Constitution Maps *[Fig. 28-29]*

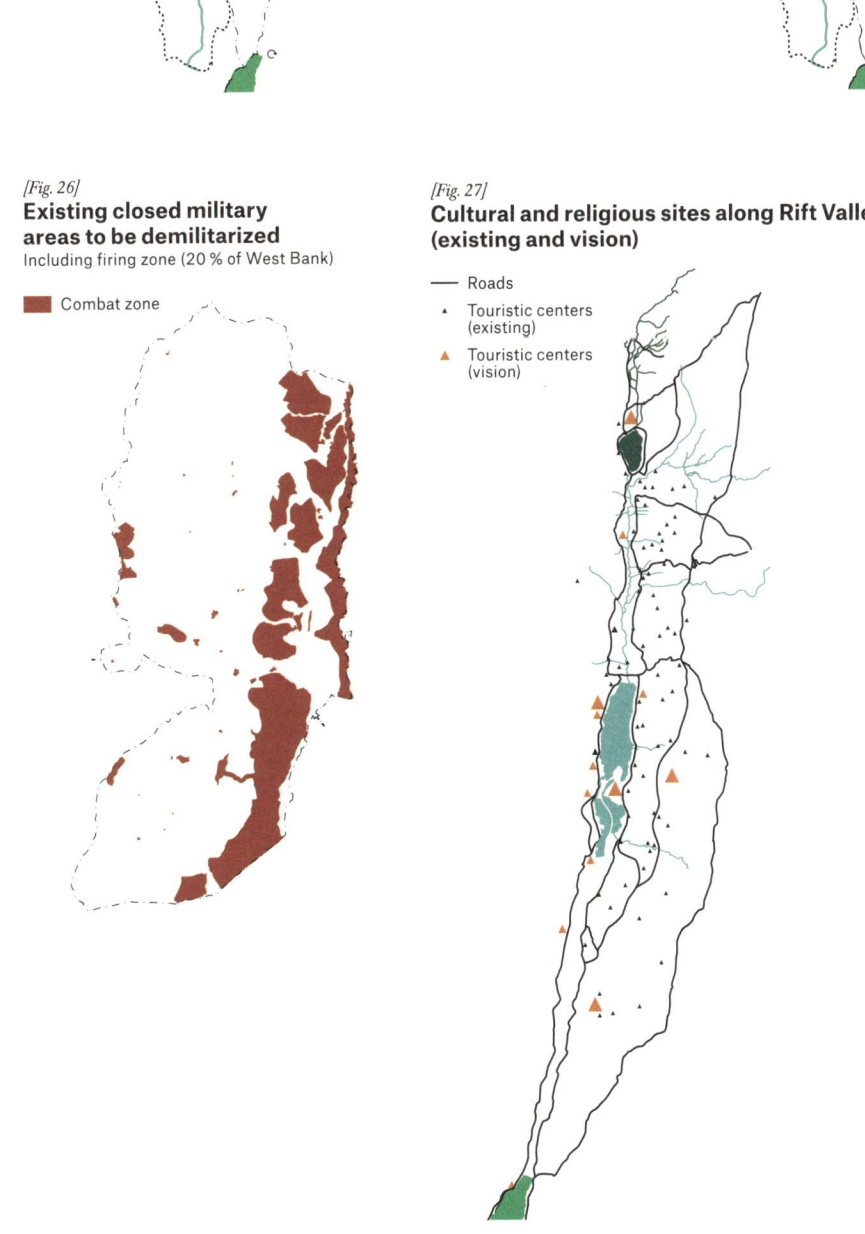

[Fig. 24]
**Water infrastructures (existing)**

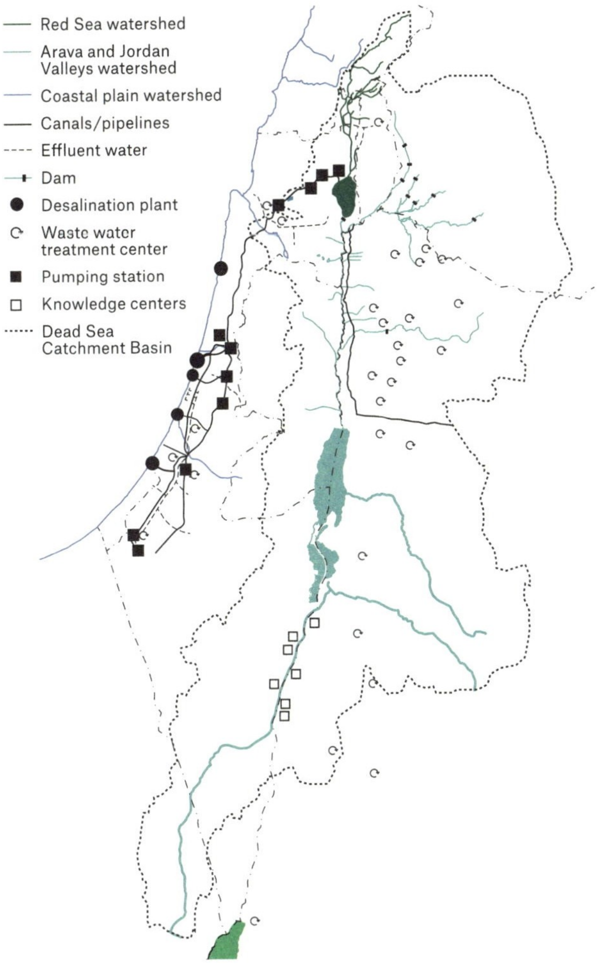

— Red Sea watershed
— Arava and Jordan Valleys watershed
— Coastal plain watershed
— Canals/pipelines
--- Effluent water
↦ Dam
● Desalination plant
↻ Waste water treatment center
■ Pumping station
□ Knowledge centers
⋯ Dead Sea Catchment Basin

[Fig. 25]
**Water infrastructures (vision)**

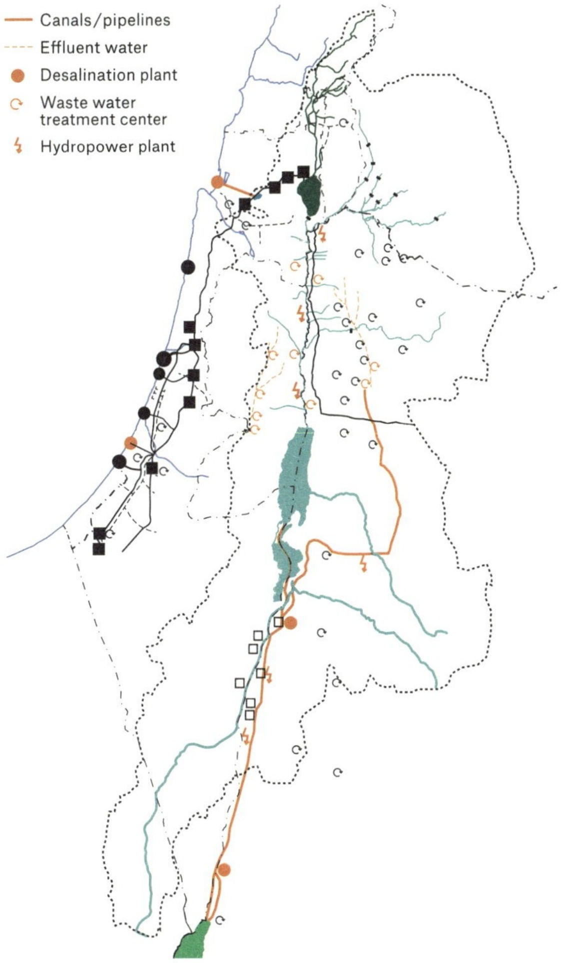

— Canals/pipelines
--- Effluent water
● Desalination plant
↻ Waste water treatment center
⚡ Hydropower plant

[Fig. 26]
**Existing closed military areas to be demilitarized**
Including firing zone (20 % of West Bank)

▬ Combat zone

[Fig. 27]
**Cultural and religious sites along Rift Valley (existing and vision)**

— Roads
▴ Touristic centers (existing)
▲ Touristic centers (vision)

Territory: Jordan Rift Valley    41

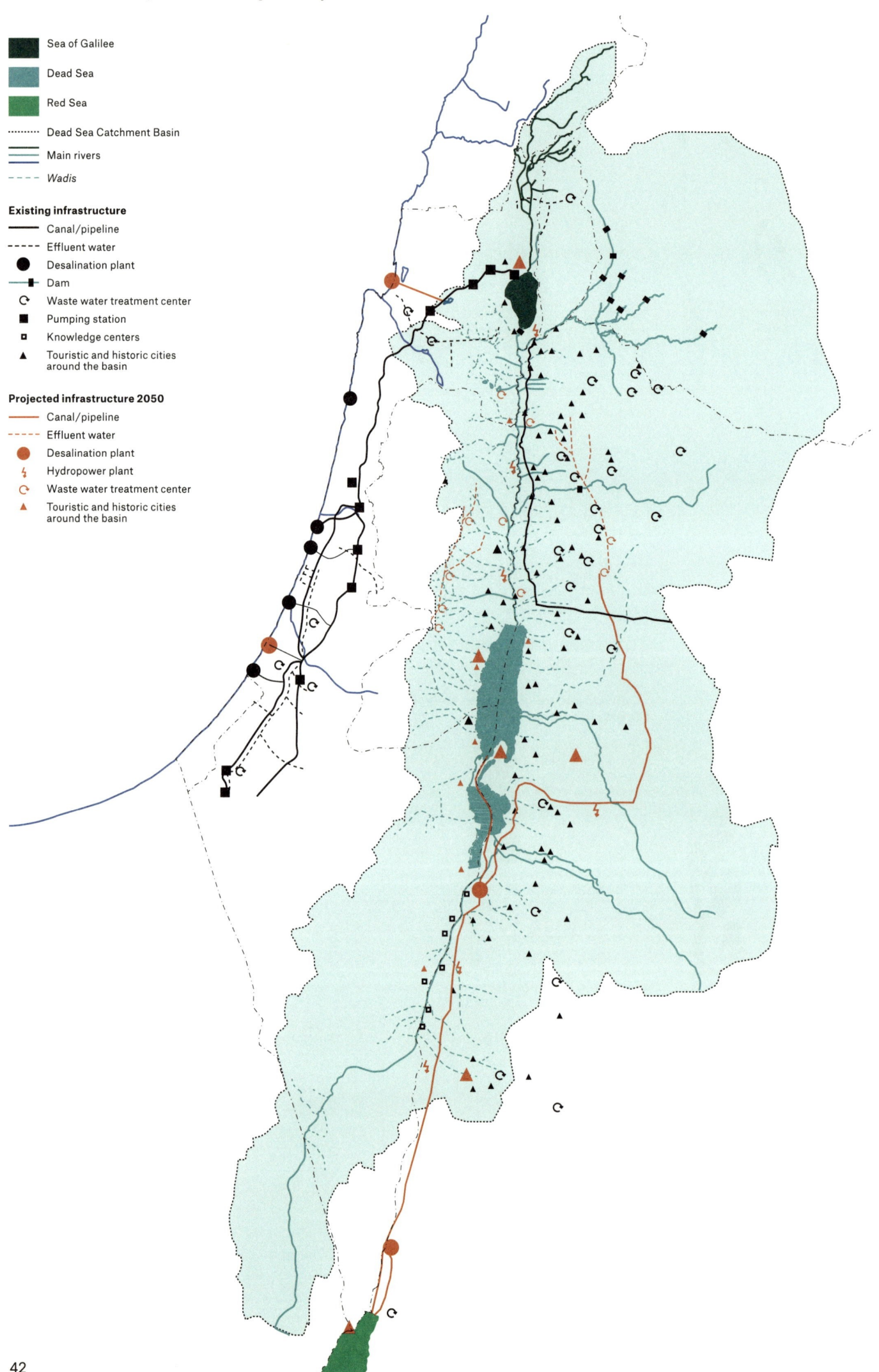

[Fig. 28]
**The Jordan Rift Valley: A Water Management System**

[Fig. 29]
**The Jordan Rift Valley: A Revitalized Region**

- Sea of Galilee
- Dead Sea
- Red Sea
- Jordan Rift Valley
- Main rivers
- Wadis
- Canal/pipeline existing and new
- Dam
- Roads
- Existing agricultural fields
- Potential region for agriculture intensification along the Jordan Valley
- Potential region for agriculture intensification in the south Arava Valley

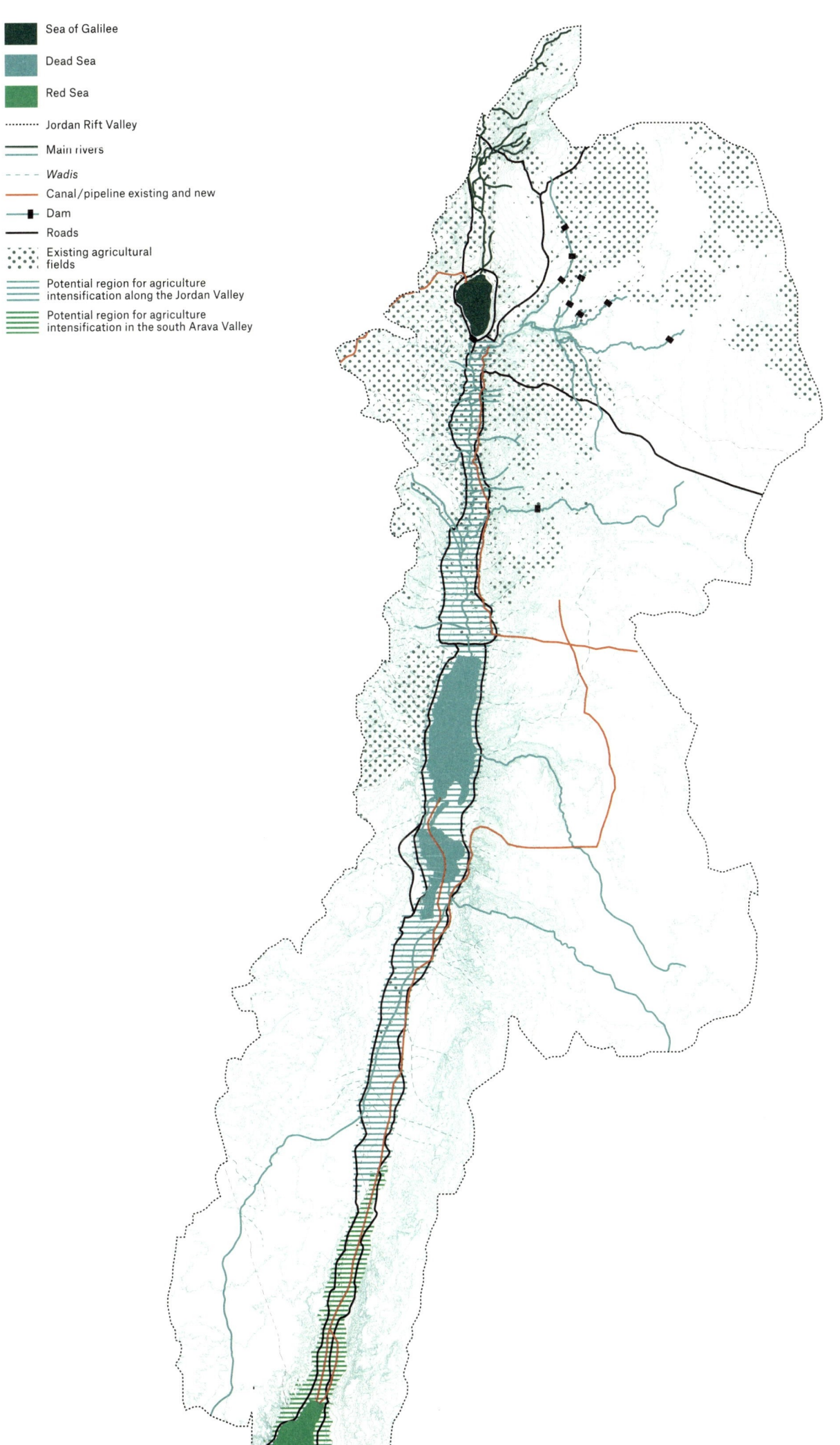

Territory: Jordan Rift Valley 43

# Territory

The Negev Desert: A Productive Landscape

1. Urbanized Desert                              44
2. Threatened Ecosystems               52
3. Constitution: A Productive Landscape    56

# 1. Urbanized Desert

Despite the increasing aridity of the Negev, the region is urbanized and productive, yielding industry, agriculture, and infrastructure and catalyzing further advancement in research and technology. With the advent of the planned railroad connection from the Mediterranean to the Red Sea, the Negev will also act as a trade route for the Middle East.

## 1.1. Open land

The Negev, *Al-Naqab* in Arabic, is a desert and semi-desert stretching across southern Israel to the Red Sea. On a larger scale it belongs to the Saharo-Arabian region and the desert belt that extends from the Sahara over the great Arabian desert to the desert of Sind in India.

The Negev covers over half of Israel, a vast area of 12,000 square kilometers, which represents 57 percent of the Israel's territory. This proportion can be compared to Switzerland, where 65 percent of the territory is covered by the Alps.

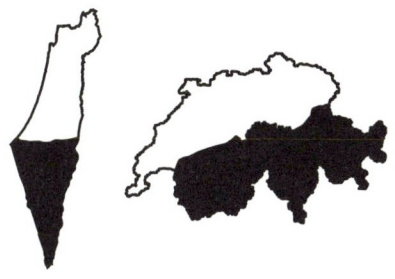

**The Negev Desert:** 57 % of 22,072 sq. km
**Swiss Alps:** 65 % of 41,285 sq. km

### 1.1.1. Rocky landscape

The Negev is a rocky desert. The northern region is a high plateau carved by deep *wadis*, whereas toward the south the desert merges into the Sinai Peninsula, a land bridge between Asia Minor and North Africa.

The rocky landscape of the Negev Desert

### 1.1.2. Arid climate

According to Thornthwaite's moisture studies the Negev has an arid climate. Wladimir Köppen and Rudolph Geiger define the Negev as a hot desert with winter rainfall. The annual average precipitation in the Negev is between 25 and 200 millimeters. The sparse and highly irregular rainfalls are related to the "lows" that occur during the winter season over the Mediterranean but only rarely reach the Negev. *[Fig. 1–3]*

The Negev can be divided into climatic sub-regions that impact their land use. *[Fig. 4]* The coastal strip, bounded by the Mediterranean on the west, is subdesertic with mild winters and warm summers. Although climatic conditions are similar to the coastal plains in the north, the average rainfall is lower. The central Negev highlands, lying between 100 meters to 500 meters above sea level, have the climate of a temperate desert, with cool winters and warm summers. The mountain region lies above 500 meters, where dry hot summers and cold winters prevail. The Arava Valley stretches from the Red Sea to the Dead Sea. Its climate is characterized by a dry season lasting the whole year, a high annual mean temperature, and low relative humidity.[1]

## 1.2. Colonized territory

Contrary to the preconceived ideas of the Negev as a harsh, hostile, untouched natural landscape, the region can be described as a productive urbanized territory. It comprises large industrial sites, agricultural regions, public and military infrastructures, planted forest, railways, and energy fields. Nevertheless, it is only inhabited by 8.1 percent of Israel's total population. *[Fig. 5]*

### 1.2.1. Nomadism: Land of Bedouins

The first recorded nomadic settlement in Sinai dates back 4,000 to 7,000 years.[2] Bedouin sedentarization began under Ottoman rule. The Bedouins' nomadic lifestyle was viewed as a threat to the state's control. A new Ottoman law was brought into force to provide the administration with "special powers of control of nomadic or semi-nomadic tribes with the object of persuading them towards a more settled way of life."[3]

Prior to the founding of Israel, the population of the Negev consisted almost entirely of 110,000 Bedouins.[4] After the war in 1948 only 11,000 remained. The rest had fled or were expelled to Jordan, the Sinai Peninsula, the Gaza Strip, or the West Bank. The first Israeli government, headed by Prime Minister David Ben-Gurion, opposed the return of the Bedouin from Jordan and Egypt. Most of the Bedouin land fell under the Ottoman classification as "non-workable" *mawat* land and thus belonged to the state under Ottoman law. Israel nationalized most of the Negev's lands, using the Land Rights Settlement Ordinance from 1969.

Between 1968 and 1989 the state established urban townships for the housing of deported Bedouin tribes and promised the Bedouin services in exchange for the renunciation of their ancestral land.[5]

Within a few years, half of the Bedouin population moved into the seven townships built for them by the Israeli government. The largest Bedouin locality in Israel is the city of Rahat, established in 1971. Today 160,000 Bedouins live in the Negev. They represent 25 percent of the Negev's population.[6] *[Fig. 6]*

### 1.2.2. Zionism: The great Negev asset

Jews represent the remaining 75 percent of the Negev's population. This over-representation is the result of the pioneering ideology of "conquering the desert" or "making the desert bloom," as envisioned by Ben-Gurion.[9]

> The Negev is a great Zionist asset, with no substitute anywhere in the country. First of all, it constitutes half of the State of Israel. ... The Negev is a desolate area which is currently empty of people, and therein lies its importance. What it lacks is water and Jews. It has the potential to be densely populated, even amounting to millions. ... [T]wo million Jews can be settled there with agriculture, and two million with industry.[10]

### 1.2.3. Agriculture: Make the desert bloom

Ben Gurion saw the desert's settlement possibilities if the inhabitants would take on the challenge of developing agriculture and industry. *[Fig. 7]* The initiative can be described by the following subcategories:

Coastal sub-region crop farming:
One of Ben-Gurion's early decisions was to construct the National Water Carrier transferring water from the Sea of Galilee to the northern Negev.

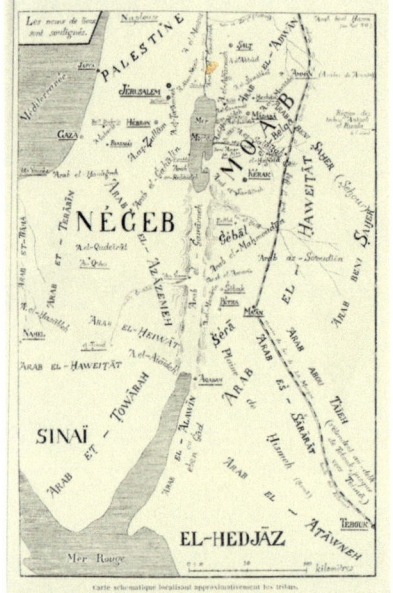
Bedouin tribes in 1908 [7]

Bedouin settlements along the *wadis* [8]

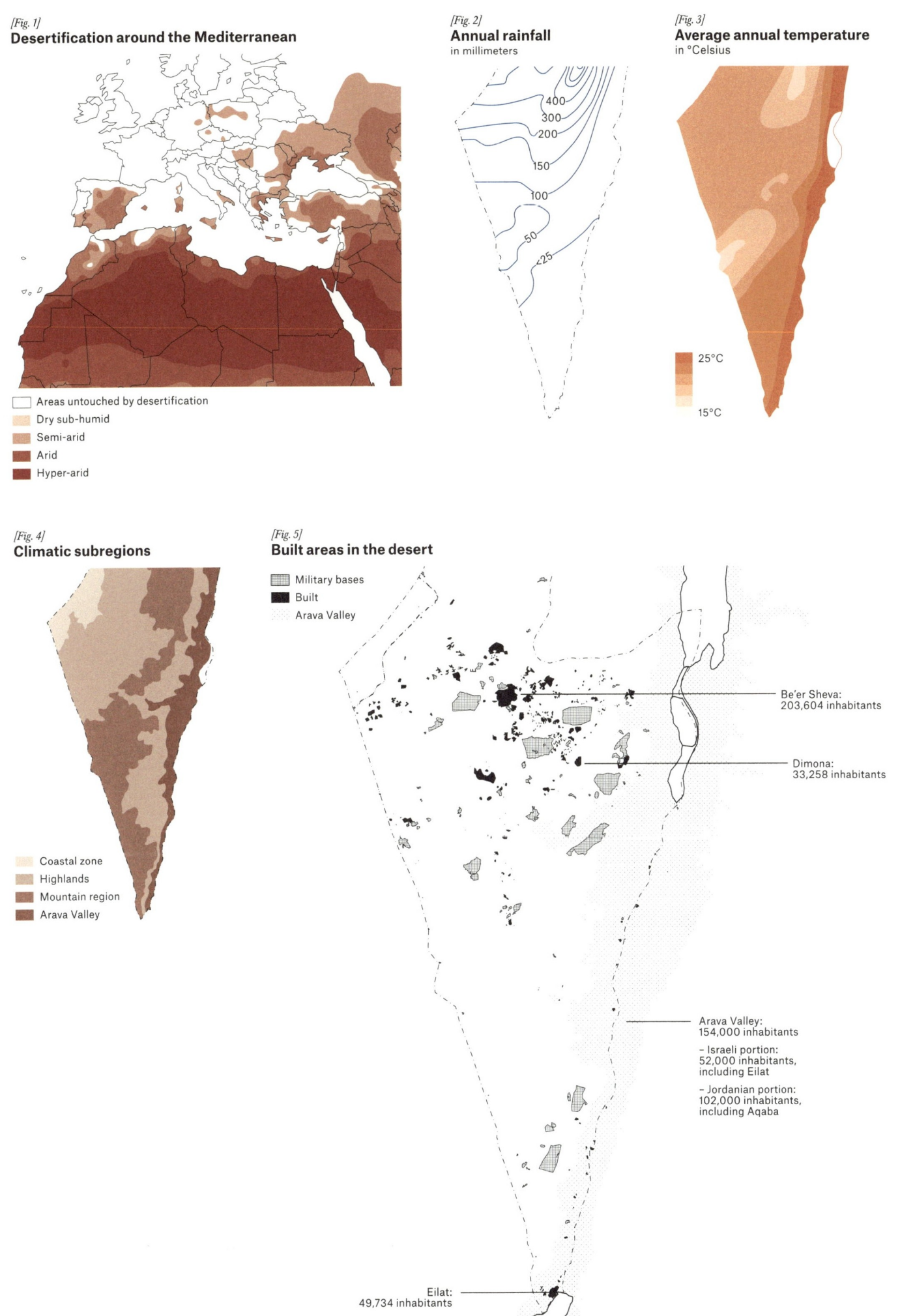

Territory: Negev Desert

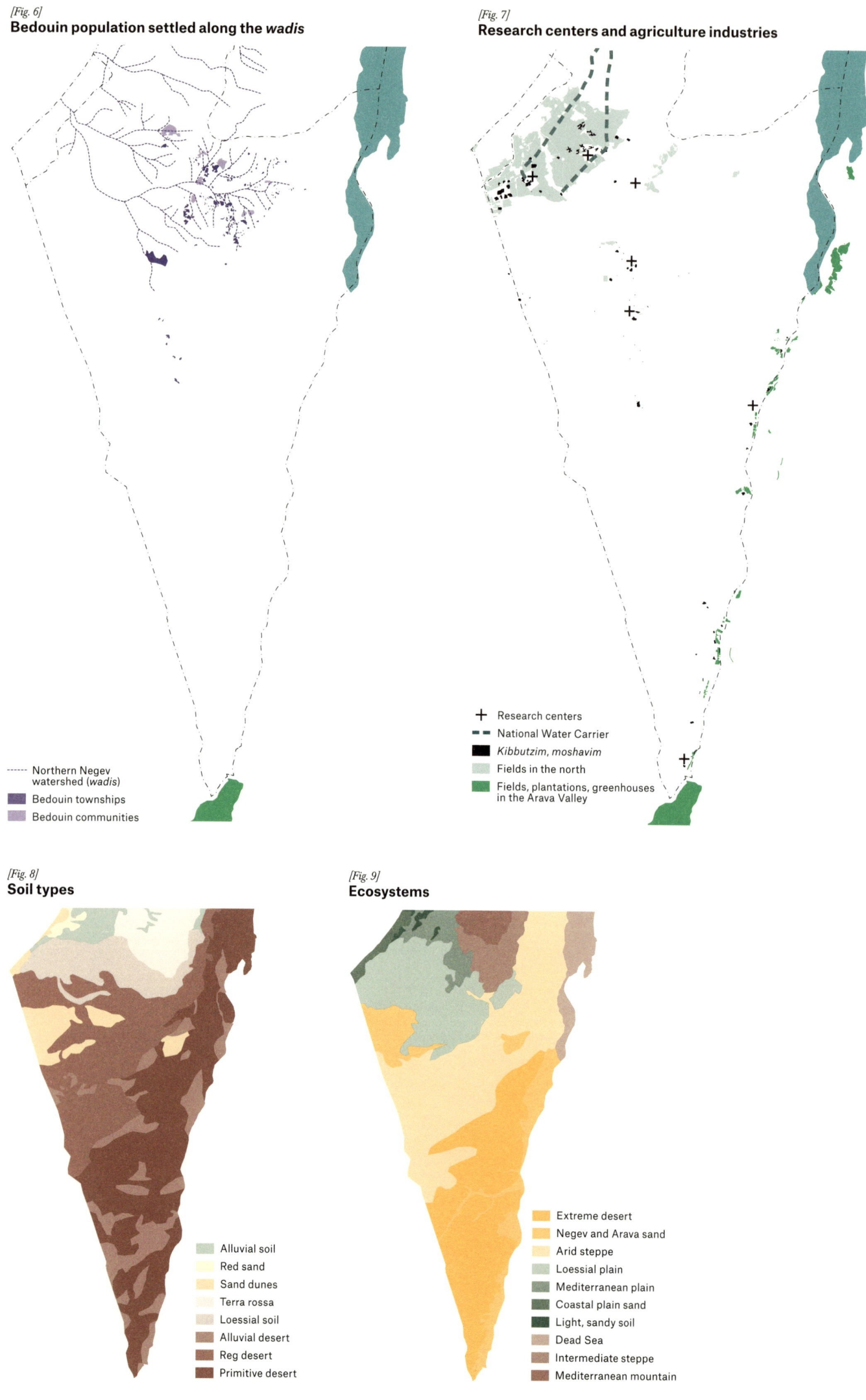

[Fig. 6]
**Bedouin population settled along the wadis**

- - - - - Northern Negev watershed (wadis)
- Bedouin townships
- Bedouin communities

[Fig. 7]
**Research centers and agriculture industries**

+ Research centers
- - - National Water Carrier
- Kibbutzim, moshavim
- Fields in the north
- Fields, plantations, greenhouses in the Arava Valley

[Fig. 8]
**Soil types**

- Alluvial soil
- Red sand
- Sand dunes
- Terra rossa
- Loessial soil
- Alluvial desert
- Reg desert
- Primitive desert

[Fig. 9]
**Ecosystems**

- Extreme desert
- Negev and Arava sand
- Arid steppe
- Loessial plain
- Mediterranean plain
- Coastal plain sand
- Light, sandy soil
- Dead Sea
- Intermediate steppe
- Mediterranean mountain

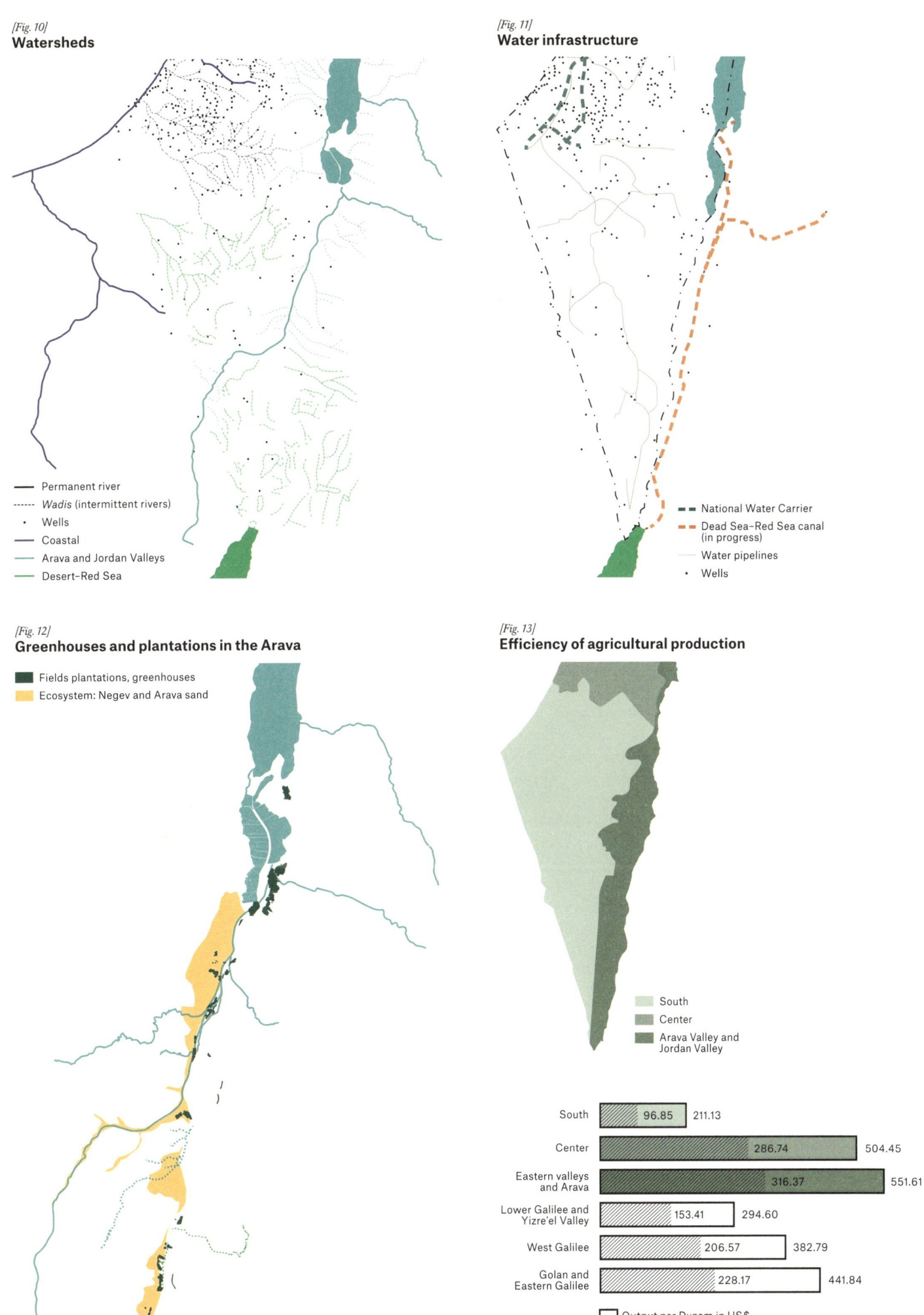

[Fig. 10]
**Watersheds**

— Permanent river
···· Wadis (intermittent rivers)
· Wells
— Coastal
— Arava and Jordan Valleys
— Desert–Red Sea

[Fig. 11]
**Water infrastructure**

– – National Water Carrier
– – Dead Sea–Red Sea canal (in progress)
— Water pipelines
· Wells

[Fig. 12]
**Greenhouses and plantations in the Arava**

■ Fields plantations, greenhouses
■ Ecosystem: Negev and Arava sand

[Fig. 13]
**Efficiency of agricultural production**

■ South
■ Center
■ Arava Valley and Jordan Valley

| Region | Gross value added per Dunam in US$ | Output per Dunam in US$ |
|---|---|---|
| South | 96.85 | 211.13 |
| Center | 286.74 | 504.45 |
| Eastern valleys and Arava | 316.37 | 551.61 |
| Lower Galilee and Yizre'el Valley | 153.41 | 294.60 |
| West Galilee | 206.57 | 382.79 |
| Golan and Eastern Galilee | 228.17 | 441.84 |

☐ Output per Dunam in US$
▨ Gross value added per Dunam in US$

Territory: Negev Desert  49

Aquaculture at the Kibbutz Ketura

Palm tree plantation in the Arava Valley

Greenhouse tents in the Arava Valley

This project enabled the development of intensive agriculture, based on traditional crop farming.

Nevertheless, the economic capacity of agricultural production in this area is lower than the national average and is called into question today. This is due to the relative remoteness of the region, the poor quality of the soil, and extensive water consumption for irrigation. According to the Agricultural Survey of Israel, the agricultural production in the Negev is the least efficient, both in terms of output and gross value added. [Fig. 8–11]

Arava Valley plantations and greenhouses:
In contrast, the high-tech farms and the date palm plantations prevailing in the landscape of the Arava Valley are highly productive. This region alone produces about 60 percent of the total Israeli export of fresh vegetables and about 10 percent of the cut flowers exported.[11] The production is intensive due to the common use of greenhouses, the rich fossil reservoir of brackish water, the relatively warm winters (which create an advantage in seasonal production[12]), and the technology and knowledge that make Israel a leader in desert farming. [Fig. 12–13]

### 1.2.4. Knowledge: The role of the frontrunner

Ben Gurion's vision for the Negev would not have been possible without the advances of research and new technology. The Negev became the experimental ground for Israel's scientific endeavors and the development of new areas of research that would benefit the population in the north: namely, the desalination of seawater; the exploitation of solar energy and wind power; the management of scarce rain water; and the analysis of the local vegetation.[13]

Over the past 25 years agricultural output has increased sevenfold[14] with hardly any increase in the amount of water used. This reflects technological advances of different types: water efficiency (up by more than 30 percent), and crops with higher yields and market value. To reduce water consumption for agriculture, advanced water-saving techniques were applied, notably the drip system, which directs the water flow straight to the root zone of plants. In addition, computerized irrigation systems were introduced, and climate-controlled greenhouse agriculture was significantly expanded.

The Ben-Gurion University is at the center of this desert-specific knowledge. It was established in 1969 as the University of the Negev with the aim of promoting the development of the area. It consists of five campuses, numerous academic departments and units, research institutes, and interdisciplinary research centers scattered throughout the whole region of the Negev.

### 1.2.5. Trade: Land bridge on the Silk Road

Another asset of the Negev is its strategic location on the Silk Road between two important trading regions: the Mediterranean basin and the Middle East/India/Asia. [Fig. 14]

A project for a new high-speed railway for passengers and commercial freight between Eilat on the Red Sea and Ashdod on the Mediterranean will intensify the region's activity. [Fig. 15] It will be an alternative to the land shipping route and will thereby avoid the Suez Canal. The port of Eilat will gain importance, and Eilat itself, with its new airport, is potentially developing into a metropolitan area. The Negev will also benefit from this infrastructure in terms of tourism attractiveness, transport of goods, and improved access for future residents.

## 2. Threatened Ecosystems

Israel's government intends to react to the growing public pressure around the issue of high living costs of the middle class by releasing more land in the north for residential building. The urbanization pushes agriculture, industries, and military bases into the desert. Global warming, polluting manufacture, agriculture, and afforestation are threatening the fragile ecosystem of the Negev and Bedouin culture.

### 2.1. Desertification

Situated on the edge of a desert zone, Israel is strongly affected by climate change, and a significant mean temperature increase causing droughts and floods is predicted. By 2050, the northward shift of the desert zone is expected to be 300 to 500 kilometers. As a consequence, arable land at the edge of the Negev may slowly transform into desert landscapes. B. A. Portnov and U. N. Safriel explain how agriculture and heavy industries are always the main causes of desertification:

> [T]hey cause land degradation due to soil erosion, soil and water salinisation, and loss of biodiversity. Population and urbanisation pressure is thus putting more drylands at risk of further desertification. These processes are bound to intensify in Israel, and probably also in many other Mediterranean countries. The first victim of desertification caused by agriculture is agriculture itself. As a result, dryland agriculture is often abandoned, leaving behind an ecosystem that ceases to provide environmental services, and is costly or even impossible to rehabilitate. Thus, by pushing agriculture from non-desert to desert, not only agriculture itself may be doomed, but also alternative uses of the desert, such as conservation of biodiversity, recreation, eco-tourism and tourism, are excluded.[15]

Due to a sustained accelerated population growth, urbanization will eventually also increase in the desert, but by then further desertification and pollution will also have taken place.

### 2.2. Dumping ground

The Negev is not only being exploited in terms of natural resources, but also serves as a site for numerous chemical industries. This development leads to serious side effects of water, soil and air pollution and affecting the health of the nearby population. Negligence and non-regulation in waste management pose an even higher risk of large scale contamination.

Noam Industrial Park [19]

Eilat N. Shkhoret Industrial Park

Dudaim landfill [23]

### 2.2.1. Chemical industry

Although Israel has few natural resources compared to nearby oil-producing countries, it is a major player in the production of fertilizers, bromine, refined oils, petrochemicals, pharmaceuticals, and cosmetics[16]. The Dead Sea and the Negev are the region's two major locations for mineral extraction and chemical industries. *[Fig. 16]*

The main chemical activity is phosphate rock extraction. Most of the world's agriculture enterprises depend on this mineral as a source of phosphorous for fertilizer to enhance soil productivity; there are about 20 deposits in the Negev region.[17] One of the biggest deposits, Har Nishpe, is located near En Yahav.

In addition to mining, 29 large industrial sites are located in the Negev.[18] The largest, Ne'ot Hovav, located in the Ramat Hovav area, is made up of 19 chemical factories, including a pesticide plant, a pharmaceutical plant, and a bromine plant. Most of those plants produce large quantities of wastewater, with a composition and concentration of hazardous substances that are difficult to treat. *[Fig. 17]*

### 2.2.2. Waste

Besides these polluting industries, the Negev is also home to most of the country's waste disposal facilities. 40 percent of the country's hazardous waste from industrial plants is disposed of at Ramat Hovav, Dudaim, or other sites.

After the sorting process, dry waste is turned into energy, organic waste is used as raw material for compost, and the remainder is poured into a landfill[21] or sent to other plants in the country.

Unfortunately, along with this recycling process, evaporation ponds are also still commonly used. These pollute the air, and cancer-causing chemicals leak into the soil and water. According to Israeli environmentalist Alon Tal, the waste is not pretreated before being transported to the site. Storage facilities are weak, barrels are often rusted, toxic residues unlabeled, and reactive materials stored near containers of cyanide.[22]

In this sector regulation is not rigid enough. The environmental consequences of these negligent practices are extremely severe. The pollution causes high levels of contamination of the ground water and incidence of cancers in nearby residents. According to environmentalist Batia Sarov, an explosion in Ramat Hovav, with the concentration of so many industries, could contaminate not simply local Negev residents but all of Israel and many of its Middle Eastern neighbors. The contamination level would be similar to that of a nuclear explosion.[24]

## 2.3. Tightening Bedouins' land

The Bedouins who are located in the northern region and exposed to the polluting industries are its main victims.

Still another condition is impacting this nomadic community. The "open" desert is subject to large governmental plans[25] defining regions in the desert, such has nature reserves or forest, where building or grazing are forbidden. The Bedouins' space is shrinking, which threatens their capacity to conduct a nomadic lifestyle.

*[Fig. 14]*
**Silk Road**

— Maritime routes
— Main Silk Road
• Cities

*[Fig. 15]*
**"Red-Med" project**
Railway between Eilat on the Red Sea to Ashdod on the Mediterranean Sea, bypassing the Suez Canal

— Maritime routes
— Red-Med railway
• Cities

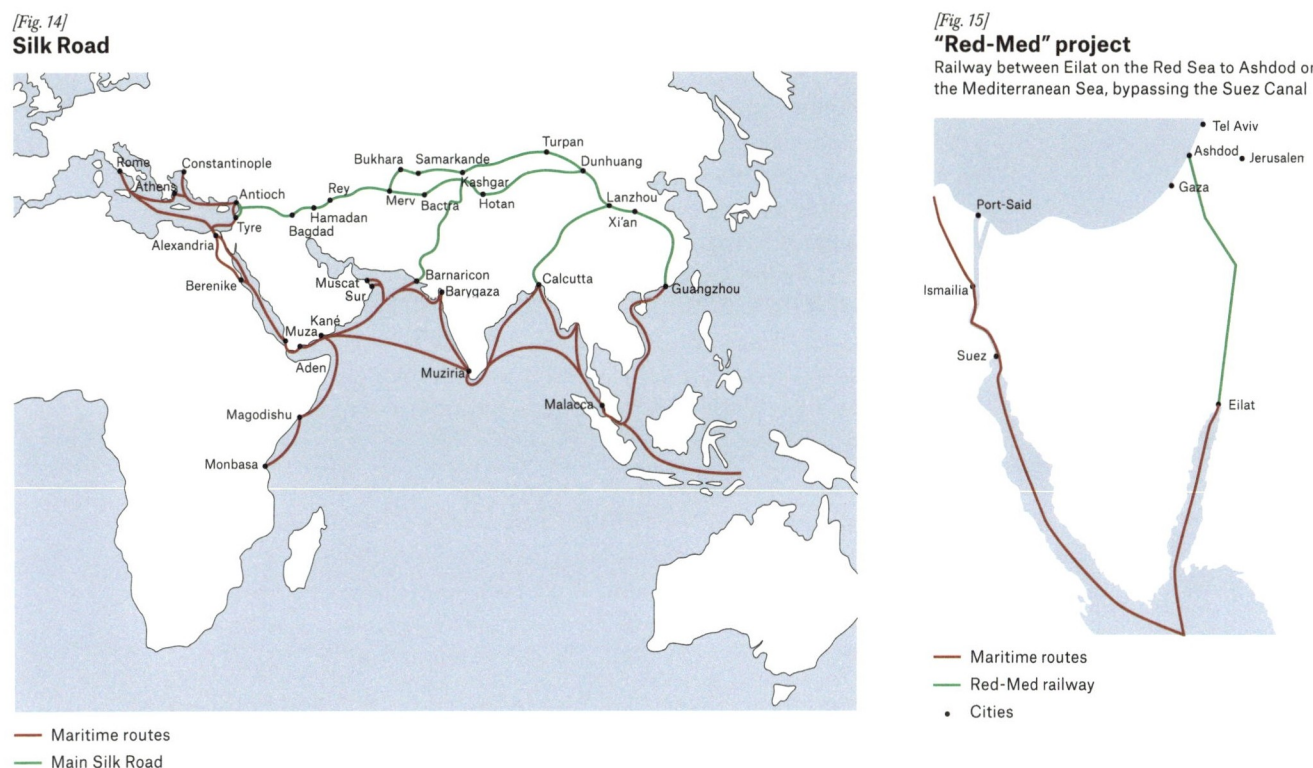

*[Fig. 16]*
**Export of agricultural inputs in 2000**
in millions of US$

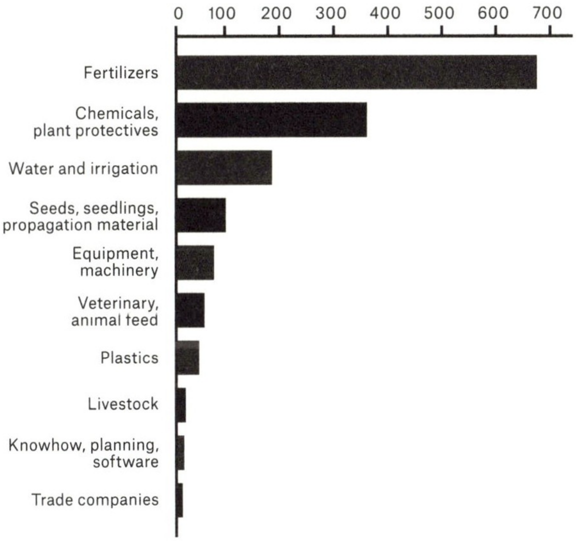

*[Fig. 17]*
**Industries in the Negev**

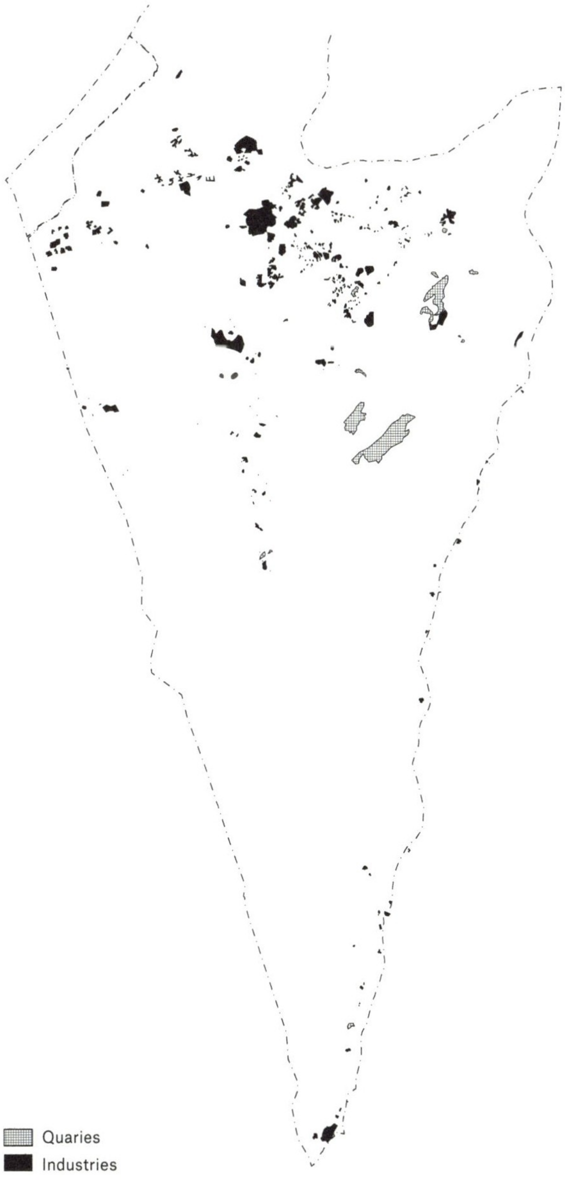

▦ Quaries
■ Industries

Territory: Negev Desert   53

### 2.3.1. Controversial forests

One of the governmental plans putting pressure on the Bedouins' land is the afforestation initiative.

During the past 50 years Israel has planted over 260 million trees in an effort to improve the landscape and to stop desertification. The afforestation plan has a long history; Israel has been planting trees ever since Jews have been moving to the region. At the beginning the impulse was pragmatic (to prevent erosion), political (to assert Jewish ownership), and ideological (to transform the dry Arab landscape into something more European, more familiar and hospitable).[26, 27] [Fig. 18]

After the 1948 war the afforestation project took a different turn. Chaim Blass, who worked at the Jewish National Fund, explained the motivation:

> Foresting really began with the first kibbutzim. ... There were two ideological goals to the initiative. First, to help the economies of the kibbutz. But there was also a practical element: holding the lands, so that they wouldn't revert to Arab hands. And tree planting was a good way to achieve it. First of all, British law protected trees, which provided some legitimacy. And there was no activity that could hold land as cheaply as forestation.[28]

A large afforestation master plan was approved in 1995. It embraces a total of 162,000 hectare of woodlands and open areas—over 15 percent of Israel's total land area north of Be'er Sheva, in which most of the Negev's population is concentrated.[29] The Bedouins and the exiled Palestinian residents of the Negev suffer from this present afforestation situation. The use of foreign tree species, which are often heavier water consumers than the indigenous species, enhances desertification.

This observation has also been made by Professor Eyal Weizman, who sees in the afforestation project a plan to move the line delineating the desert. As a consequence the palestinian population is systematically evicted from their villages situated in the proximity of this line.[30]

### 2.3.2. Nature reserves

The quadrupling of the population, the rise in the standard of living, and the vast expansion of tourism, have brought large numbers of hikers and trippers to the countryside. To protect the flora and fauna, another plan called the "National Parks and Nature Reserves Act" was approved by the Israeli Knesset in 1963. Since 1998 the Israel Nature and Park Authority has been in charge of this act, and the new authority's aim is "to preserve Israel's green areas in the face of rapid urban development, increasing transportation needs, and the steep growth of Israel's population".[31]

There are 380 nature reserves in Israel, which represent 6,130 kilometers[32] or 27 percent of the overall land. In the Negev, nature reserves and forests cover almost half of the territory. [Fig. 18] Nature conservation deals, by definition, with minimizing changes in the ecosystem, usually by excluding human interference and stabilizing a desired situation. As a consequence, the designated areas are off limits for building and even for Bedouins who had previously lived there. In fact, the designation of land as nature reserves often masks policies of land confiscation, as well as confiscation of the livestock of the Bedouin communities and Palestinian home demolitions.[33]

[Fig. 18]
**Forest and nature reserves in the Negev**

Forests
Nature reserves

[Fig. 19]
**Military bases and firing zones**

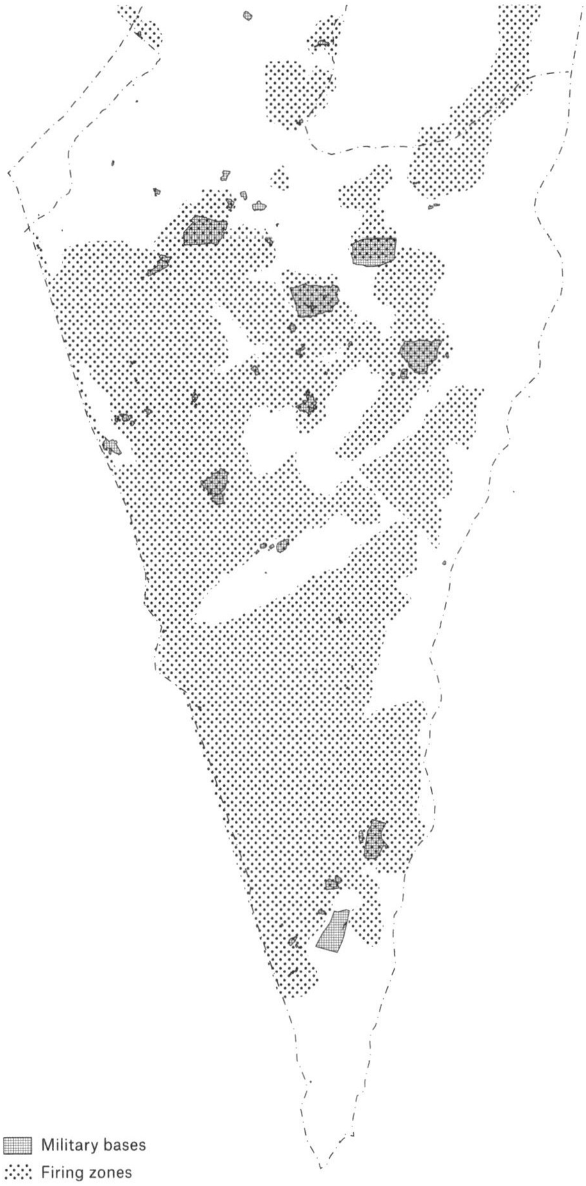

Military bases
Firing zones

Territory: Negev Desert

### 2.3.3. Firing zones

Part of the plan to free up space in northern Israel is to relocate and build new military megabases (with 12,500 personnel and civilian staff) in the desert.[34]

Firing zones were initially established as a means of land control. *[Fig. 19]* Now they are being used to create an environment so hostile that Bedouins are forced to leave the area. *[Fig. 20]*

The Israeli policy to occupy the desert through settling and cultivation as well as applying restrictions to large open spaces has drastically reduced the capacity of the Bedouin communities to conduct a nomadic lifestyle. The desertification reduces the area of the desert where their activities can be carried out. They are now pushed to the north or forced to settle in Bedouin towns. Hopefully this condition will be reversed by the recent governmental measures to help these communities by offering a basic health and education infrastructure, as well as recognizing some of the Bedouin villages.

A view of the new Combined Military Training Bases in the Negev Desert, near Be'er Sheva. The vacated Israel Defense Force bases in the central region will be earmarked for the general housing market.[35]

# 3. Constitution: A Productive Landscape

This constitution attempts to identify new landscapes that are generated by post-industrial agriculture in arid zones and to define three different ecologies.

Each ecology corresponds to a set of geographical, urban, cultural, and technical conditions. Contrary to the common reading of the Negev as a hostile and worthless territory, the three ecologies intend to amplify the area's richness and intrinsic value.

Targeting specific activities, all three ecologies are interconnected through a grid of existing and new infrastructures.
Expertise as a steering element: The territory of the Negev Desert lends itself as a place for innovative experiments on correcting the "image of desertification as an unstoppable monster slowly consuming the world's fertile lands, plants, livestock and people."[36] Having already gained expertise in managing drylands, Israel could emphasize its pioneering role and support other regions affected by desertification with its knowledge and technologies.

The constitution "Three Negev Ecologies" is a proposal to invert the common perception of this landscape by foregrounding its character and potential.

## 3.1. Loessial plain: Bedouin heritage

This ecology is linked to the loessial plain ecosystem and part of the highland and mountain climate zone. The region is characterized by the traditional farming of the semi-nomadic communities specializing in husbandry. Bedouin know-how and experience with this territory characterized by very low precipitation, wind, and erosion of the loessial soil is key to successful future management of dry zones. *[Fig. 21]*

The project proposes to intensify the *wadi* network as a structure for the Bedouins to define their territory. Their development is highly bound

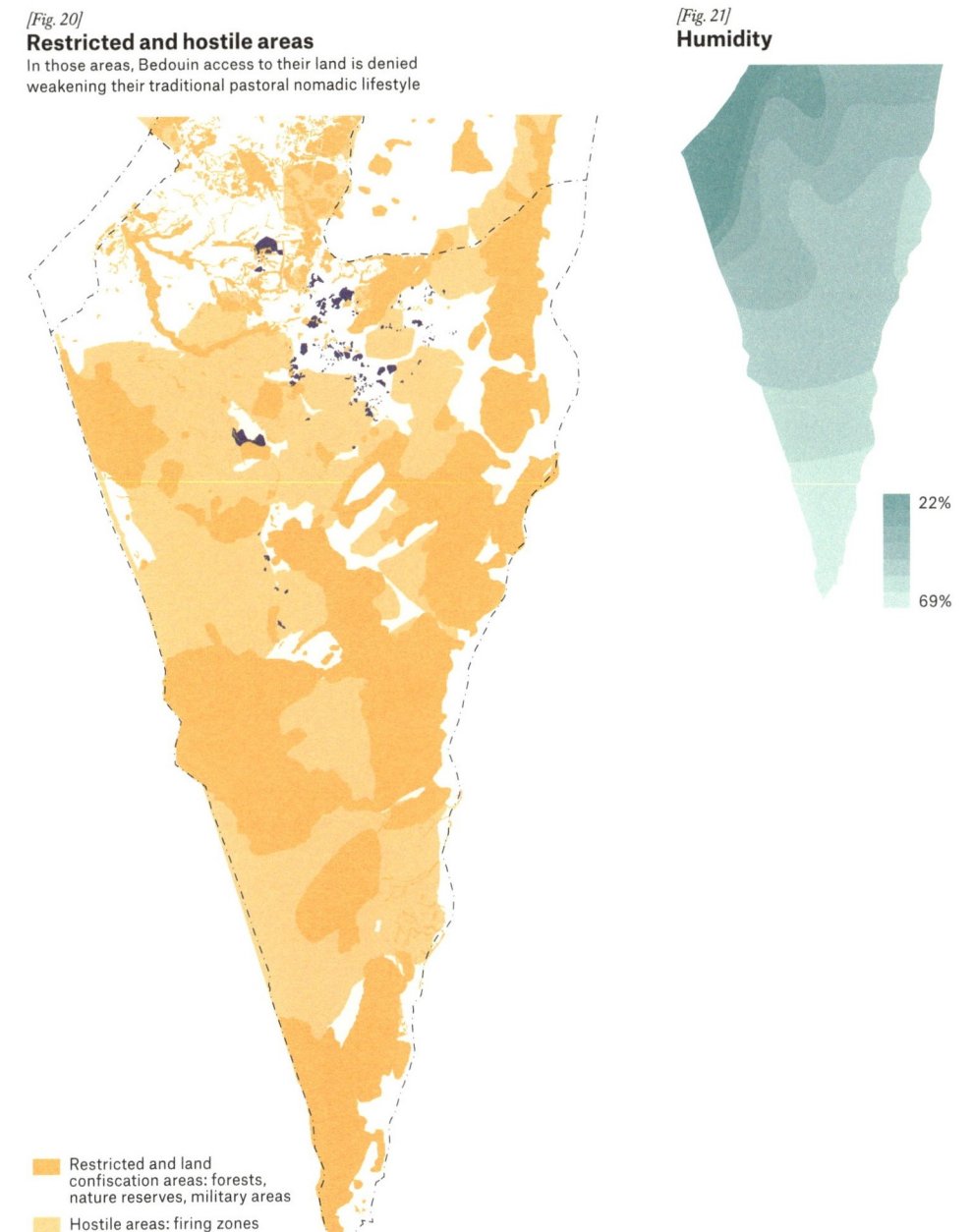

*[Fig. 20]*
**Restricted and hostile areas**
In those areas, Bedouin access to their land is denied weakening their traditional pastoral nomadic lifestyle

▨ Restricted and land confiscation areas: forests, nature reserves, military areas
▨ Hostile areas: firing zones
▨ Bedouin communities

*[Fig. 21]*
**Humidity**

22%
69%

Territory: Negev Desert

Liman irrigation system **37**

Project Wadi Attir's ecosystem restoration initiative is counteracting desertification. **38**

to the soil and water. Rather than relocating and concentrating these communities, the project encourages Bedouins to set up along this watershed ecosystem where they can proceed with their activities. Proximity to larger towns allows for a younger generation to choose between staying in the family's living traditions or moving to the cities.

## 3.2. Extreme desert and arid steppe: Energy field

Parts of the most hostile areas of the Negev are designated for the production of renewable energies. Since this production is based on solar panels and windmills the energy fields are chosen following geographical and climatic criteria such as high solar radiation and wind forces. The proposed areas exclude bird-migration corridors and existing Bedouin settlements. [Fig. 22–24]

## 3.3. Arava Valley: Plantation grid and greenhouse garden

As explained in Paragraph 1.2.3., the economic capacity of intensive crop fields in the northern Negev is lower than the national average. It cannot be sustained neither economically nor ecologically. The proposal is to reduce the impact of intensive agriculture in the north by focusing and intensifying production in the Arava Valley.

This ecology describes the area situated in the flatlands along the Rift Valley south of the Dead Sea. The combination of soil type and climate allows for an intensification of agriculture to balance the loss in the northern region. Alluvial sand deposits offer flatland in the north for controlled-environment agriculture. For reasons of shading and because of the significant drop in temperature at night, the production relies on greenhouses. These high-tech greenhouse garden farms will produce the major share of the national production of vegetables.

In the southern part of the Arava Valley, where precipitation drops to under 50 millimeters per year, an intensification of the plantation grid can be considered. It consists mainly of palm tree crops—a crop that grows well in brackish water.

The urbanization of this region should follow the linear agricultural development that takes place along the Israeli and Jordanian roads, contrasting with the mountainous desert landscapes that frame the site.

The Negev Desert: Constitution Maps [Fig. 25–26]

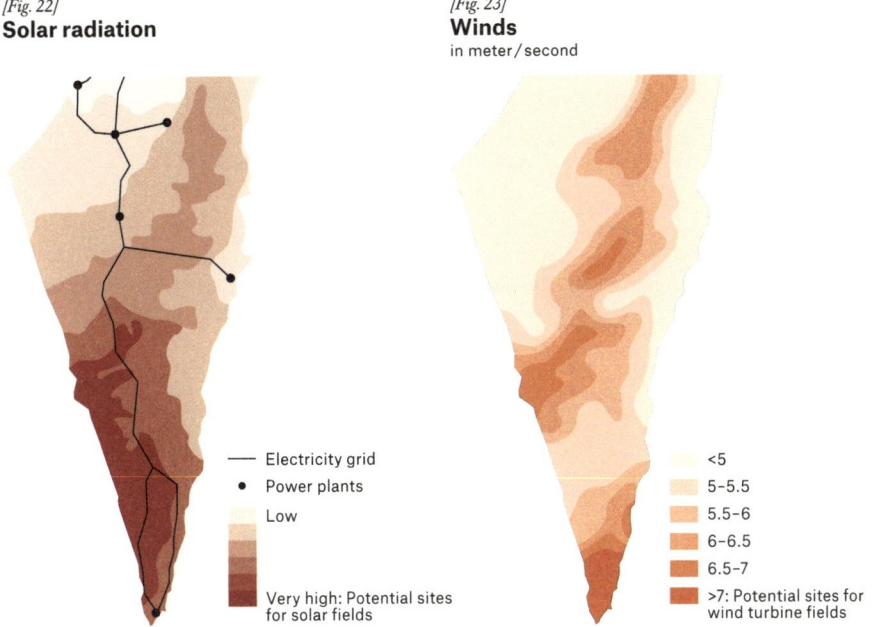

*[Fig. 22]*
**Solar radiation**

— Electricity grid
• Power plants
Low
Very high: Potential sites for solar fields

*[Fig. 23]*
**Winds**
in meter/second

<5
5-5.5
5.5-6
6-6.5
6.5-7
>7: Potential sites for wind turbine fields

*[Fig. 24]*
**Migration routes of soaring birds in the Middle East**

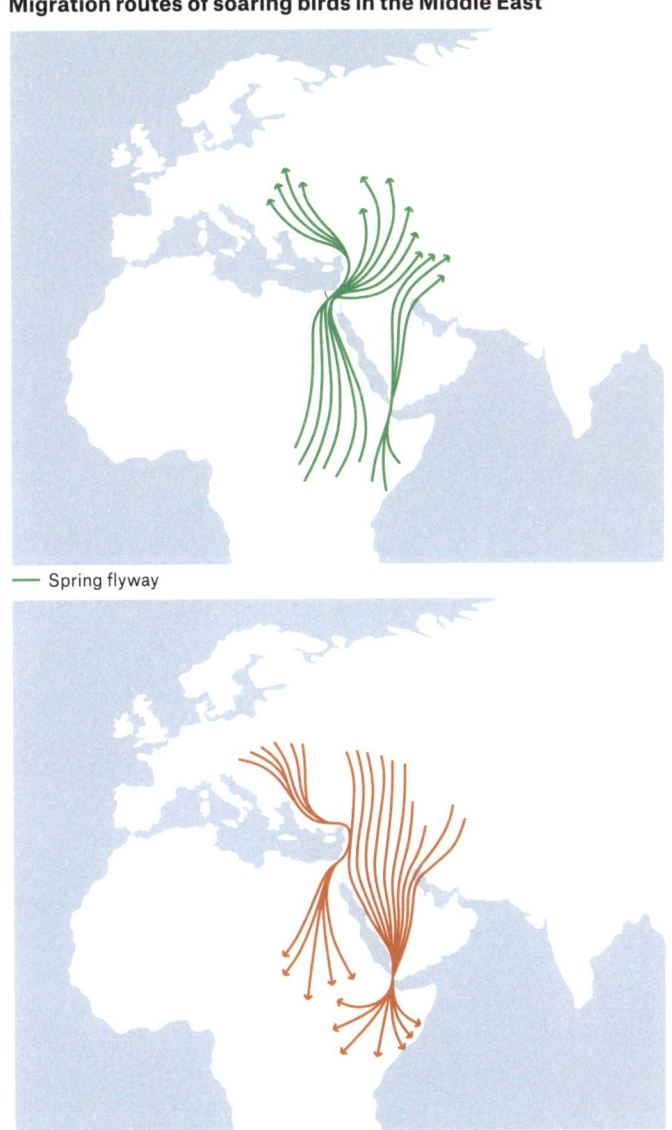

— Spring flyway

— Autumn flyway

Territory: Negev Desert

[Fig. 25]
**The Negev Desert: Urbanized Desert**

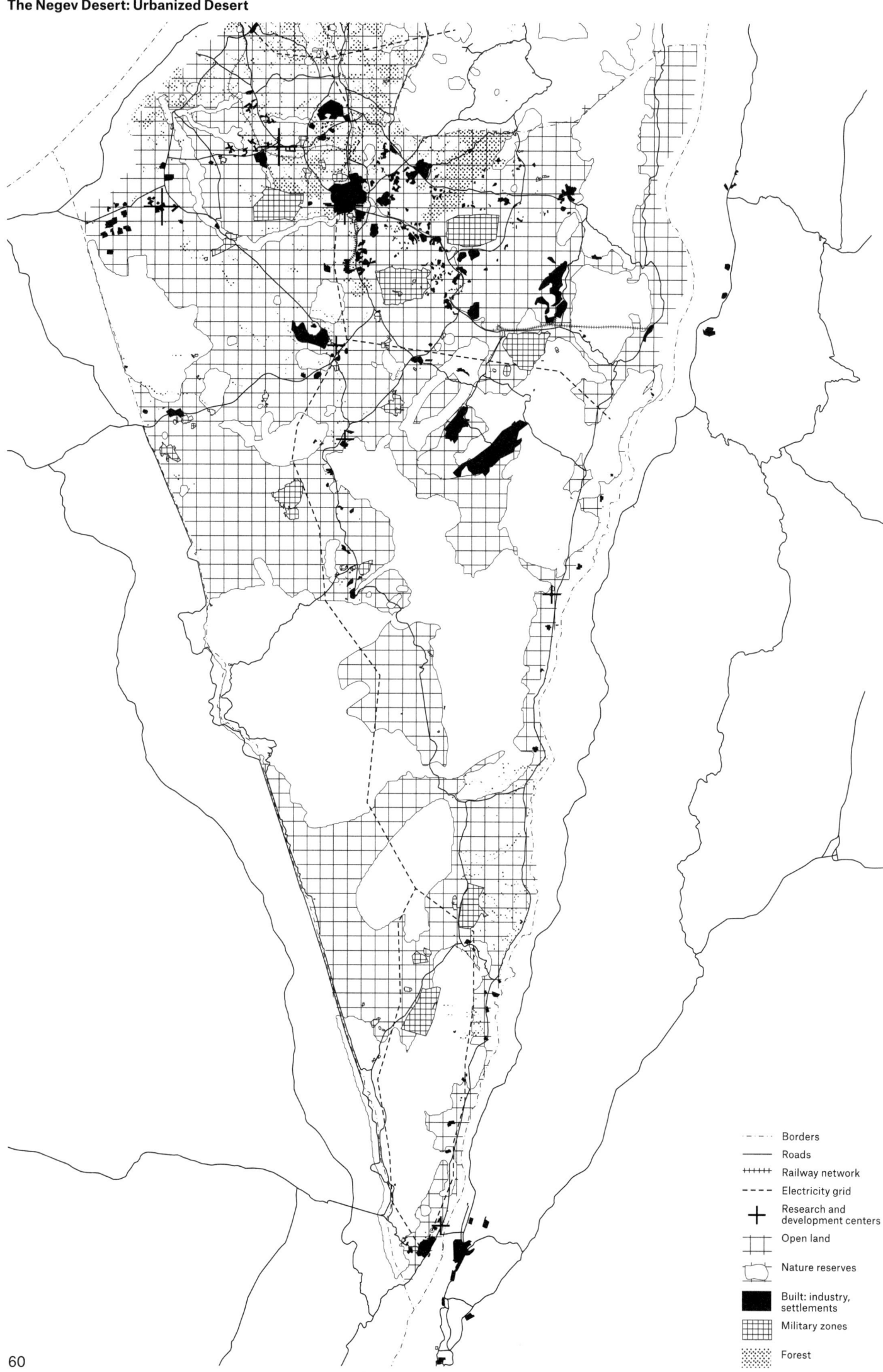

- — - — Borders
- ——— Roads
- +++++ Railway network
- - - - - Electricity grid
- + Research and development centers
- Open land
- Nature reserves
- Built: industry, settlements
- Military zones
- Forest

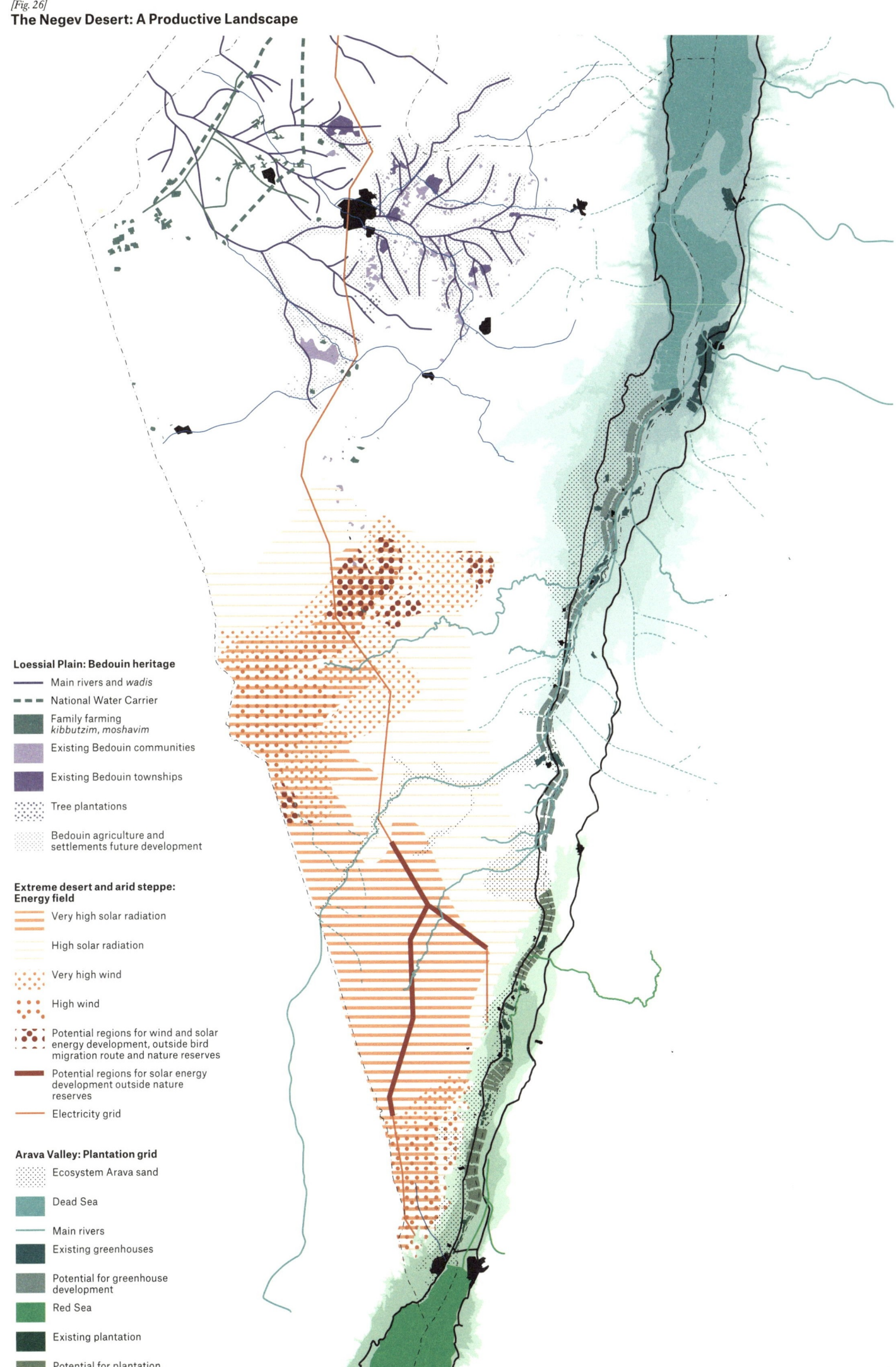

[Fig. 26]
**The Negev Desert: A Productive Landscape**

Territory: Negev Desert

# Territory

## The Coastal Plain: A Metropolitan Landscape

1. Israel's Growth Pattern     63
2. Open Space Under Threat     66
3. Constitution: A Metropolitan Landscape     66

# 1. Israel's Growth Pattern

Anti-urban sentiment, originating in the longing for a rural-agrarian life, has been a leitmotif of Jewish settlement in Palestine since the late nineteenth century. This frame of mind persisted after the establishment of the Jewish State in 1948 until the 1990s when it was challenged by large immigration waves from the former Soviet Union and Ethiopia. Today 74 percent of Israel's population (6.3 million) are based in one of the 4 metropolitan areas of the country (Tel Aviv, Jerusalem, Haifa, and Be'er Sheva). The rest of the population is mostly dispersed in medium- and low-density towns located mainly in the northern half of Israel.

## 1.1. Israel's dispersal policies

Starting in the 1880s, Jews settling in Palestine tried to establish as many agricultural areas as possible. This served several purposes. First, it was in line with Zionist ideology, which promoted getting the Jewish population in touch with a rural-agrarian life. Second, there were strategic defense objectives. Establishing these settlements provided a way of defending territorial claims. However, due to British restrictions on Jewish building, the Jewish population became highly concentrated along a narrow coastal strip, especially in Tel Aviv and Haifa, and within the city of Jerusalem. [Fig. 1]

Since the establishment of Israel, the population dispersal policy, endorsed by every government, has remained a key component of security, housing, economic, and land-use policy.[1] The physical planning of Israel, starting with Ariel Sharon's first National Outline Plan[2] in 1953, is based on this premise of decentralization. Until the 1990s the country's population and industries were planned to be dispersed in small-to medium-sized cities throughout the country, supported by a new transportation infrastructure. [Fig. 2-3]

## 1.2. Urbanized coastal plain

The coastal plain is the most urbanized region as well as one of the most productive agricultural areas in Israel. The population in this region is rapidly growing, making affordable living space scarce. Pressure to develop land is therefore not limited to cities and towns alone, but extends beyond the urban periphery into areas generally reserved for agriculture. In a country with a majority of the landmass located in arid to semi-arid zones, this creates a fierce competition between land uses.

The coastal plain features a broad range of urban typologies, ranging from low-density *kibbutzim* and medium-density towns to high-density metropoles. These typologies reveal Israel's different layers of cultural and political strategies over time. [Fig. 4-5]

### 1.2.1. Tel Aviv metropolitan area

Tel Aviv metropolitan area has 3.8 million[3] inhabitants and is home to almost half of Israel's population[4]. The area stretches over 1,685 square

Tel Aviv

kilometers from Netanya in the north to Ashdod, roughly 60 kilometers further south. With an average official density of 22 inhabitants per hectare most citizens of the Tel Aviv metropolitan area are living in rather low densities compared to metropolitan areas abroad. [Fig. 6]

The Tel Aviv metropolitan area supports 75 percent of Israeli business activity and 50 percent of Israel's total employment. These numbers show the strong monocentric nature of the country's economy. Israel is dominated by the Tel Aviv metropolitan core, and none of the secondary metropolitan areas are able to compete with Tel Aviv for national dominance. Commuters in the outer suburbs of Israel's secondary metropolitan areas such as Be'er Sheva and Haifa have increasingly looked to the Tel Aviv region for employment, tending to bypass the closer secondary metropolitan nodes.[5] [Fig. 7–8]

The search for affordable living space is the main reason for the suburbanization of Tel Aviv today. According to the Mercer Cost of Living Survey, in 2016 Tel Aviv was the most expensive city in the Middle East, and the nineteenth-most expensive city in the world.[6] With few, or week regulatory tools (i.e., the Statuary Tel Aviv Outline Plan, 2004), the urban development is heavily driven by market forces. [Fig. 9–12]

In the Tel Aviv metropolitan area, three phases of suburbanization can be differentiated. In the 1950s and 1960s it was primarily driven by state-sponsored public housing built in the urban periphery of Tel Aviv and Haifa. This changed in the late 1970s and 1980s, when the middle-class urban population started moving beyond the newly formed metropolitan areas to more distant suburban and rural areas. Sprawling low-density and single-family housing was the prevailing development type at that time. And in the 1990s *kibbutzim* and *moshavim*, which had previously resisted suburbanization, started to lose their unique cooperative structure and increasingly turned into rural suburbs.[7]

### 1.2.2. Development towns

Exemplary development town Migdal HaEmek [8]

Development towns were built in Israel in the 1950s in order to provide housing to a large influx of Jewish immigrants at the time. The aim was to counterbalance the polarity of the three large cities (Tel Aviv, Jerusalem, and Haifa) with the addition of medium-sized urban centers, while forming a gradually shifting pattern of urban-to-rural spaces. As most of these towns were initially conceived as temporary settlements (Hebrew: *ma'abarot*), their urban layout was never planned with an end in view, while their economic prospects focused mainly on work in agriculture of the surrounding areas. The settlement of homogenous ethnic groups in these new development towns, particularly from less-developed countries, led to their isolation from Israeli society. For these reasons and despite government subsidies, most of the development towns have economically fared poorly and often feature amongst the poorest Jewish areas in Israel. [Fig. 13]

### 1.2.3. Arab-majority towns

Originally the arab villages were located on the slopes of the Judaean mountains, along the *wadis* and rivers. [Fig. 14] Since Israel's founding, about 600 new Jewish communities have been established, but not a

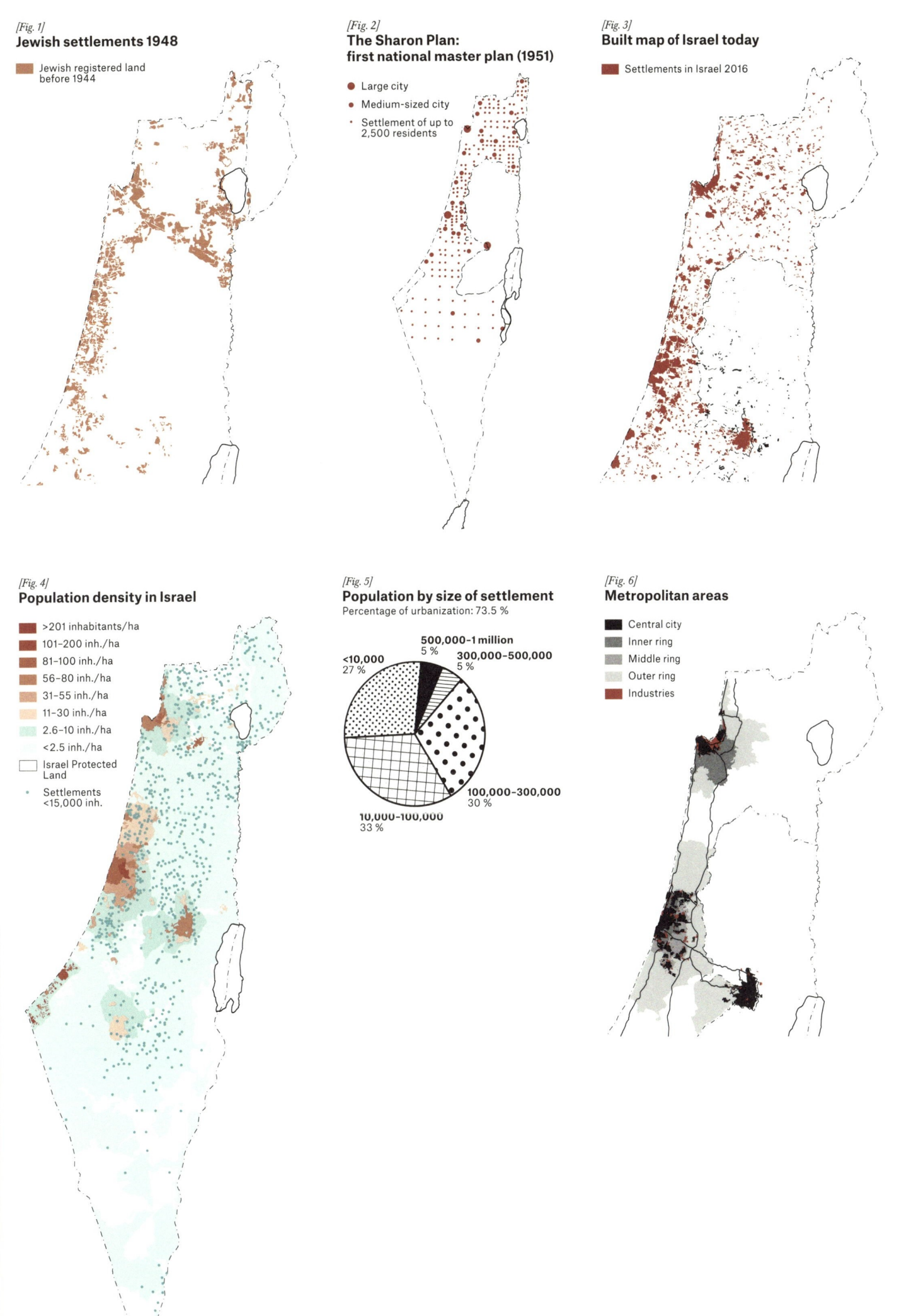

Territory: Coastal Plain

Typical Arab settlement Qalansawe

single new Arab community has been built. This is reflected in the shortage of living space in Arab municipalities. While there is a need in these communities for approximately 5,000 new housing units per year, only 1,300 building permits are issued annually.

The Israeli government tried to tackle the housing shortage in the 1980s and 1990s by instituting a policy allowing for the addition of two stories to existing two-story buildings. Consequently, Arab villages densified to four-story homes, but area infrastructures remained untouched.[9]

The socio-economic status of the 75 Arab towns in Israel is far lower than that of their Jewish counterparts. Their capacity to provide services is correspondingly lower.

## 2. Open Space Under Threat

Israel's population is projected to grow by 4.1 million from today's 8.5 million[10] to 12.6 million[11] by 2050. The greater Tel Aviv metropolitan area of Gush Dan, with a population of currently 3.7 million, is alone projected to absorb half of Israel's future population growth.

Since the conception of Tel Aviv's first master plan by Sir Patrick Geddes in the late 1920s, the city has not formulated another urban plan until today. After years of planning following only the guidelines set by the national plans, the mayor of Tel Aviv recently signed off the TA-5000 plan[12], a first Statutory Master Plan for the city of Tel Aviv through 2025. It is based on the "Vision of the City," which was approved by the city municipality in 2004 and follows the strategic guidelines that were put forth in that vision.

But the outline of the master plan is set to the political boundaries of the Tel Aviv municipality and therefore to a large extent does not take into consideration the development of the whole metropolitan area. On the contrary, some critical voices claim that the new plan, by focusing too much on the creation of new working spaces and neglecting the housing question, will actually increase the problem of the uncontrolled urban development and growth of the Tel Aviv metropolitan area. The lack of a vision on an intermediate scale between national and city plans forms the basis of the constitution "A Metropolitan Landscape."

Further urban sprawl around metropolitan areas and increasing pressure on open spaces in their proximity are to be expected. This would intensify the problem of diminishing agricultural areas, already scarce natural habitat for local fauna and flora, and the loss of recreational spaces close to urban centers.

## 3. Constitution: A Metropolitan Landscape

The constitution's objective is to outline a strategy for how to integrate half of Israel's population growth until 2050 (2 million people) into the coastal plain, while at the same time preserving and enhancing the existing open spaces.

*[Fig. 7]*
**Employment nodes**
Percentage of employed persons commuting to each metropolitan node

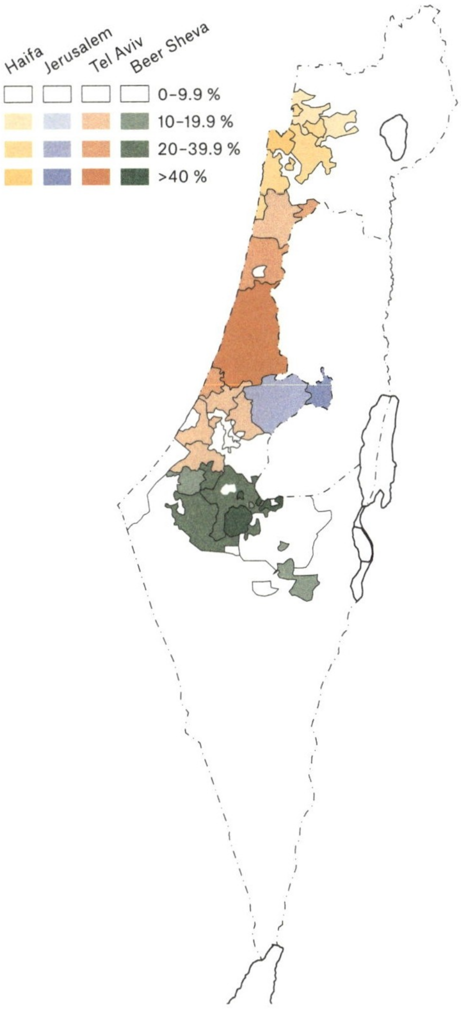

Haifa / Jerusalem / Tel Aviv / Beer Sheva
- 0–9.9 %
- 10–19.9 %
- 20–39.9 %
- >40 %

*[Fig. 8]*
**Population by size of settlement**
Communities that crossed 10 %, 20 % threshold to one of metropolitan nodes

Nahariya, Karmiel, Haifa, Yafra, Zikhron Yaakov, Binyamina, Hadera, Netanya, Tel Aviv, Ashdod, Jerusalem, Ashkelon, Mate Yahuda, Beer Sheva, Dimona

- >20 % (1995) <20 % (2008)
- 10–20 % (1995) <10 % (2008)
- <10 % (1995) 10–20 % (2008)
- <20 % (1995) >20 % (2008)
- ••• Commuting to the Haifa and Tel Aviv node
- ▬ ▬ ▬ Commuting to the Tel Aviv and Be'er Sheva node

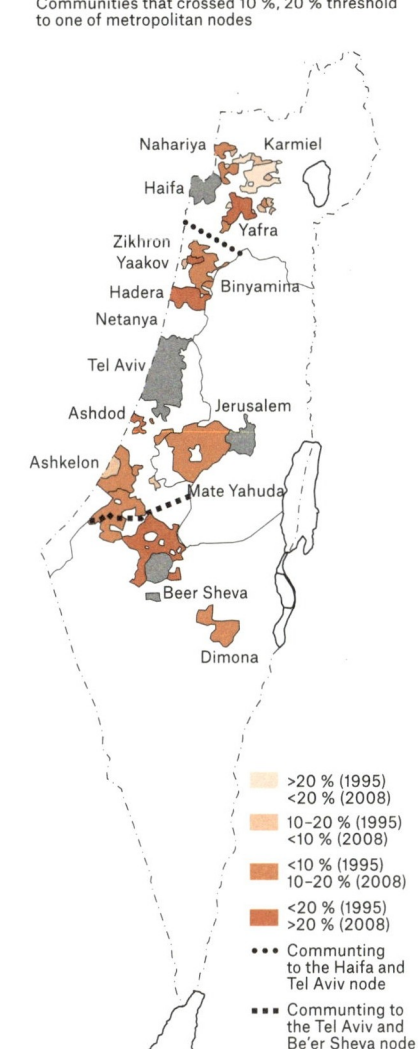

*[Fig. 9]*
**Population density Tel Aviv**

- >20,000 inhabitants/sq. km
- 15,000–20,000 inh./sq. km
- 10,000–15,000 inh./sq. km

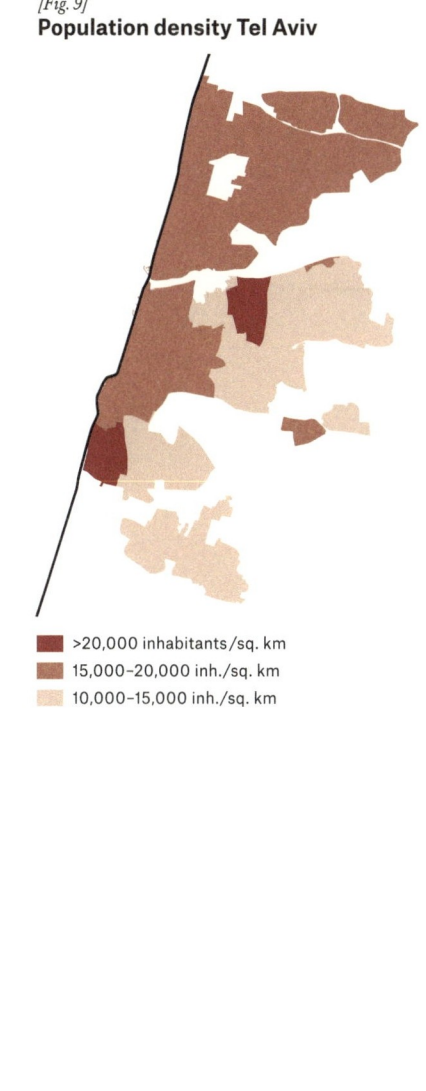

*[Fig. 10]*
**Changes in housing price indices**
Data are for January in each year

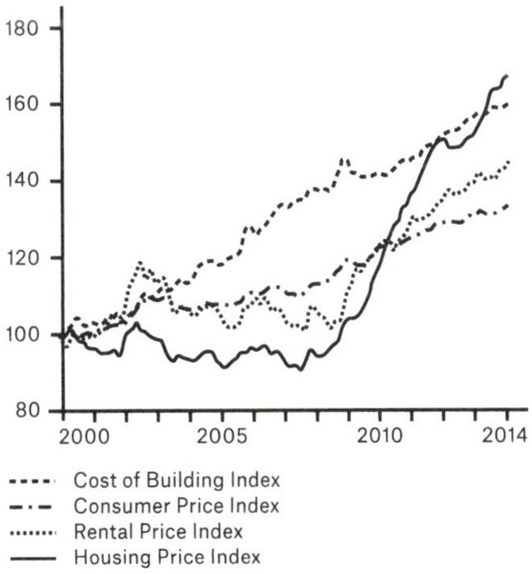

- Cost of Building Index
- Consumer Price Index
- Rental Price Index
- Housing Price Index

*[Fig. 11]*
**Duration of construction process**
in years

- Building time
- Building permits
- Marketing
- Development plans
- District committee license
- Feasability study and plan preparation for district committee

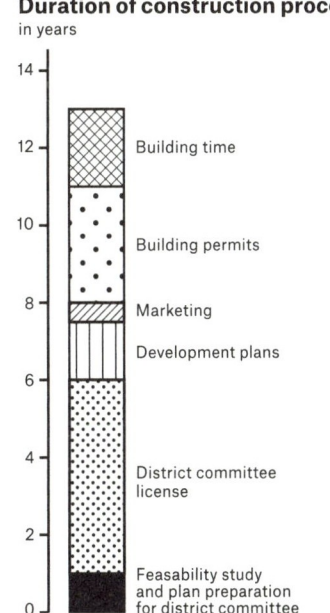

*[Fig. 12]*
**Population growth of four major cities**
in millions

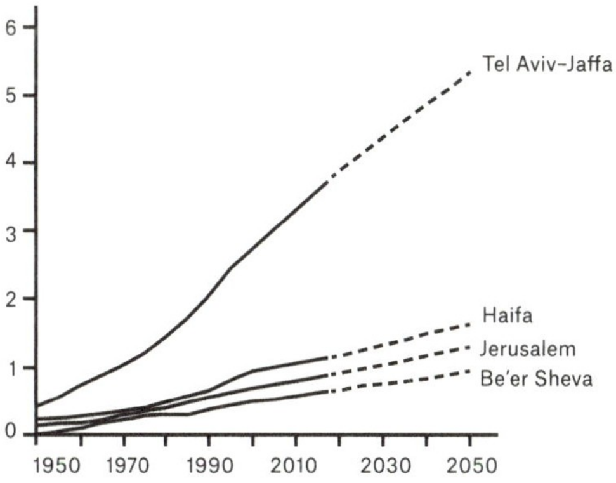

Tel Aviv–Jaffa, Haifa, Jerusalem, Be'er Sheva

Territory: Coastal Plain   67

## 3.1. Charging the void

Agriculture historically played a central role in the urbanization of Israel. Giving the Jewish people a new homeland that they can cultivate is deeply embedded in Zionist ideology. Uncontrolled urban sprawl since the 1970s has turned the pastoral landscape into a background lacking of a clear identity. As long as the open space is seen only as the negative of the built mass, it will continue to be given up easily.

The vision "A Metropolitan Landscape" puts its focus on a shift from the solely nostalgic image of the "green" boulevard to its multilayered functional aspects. On a territorial scale this constitution defines a clear geometric urban form, which is based on NOP 35, the "Integrated National Master Plan for Construction, Development and Preservation," approved in 2005 by the government. It aims at guiding spatial development on a national scale by defining metropolitan regions and non-urban zones according to five texture typologies[13] (urban, rural, mixed preserved, national preserved, coastal). *[Fig. 15]*

### 3.1.1. "Vertical spine"

Following NOP 35, this constitution also envisions a continuum of open spaces on a national scale, stretching from the Galilee to the Negev "joining the large metropolitan regions and containing open spaces of diverse character and standards—farmland, nature reserves and forests"[14] by charging the "void" with various qualities that do not conflict with the character of an open space. This means keeping these spaces free of further densification, while at the same time allocating to them functions of common interest, such as nature reserves, forests, agriculture, leisure, and public transportation. *[Fig. 16]*

### 3.1.2. "Finger parks"

All along the country's coastal plain east-west-oriented parks link a north-south-oriented "vertical spine" to the Mediterranean coastline. Unlike other urban parks, these "finger parks" are not clearly defined cut-outs of the urban fabric but continuous linear open spaces with changing identities and blurred boundaries. They follow existing dry streams or riverbeds, running perpendicular to the shoreline through the plain. As they get closer to the coastline, the open spaces turn into actual green lungs of the dense metropolitan areas. In the case of the Tel Aviv metropolitan area two of these finger parks structure the city into North, Central, and South Tel Aviv. One of the big challenges of their reconception will be the permeability and accessibility for both humans and wildlife. Today transportation infrastructures, such as highways and train tracks, placed within these voids are representing impermeable boundaries in the territory. *[Fig. 17]*

## 3.2. Densifying the built

The project identifies two strategies for a sustainable integrated population growth of about 2 million people in the metropolitan area of Tel Aviv by 2050.[15] The objective is to identify areas for future population densification, allowing the unbuilt voids to remain untouched.

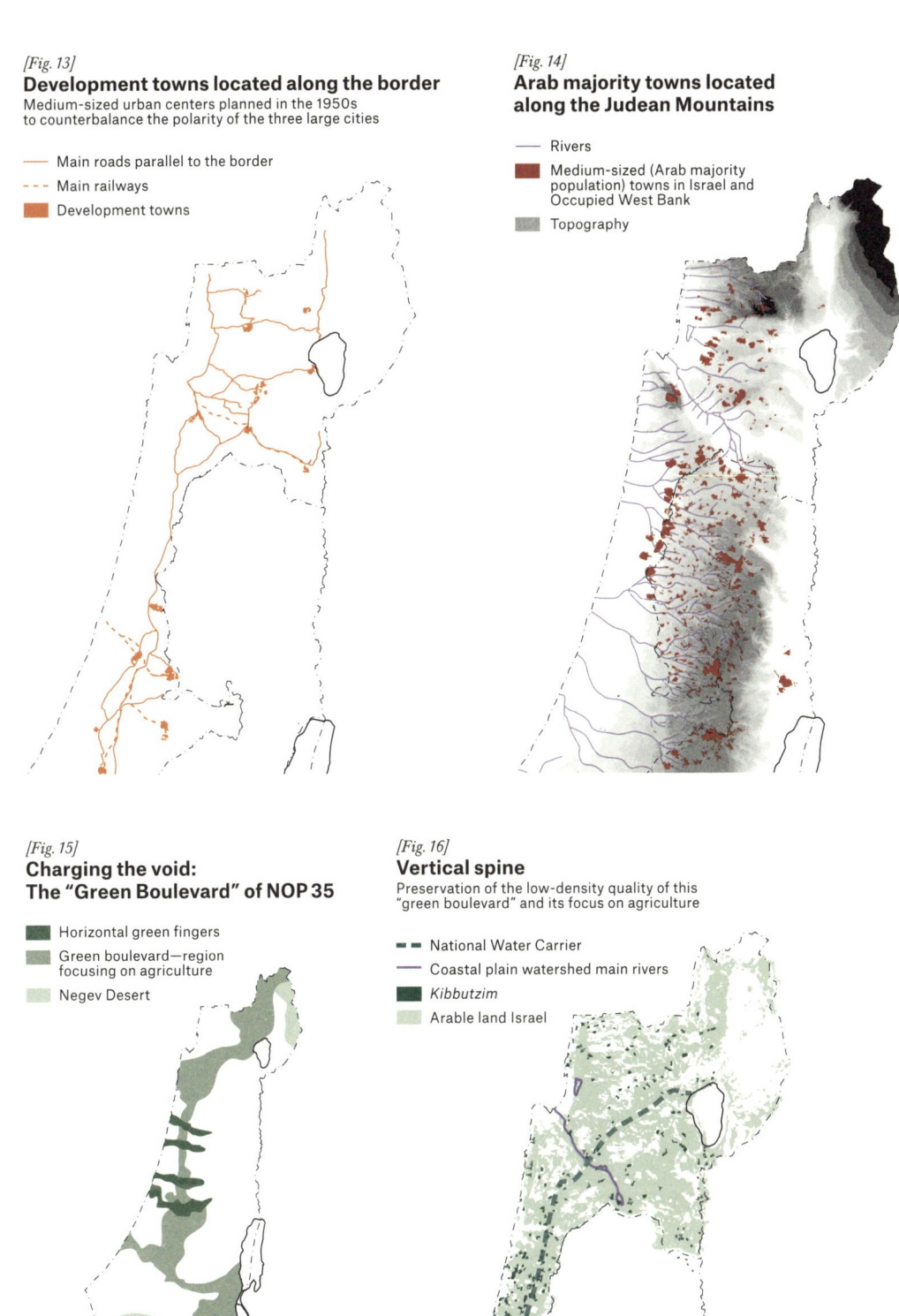

[Fig. 13]
**Development towns located along the border**
Medium-sized urban centers planned in the 1950s to counterbalance the polarity of the three large cities

— Main roads parallel to the border
--- Main railways
■ Development towns

[Fig. 14]
**Arab majority towns located along the Judean Mountains**

— Rivers
■ Medium-sized (Arab majority population) towns in Israel and Occupied West Bank
■ Topography

[Fig. 15]
**Charging the void:
The "Green Boulevard" of NOP 35**

■ Horizontal green fingers
■ Green boulevard—region focusing on agriculture
■ Negev Desert

[Fig. 16]
**Vertical spine**
Preservation of the low-density quality of this "green boulevard" and its focus on agriculture

--- National Water Carrier
— Coastal plain watershed main rivers
■ *Kibbutzim*
■ Arable land Israel

Territory: Coastal Plain    69

### 3.2.1. Linear metropolis

Many localities in the central metropolitan area of Tel Aviv show a rather low density of 100 or fewer inhabitants per hectare. Only by increasing the density up to 100–150 inhabitants per hectare could Tel Aviv absorb up to 1 million new inhabitants without further loss of open space.[16] [Fig. 18-20]

### 3.2.2. Necklace of medium-sized cities

Solely relying on the densification of existing coastal cities would put enormous pressures on their infrastructure and open spaces. The emphasis on a secondary linear network of mid-sized towns along the foot of Israel's central hills is therefore proposed. Raising the density of these mid-sized towns from today's 20–30 inhabitants per hectare to closer to 60 could absorb 1 million of the projected population and counterbalance the development along the coastal plain.

It is important to control the densification within the current city limits, as this network of towns lies along the eastern edge of the vertical spine, Israel's north-south spine defined in NOP 22. The unique situation of being surrounded by this continuous open space provides an immediate exposure to the cultural landscape of Israel, a unique quality that sets these cities apart from the suburbs of other metropolitan regions. Functionally and on a qualitative level these towns create the missing link between metropolis and countryside.

The selection of towns to be densified focuses on two types of cities in need of urban improvement: faceless and unattractive development towns, which currently act as residential dormitories to the neighboring larger cities; and towns with a majority Arab population, which are underprivileged in terms of investments in their public infrastructures. The aim is to create attractive, self-sufficient secondary poles, which act as mediating cities between metropolis and countryside. Four factors were identified to highlight the specific problems of each town: population growth/population density/education level/income. Accordingly, the cities were then grouped by these factors. In a second step, fields of actions (education/work infrastructure/public institutions/transportation) are proposed to counterbalance the analyzed specific deficiencies. [Fig. 21]

## 3.3. Ladder transportation network

Both of the urban systems described above are placed along an existing north-south transportation infrastructure. The highly urbanized coastal zone expands along Highways 2, 4, and 20, following the Mediterranean coastline. Located along the foot of Israel's central hills, existing Arab settlements and development towns line up along Highway 6. Along with adding train connections, the mostly north-south transportation infrastructure will be complemented by east-west connections within the defined open spaces. This new ladder-like transportation network allows for the creation of an encompassing metropolitan landscape in the coastal plains, which could absorb the predicted future population growth in the region. [Fig. 22]

The Coastal Plain: Territorial Constitution maps [Fig. 23-24]

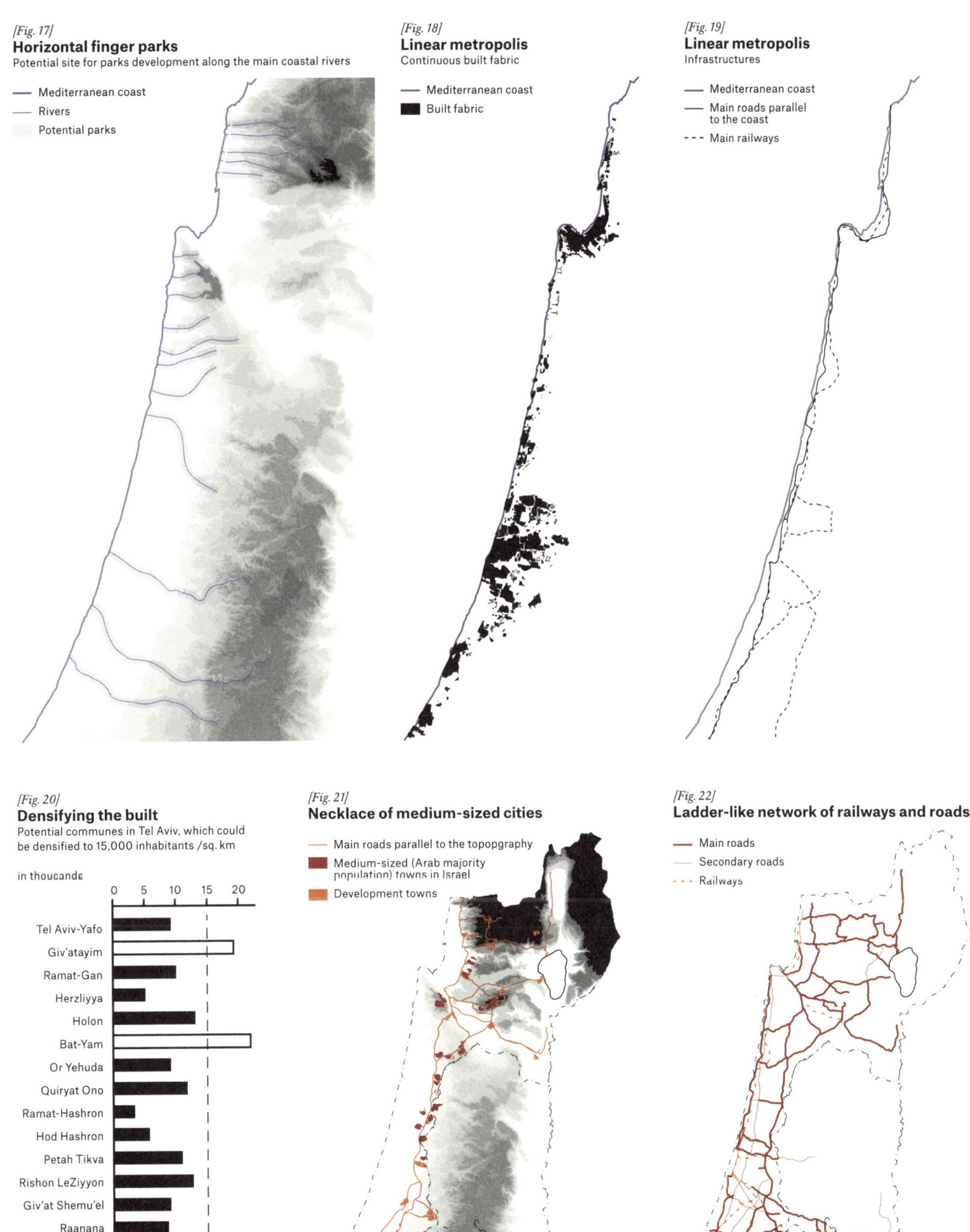

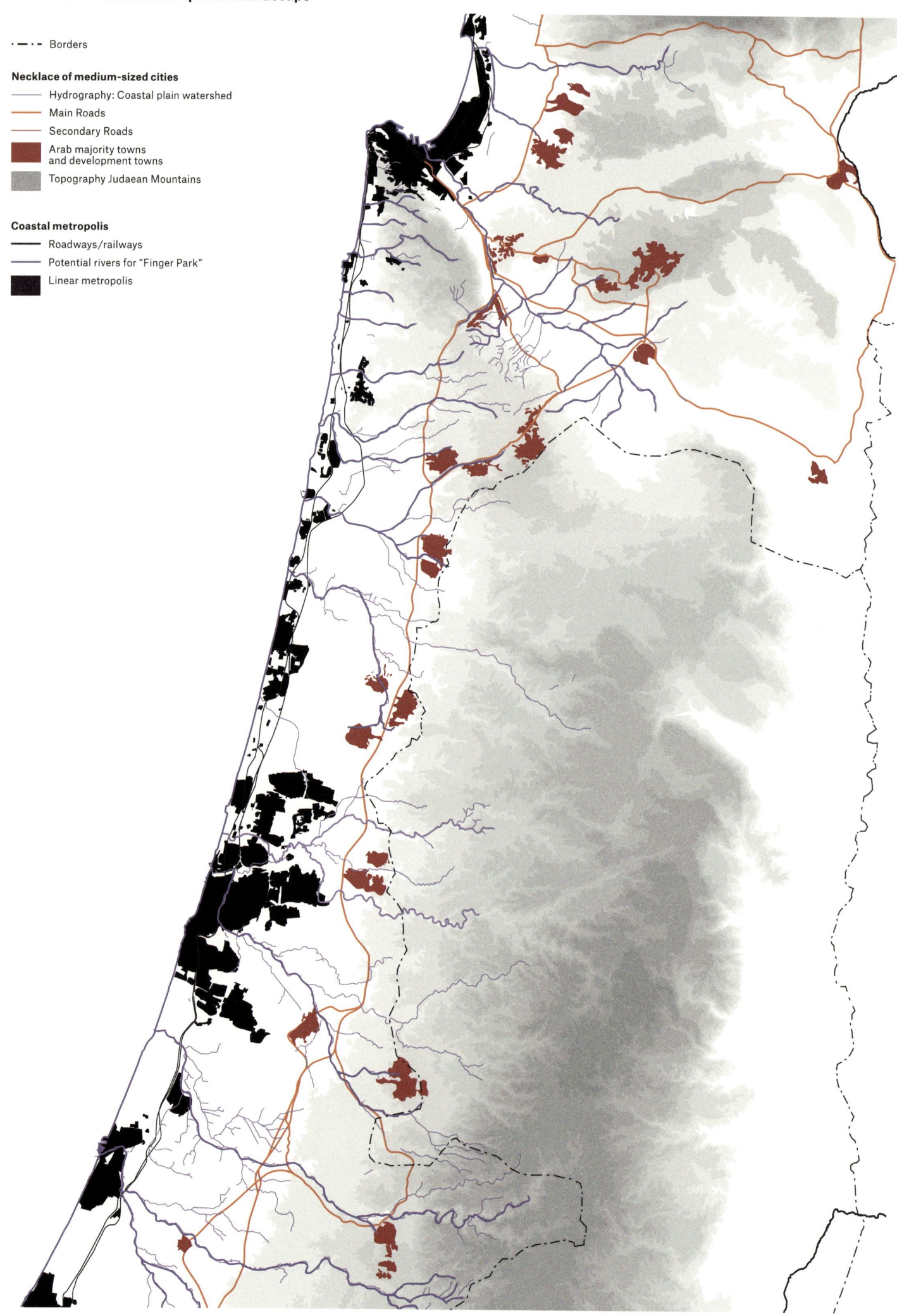

[Fig. 23]
**The Coastal Plain: A Metropolitan Landscape**

– · – · – Borders

**Necklace of medium-sized cities**
— Hydrography: Coastal plain watershed
— Main Roads
— Secondary Roads
■ Arab majority towns and development towns
■ Topography Judaean Mountains

**Coastal metropolis**
— Roadways/railways
— Potential rivers for "Finger Park"
■ Linear metropolis

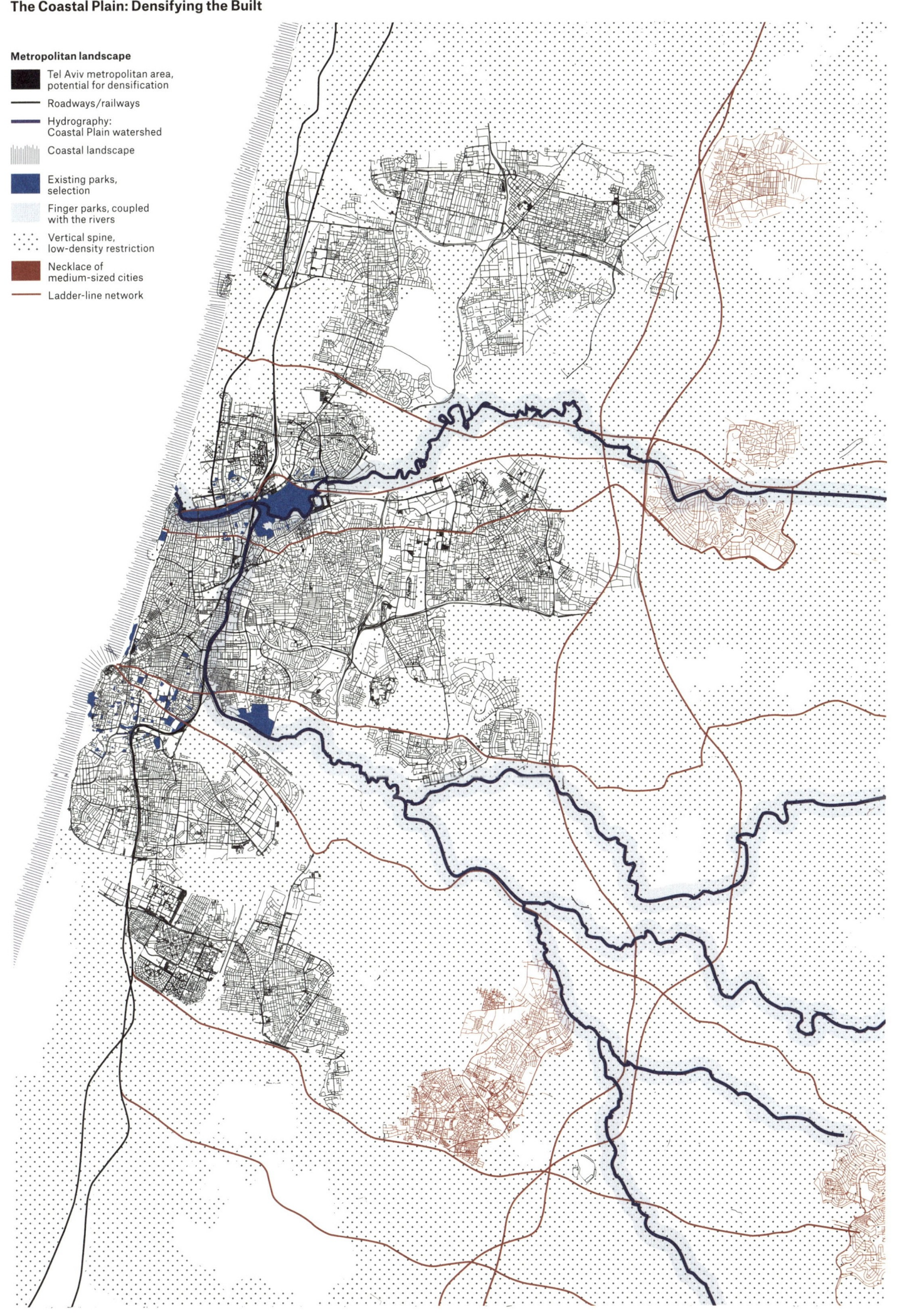

[Fig. 24]
## The Coastal Plain: Densifying the Built

**Metropolitan landscape**
- Tel Aviv metropolitan area, potential for densification
- Roadways/railways
- Hydrography: Coastal Plain watershed
- Coastal landscape
- Existing parks, selection
- Finger parks, coupled with the rivers
- Vertical spine, low-density restriction
- Necklace of medium-sized cities
- Ladder-line network

Territory: Coastal Plain  73

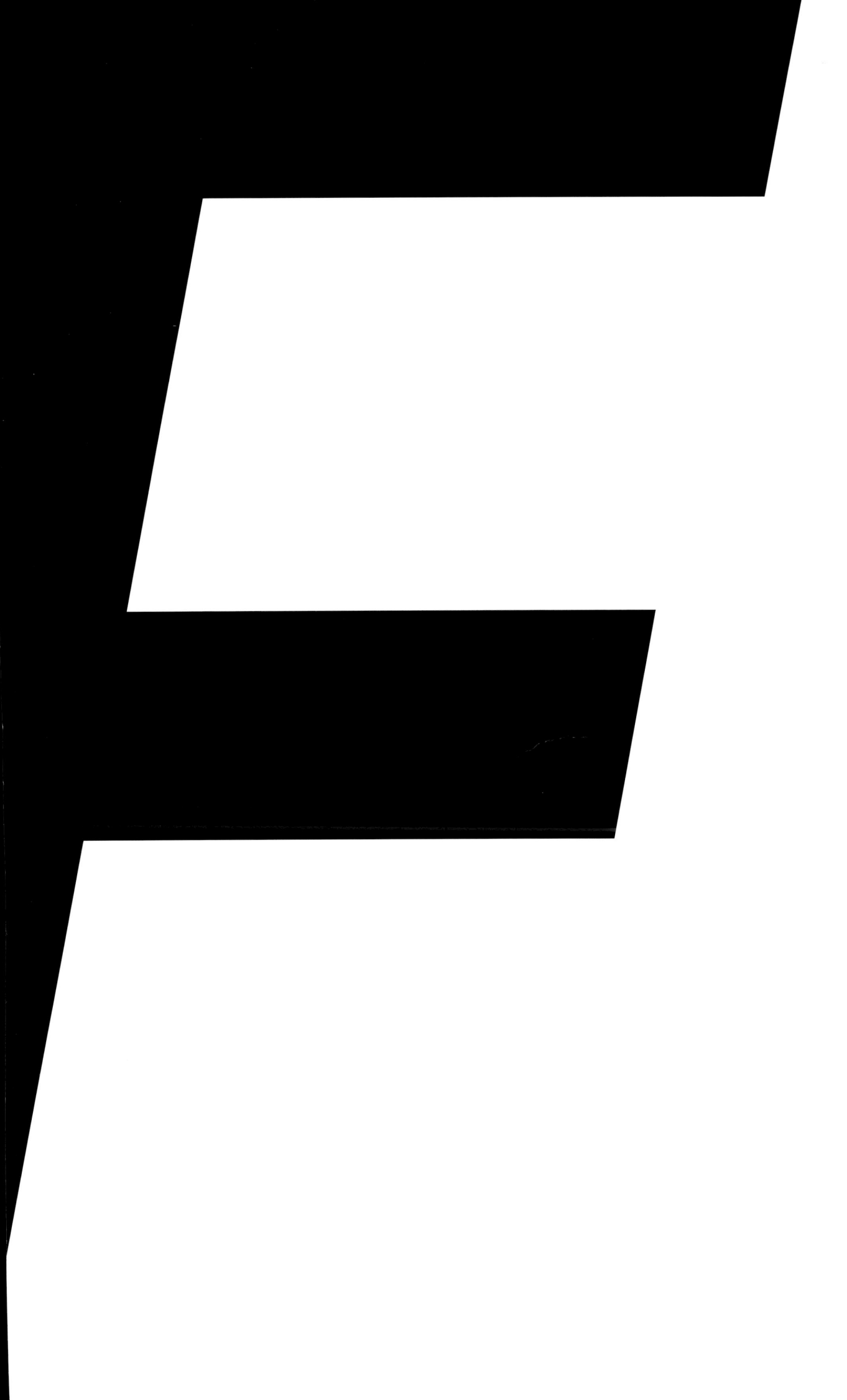

# Field

1 11th–12th of Dec: Tel Aviv
2 12th–14th of Dec: Jerusalem, Bethlehem
3 14th of Dec: Negev–Eilat
4 15th of Dec: Arava Valley–Ein Gedi
5 16th of Dec: Jordan Valley–Yzreel Valley
6 17th of Dec: Sea of Galilee–Acre
7 18th of Dec: Haifa–Symposium
   19th of Dec: Haifa–Symposium
   20th of Dec: Reviews Feasibility Study 1, Technion, Haifa

w from the Azrieli Observatory tower in Tel Aviv

Bat Yam City Hall entrance

Bat Yam City Hall. Project by Zvi Hecker and Alfred Neumann built in 1963, today used as a municipality building in Tel Aviv

Bat Yam City Hall foyer

A Bedouin community along the Auja *wadi* in Occupied West Bank

Irtas hills and agriculture structures along a *wadi* in Occupied West Bank

Typical housing typology in Tel Aviv

Abandoned infrastructure along the Dead Sea, in Area C, Occupied West Bank

Field 81

This page: Western Wall in Occupied East Jerusalem
Left page: Watch tower and Israeli-West Bank separation wall in Bethlehem, Occupied West Bank

This page: Street in the Old City in Occupied East Jerusalem
Previous page: The Dome of the Rock (Qubbat al-Sakhrah, Kippat ha-Sela), an Islamic Shrine located on the Temple Mount in the Old City of Occupied East Jerusalem

Israeli-West Bank separation wall outside Jerusalem, Seam Zone, Occupied West Bank

Solomon's Pools, part of a complex ancient water system that provided water to Jerusalem and Herodium, Occupied West Bank

The Gilo Housing project built by Arieh & Eldar Sharon in 1973 on the surrounding hilltops of Jerusalem, Seam Zone, Occupied West Bank

Ben-Gurion Research Institute of Israel and Zionism in the Negev

This page: Project Wadi Attir, a sustainable farm of a Bedouin community in the Negev desert
Previous page: Canyon in Ein Advat National Park in the Negev Desert

Electricity grid and Bedouin settlements in the northern Negev region

Project Wadi Attir, olive tree plantation

Negev Desert

Rocky landscape of the Ein Avdat National Park

Negev Desert infrastructures

Field 95

A 40-megawatt solar field at Kibbutz Ketura in the southern Arava Valley

This page: Micro algae production of antioxidants used in the health industry at Kibbutz Ketura
Right page: Medjool date plantation at Kibbutz Ketura, Arava Valley

This page: Greenhouses of Moshav Ein Yahav in the Arava Valley
Previous page: Green house tent for vegetable and herb production at Moshav Ein Yahav

Dead Sea factory, terminal for potash extraction mainly used in fertilizers

This page: Restricted access to the Dead Sea due to sinkhole formations
Left page: View of the Dead Sea and the sinkholes from the Ein Gedi National Park

Western Wall and walkway to access the Temple Mount in Occupied East Jerusalem

Jordanian army across Jordan River at the traditional baptism site of Jesus

Fabrizio Barozzi, Alberto Veiga, José Zabala
**Barozzi Veiga**

Paperback, 312 pages, 282 ills and plans
22 × 29 cm
978-3-906027-52-4 English
sFr. 49.00 | € 48.00 | £ 35.00 | $ 49.00

**The Barcelona-based firm Barozzi Veiga, winners of the 2015 Mies van der Rohe Award**

Irénée Scalbert, 6a architects
**Never Modern**

Paperback, 176 pages, 64 ills, 14 × 21 cm
978-3-906027-24-1 English
sFr. 24.00 | € 24.00 | £ 20.00 | $ 29.00

"**Never Modern** is a significant achievement in architectural publishing." *Architecture Today*

Edelaar Mosayebi Inderbitzin Architects (eds)
**Garden**

Paperback, 72 pages, 25 ills, 23 × 29 cm
978-3-03860-079-4 English
978-3-03860-078-7 German
sFr. 29.00 | € 29.00 | £ 25.00 | $ 29.00

**An arcane reflection on the garden as a topos by Zurich-based Edelaar Mosayebi Inderbitzin Architects**

Angelika Fitz, Katharina Ritter, Architekturzentrum Wien Az W (eds)
**Assemble**
How We Build

Paperback, 160 pages, 91 ills
16.5 × 24 cm
978-3-03860-077-0 English / German
sFr. 29.00 | € 29.00 | £ 25.00 | $ 29.00

**The first comprehensive insight into the work and selected projects of the London-based architecture collective Assemble, winners of the 2015 Turner Prize.**

 PARK BOOKS

Oliver Elser, Philip Kurz, Peter Cachola Schmal (eds)
## SOS Brutalism
A Global Survey

Hardback with paperback supplement, approx. 716 pages in total, 1,200 ills
22.5 × 27.5 cm
978-3-03860-075-6 English
978-3-03860-074-9 German
sFr. 69.00 | € 68.00 | £ 60.00 | $ 69.00
**November 2017**

**A groundbreaking global survey of Brutalist architecture, based on collaborative research by Deutsches Architekturmuseum DAM and Wüstenrot Foundation**

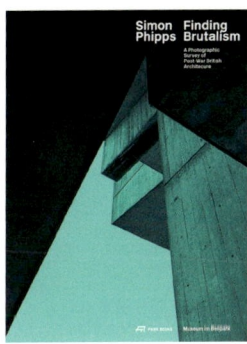

Hilar Stadler, Andreas Hertach (eds)
## Simon Phipps Finding Brutalism
A Photographic Survey of Post-War British Architecture

Hardback, 258 pages, 230 ills
20 × 25.5 cm
978-3-03860-063-3 English
978-3-03860-064-0 German
sFr. 39.00 | € 38.00 | £ 32.00 | $ 39.00

**A striking selection from Simon Phipps's unique documentation of British Brutalism.**

Rafi Segal
## Space Packed
The Architecture of Alfred Neumann

Hardback, 376 pages, 422 ills,
18.5 × 24.5 cm
978-3-03860-055-8 English
sFr. 49.00 | € 48.00 | £ 45.00 | $ 49.00

**Work and vision of a master of Modernism, who has influenced generations of architects in Israel, yet himself has largely been forgotten.**

www.park-books.com

**A unique, extensive, and richly illustrated survey of Northern Italy's modernist architecture, featuring some 200 buildings: useful guidebooks for architects and architecture lovers alike**

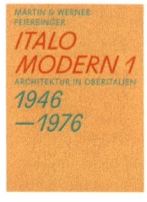

Martin and Werner Feiersinger
**Italomodern 1**
Architecture in Northern Italy 1946–1976

Paperback, 352 pages, 339 ills
16.5 × 22 cm
978-3-03860-028-2 English
978-3-906027-98-2 German
sFr. 45.00 | € 45.00 | £ 32.00 | $ 45.00

Martin and Werner Feiersinger
**Italomodern 2**
Architecture in Northern Italy 1946–1976

Paperback, 552 pages, 525 ills
16.5 × 22 cm
978-3-03860-029-9 English
978-3-906027-99-9 German
sFr. 49.00 | € 48.00 | £ 35.00 | $ 49.00

Manuel Herz (ed.)
Photographs by Iwan Baan
**African Modernism**
The Architecture of Independence. Ghana, Senegal, Côte d'Ivoire, Kenya, Zambia

Hardback (flexicover), 640 pages, 1209 ills and plans, 23.5 × 32 cm
978-3-906027-74-6 English
sFr. 69.00 | € 68.00 | £ 55.00 | $ 79.00

**"This gorgeous book introduces us to an extraordinary collection of unfamiliar buildings."** *Financial Times*

Tanja Herdt
**The City and the Architecture of Change**
The Work and Radical Visions of Cedric Price

Paperback, 206 pages, 100 ills, 17 × 24 cm
978-3-03860-045-9 English
978-3-03860-050-3 German
sFr. 49.00 | € 48.00 | £ 40.00 | $ 49.00

**Witty and inspiring: the designs, ideas, and thinking of British architect and urbanist Cedric Price**

PARK BOOKS

Iñaki Ábalos
## The good life
A guided visit to the houses of modernity

Paperback, 256 pages, 116 ills
15.5 × 21 cm
978-3-03860-051-0 English
sFr. 39.00 | € 38.00 | £ 35.00 | $ 39.00

**New and revised edition of Iñaki Ábalos's highly acclaimed book on seven iconic 20th-century houses, some actually built, others merely imagined or realized as film sets**

Eve Blau, Ivan Rupnik
## Baku—Oil and Urbanism

Hardback, approx. 320 pages, 270 ills
18 × 26 cm
978-3-03860-076-3 English
sFr. 49.00 | € 48.00 | £ 40.00 | $ 49.00
**March 2018**

**The first-ever comprehensive study on the close interplay of oil industry and urbanism, also featuring a new photo essay by Iwan Baan**

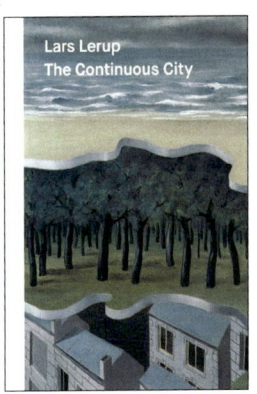

Lars Lerup
## The Continuous City
Fourteen Essays on Architecture and Urbanization

Hardback, 220 pages, 21 ills
14.5 × 21.5 cm
978-3-03860-066-4 English
sFr. 39.00 | € 38.00 | £ 35.00 | $ 39.00

**The architect as hunter-gatherer: Lars Lerup and his concept of the modern city.**

www.park-books.com

Harry Gugger, Barbara Costa, Salomé Gutscher, Stefan Hörner, Charlotte Truwant (eds)
## Israel Lessons
Industrial Arcadia. Teaching and Research in Architecture

Paperback, approx. 200 pages, 340 ills
21 × 31 cm
978-3-03860-087-9 English
sFr. 49.00 | € 48.00 | £ 40.00 | $ 49.00
**November 2017**

**A critical look at agriculture's role in territorial appropriation and domestication, urbanization, and creating a national homeland narrative for territory that today is the state of Israel**

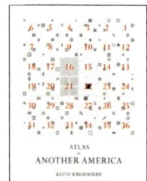

Keith Krumwiede
## Atlas of Another America
An Architectural Fiction

Hardback, 272 pages, 522 ills
24 × 32.5 cm
978-3-03860-002-2 English
sFr. 49.00 | € 48.00 | £ 35.00 | $ 49.00

**The single-family home, pinnacle of the American Dream and the ultimate status symbol of the American middle class: an architectural satire**

Yona Friedman, Manuel Orazi
## Yona Friedman
## The Dilution of Architecture

Paperback, 582 pages, 761 ills, 17 × 24 cm
978-3-906027-68-5 English
sFr. 49.00 | € 48.00 | £ 35.00 | $ 49.00

**The lasting inspiration of Yona Friedman, Hungarian-French avant-garde urbanist, architect, theoretician, and artist**

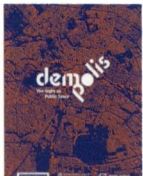

Barbara Hoidn (ed.)
## Demo:Polis
The Right to Public Space

Hardback (flexicover), 288 pages, 492 ills
21.5 × 27.5 cm
978-3-03860-005-3 English
978-3-03860-004-6 German
sFr. 49.00 | € 48.00 | £ 35.00 | $ 49.00

**Negotiating the future of public space: use, design, participation. A catalog by the Academy of Arts Berlin**

Christian Bjone
**Almost Nothing**
100 Artists Comment on the Work of Mies van der Rohe

Hardback, approx. 226 pages, 221 ills
21.5 × 28 cm
978-3-03860-080-0 English
sFr. 49.00 | € 48.00 | £ 45.00 | $ 49.00
**March 2018**

**Artworks inspired by Mies van der Rohe by international artists such as Alexander Calder, Christo & Jeanne-Claude, Isa Genzken, Yves Klein, Sarah Morris, Kurt Schwitters, Thomas Ruff, Ed Ruscha, and others**

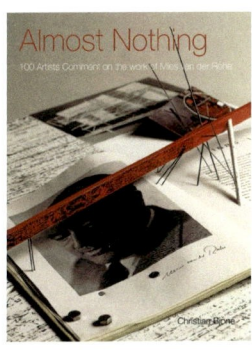

Dominique Boudet (ed.)
**New Housing in Zurich**
Typologies for a Changing Society

Paperback, approx. 256 pages, 700 ills and plans, 24 × 30 cm
978-3-03860-042-8 English
978-3-03860-043-5 French
978-3-03860-041-1 German
sFr. 69.00 | € 68.00 | £ 60.00 | $ 75.00
**November 2017**

**A comprehensive survey of co-operative housing projects in Zurich, featuring in detail some fifty recent designs that have had a major impact on the city's urban life**

Kornel Ringli
**Designing TWA**
Eero Saarinen's Airport Terminal in New York

Hardback, 224 pages, 240 ills
21.5 × 28 cm
978-3-906027-75-3 English
978-3-906027-83-8 German
sFr. 39.00 | € 38.00 | £ 30.00 | $ 39.00

**The iconic monograph on Eero Saarinen's iconic TWA terminal, named one of the Most Beautiful Swiss Books of 2015**

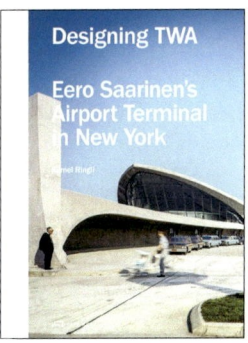

www.park-books.com

Diogo Seixas Lopes
## Melancholy and Architecture
On Aldo Rossi

Hardback, 232 pages, 32 ills
15.5 × 23.5 cm
978-3-906027-47-0 English
sFr. 39.00 | € 38.00 | £ 30.00 | $ 39.00

**"An absorbing and persuasive discussion of the relationship between emotion and architecture that applies more widely than to Rossi alone."** *Cassone-art.com*

Aberrant Architecture, David Chambers, Kevin Haley (eds)
## Wherever You Find People
The Radical Schools of Oscar Niemeyer, Darcy Ribeiro and Leonel Brizola

Paperback, 192 pages, 91 ills, 16 × 24 cm
978-3-03860-026-8 English
sFr. 39.00 | € 38.00 | £ 28.00 | $ 39.00

**The compelling story of a unique and bold, yet little known, experimental public-education project in Rio de Janeiro**

Kersten Geers, Jelena Pančevac, Andrea Zanderigo (eds)
## The Difficult Whole
A Reference Book on Robert Venturi, John Rauch and Denise Scott Brown

Hardback, 216 pages, 302 ills, 21 × 30 cm
978-3-906027-84-5 English
sFr. 49.00 | € 48.00 | £ 35.00 | $ 49.00

**Robert Venturi's idea of the "difficult whole" re-evaluated in the context of his work**

Giovanna Borasi (ed.)
## AP 164: Ábalos & Herreros
Selected by Kersten Geers and David Van Severen, Juan José Castellón González, Florian Idenburg and Jing Liu, with an interpretation in photographs by Stefano Graziani

Paperback, 208 pages, 384 ills, 24 × 31 cm
978-3-03860-006-0 English
978-3-03860-030-5 Spanish
sFr. 39.00 | € 38.00 | £ 30.00 | $ 39.00

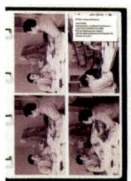

**The influential work of Ábalos & Herreros re-interpreted by their contemporaries, collaborators, and students**

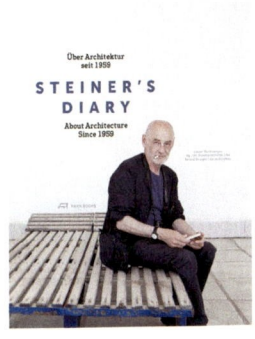

Kunstuniversität Linz (ed.)
### Steiner's Diary
About Architecture since 1959

Hardback (flexicover), 400 pages, 360 ills
24.5 × 30 cm
978-3-03860-032-9 English / German
sFr. 49.00 | € 48.00 | £ 35.00 | $ 49.00

**A succinct review of forty years of observing contemporary architecture: writings and interviews by Dietmar Steiner, one of Austria's most eminent architectural publicists**

Le Corbusier
### Precisions on the Present State of Architecture and City Planning

Hardback, 408 pages, 133 ills
15.5 × 24.5 cm
978-3-906027-65-4 English
sFr. 29.00 | € 29.00 | £ 25.00 | $ 29.00

**Perhaps Le Corbusier's most influential book in a new facsimile reprint edition, featuring for the first time and in color the complete drawings from his 1929 South American lecture series**

### CARTHA—On Making Heimat

Paperback, 128 pages, 15.8 × 10.5 cm
978-3-03860-053-4 English
sFr. 19.00 | € 19.00 | £ 18.00 | $ 20.00

**How can migrants settle and feel at home far away from their native environment? This book offers essential contributions to the international discourse on migration issues in contemporary architecture and urban design.**

www.park-books.com

Mikael Bergquist, Olof Michélsen
**Josef Frank—Spaces**

Hardback, 144 pages, 215 ills, 14 × 23 cm
978-3-03860-018-3 English
sFr. 39.00 | € 38.00 | £ 30.00 | $ 39.00

The single-family houses of a legendary European modernist

Janne Ahlin
**Sigurd Lewerentz, architect**
1885–1975

Hardback, 204 pages, 336 ills
20.5 × 33 cm
978-3-906027-48-7 English
sFr. 64.00 | € 64.00 | £ 50.00 | $ 75.00

The classic monograph on Sweden's pre-eminent architect, Sigurd Lewerentz, complemented with a new essay by renowned architect and scholar Wilfried Wang

Paulo Providência
**Paulo Providência—
Architectonica Percepta**
Texts and Images 1989–2015

Paperback, 232 pages, 159 ills and plans,
14 × 22 cm
978-3-03860-024-4 English
sFr. 39.00 | € 38.00 | £ 30.00 | $ 40.00

Insights into the manifold designs and the thinking of one of Portugal's most significant contemporary architects

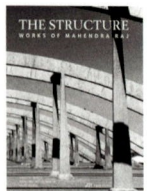

Vandini Mehta, Rohit Raj Mehndiratta,
Ariel Huber (eds)
**The Structure**
Works of Mahendra Raj

Hardback, 428 pages, 570 ills
19.5 × 25.5 cm
978-3-03860-025-1 English
sFr. 69.00 | € 68.00 | £ 50.00 | $ 70.00

Sixty years of engineering: Mahendra Raj's extraordinary structures in India and the Middle East

## Neri & Hu Design and Research Office
Works and Projects

Hardback, approx. 256 pages, 351 ills and plans, 21.5 × 27 cm
978-3-906027-89-0 English
sFr. 59.00 | € 58.00 | £ 45.00 | $ 65.00
**November 2017**

**The first monograph on internationally celebrated, Shanghai- and London-based Neri & Hu Design and Research Office.**

Alice Grahame, Taran Wilkhu
## Walters Way & Segal Close
The Architect Walter Segal and London's Self-Build Communities. A Look at Two of London's Most Unusual Streets

Hardback, 232 pages. 161 ills
20.5 × 25.5 cm
978-3-03860-049-7 English
sFr. 39.00 | € 38.00 | £ 30.00 | $ 40.00

**The story of two tiny roads in Lewisham, south London, and of German-British architect Walter Segal's designs for twenty self-build homes they contain**

William O'Brien Jr. (ed.)
## Room for Artifacts
The Architecture of WOJR

Hardback, 240 pages, 151 ills, 20 × 27 cm
978-3-03860-027-5 English
sFr. 49.00 | € 48.00 | £ 35.00 | $ 50.00

**Based in Cambridge, MA, WOJR have won various awards, including the 2010 Design Biennial Boston Award and the 2011 Architectural League Prize for Young Architects and Designers**

www.park-books.com

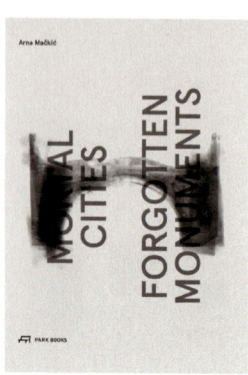

Arna Mačkić, Rosa te Velde (eds)
# Mortal Cities & Forgotten Monuments

Hardback, 160 pages, 154 ills, 17 × 23 cm
978-3-03860-009-1 English
sFr. 49.00 | € 48.00 | £ 35.00 | $ 50.00

A revealing study on the potential of architecture and urban design to reconcile people in war-ravaged regions with the loss of urban structure and cultural symbols

---

Prices quoted in Swiss francs are recommended retail prices valid in Switzerland only including VAT.
Prices quoted in Euros are fixed retail prices valid in Germany only including VAT. For all other countries

Scheidegger & Spiess
Kunst | Fotografie | Architektur

Nadine Olonetzky (ed.)
## Meinrad Schade—War without War

Photographs of the Former Soviet Union

Hardback, 264 pages, 161 ills, 22 × 27 cm
978-3-85881-452-4 English / German
sFr. 54.00 | € 54.00 | £ 40.00 | $ 60.00

An impressive account of life oscillating between war and peace, and a study on the effect of historic events on the individual

Nanni Baltzer, Martino Stierli (eds)
## Before Publication
Montage in Art, Architecture, and Book Design. A Reader

Hardback (flexicover), 144 pages, 60 ills
16 × 22 cm
978-3-03860-022-0 English
sFr. 39.00 | € 38.00 | £ 30.00 | $ 39.00

**Photographer Ed Ruscha, designer Muriel Coopers, and Dadaist Tristan Tzara: the practice of montage in art, architecture, and book design.**

 PARK BOOKS

---

prices quoted are recommended retail prices only and may vary subject to local duty and taxes. All prices, dates, and descriptions are subject to change without notice.

---

Jolanda Gsponer (ed.)
## Peter Liechti—Dédications

Paperback with DVD, 184 pages, 166 ills,
17 × 22.5 cm
978-3-85881-776-1 English
978-3-85881-500-2 German
sFr. 39.00 | € 38.00 | £ 32.00 | $ 45.00

**Reflections on living and dying: Peter Liechti's last and unfinished film project Dédications.**

Martin and Werner Feiersinger (eds)

## Chandigarh Redux

Le Corbusier, Pierre Jeanneret, Jane B. Drew, E. Maxwell Fry

Paperback, 416 pages, 307 ills, 16 × 24 cm
978-3-85881-762-4 English
sFr. 49.00 | € 48.00 | £ 35.00 | $ 49.00

**A new, distinctly artistic view at Chandigarh: Werner Feiersinger's comprehensive pictorial account of the city today**

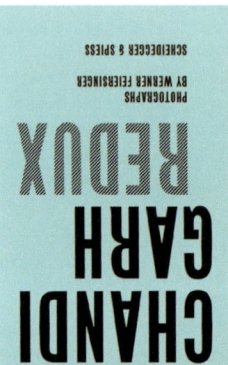

Ludovic Balland (ed.)

## American Readers at Home

A Road Trip across the United States in Interviews and Photographs

Hardback, approx. 420 pages, 512 ills, 25 × 35 cm
978-3-85881-788-4 English
sFr. 69.00 | € 68.00 | £ 60.00 | $ 69.00
February 2018

**How does our experience and perception of daily events through the media translate into personal memories?**

Charlie Koolhaas

## City Lust

Hardback, approx. 256 pages, 200 ills, 20 × 28.5 cm
978-3-85881-804-1 English
sFr. 59.00 | € 58.00 | £ 50.00 | $ 59.00
February 2018

**A visual and narrative exploration of the constantly changing global economy, pop culture codes and the implicit rules of merchandise, and of male and female role models in business-driven relationships**

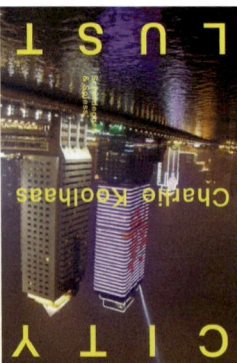

www.scheidegger-spiess.ch

Roger Wehrli, Ibon Zubiaur

### Roger Wehrli. Bilbao
Photographs since 1988

Hardback, 160 pages, 95 ills, 17 × 24 cm
978-3-85881-535-4 English / German
sFr. 39.00 | € 38.00 | £ 35.00 | $ 45.00

**Bilbao's transformation from Spain's most polluted industrial city to Europe's Capital of Culture and creative hotspot**

---

Caspar Schärer, Christian Menn (eds)

### Christian Menn—Bridges

Hardback, 352 pages, 276 ills and plans, 25.5 × 29 cm
978-3-85881-455-5 English / German
sFr. 99.00 | € 97.00 | £ 70.00 | $ 99.00

**The art of structural engineering: the bridges, vision, and philosophy of Christian Menn**

---

### Christoph Schaub—Films on Architecture

3 DVDs with booklet, 24 pages,
14 × 19.5 cm, 320 mins in total, color,
various languages, subtitles English
and French
978-3-85881-908-6 English / German
sFr. 39.00 | € 39.00 | £ 30.00 | $ 45.00

**Can architecture really be captured in film? Christoph Schaub's nine documentaries offer an answer.**

---

Anette Freytag (ed.)

### The Gardens of La Gara
An 18th-Century Estate in Geneva with Gardens Designed by Erik Dhont and a Labyrinth by Markus Raetz

Hardback, approx. 272 pages, 240 ills
19 × 27 cm
978-3-85881-802-7 English
978-3-85881-803-4 French
978-3-85881-570-5 German
sFr. 99.00 | € 97.00 | £ 85.00 | $ 99.00
November 2018

**Contemporary and historic landscape design on an 18th-century estate near Geneva**

Scheidegger & Spiess
Art | Photography | Architecture

www.scheidegger-spiess.ch

Hilar Stadler, Martino Stierli, Peter Fischli (eds)

## Las Vegas Studio
Images from the Archive of Robert Venturi and Denise Scott Brown

Paperback, 196 pages, 172 ills, 20 × 26 cm
978-3-85881-764-8 English
978-3-85881-765-5 French
sFr. 32.00 | € 32.00 | £ 25.00 | $ 39.00

**The only book in print featuring Venturi and Scott Brown's legendary Las Vegas images in full-color splendor**

Arthur Rüegg (ed.)

## René Burri. Brasilia
Photographs 1958–1997

Hardback, 224 pages, 222 ills, 23 × 31 cm
978-3-85881-307-7 English / German
sFr. 79.00 | € 77.00 | £ 60.00 | $ 85.00

**René Burri's photographic account of construction, development, and the life and people of Brasilia over four decades**

Samuel Titan Jr., Sergio Burgi (eds)

## Marcel Gautherot
The Monograph

Hardback, 256 pages, 241 ills,
23.5 × 27.5 cm
978-3-85881-777-8 English
978-3-85881-495-1 German
sFr. 49.00 | € 48.00 | £ 35.00 | $ 50.00

**An outstanding photographer rediscovered**

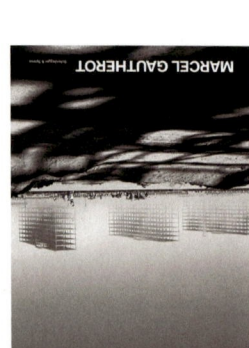

Scheidegger & Spiess
Art | Photography | Architecture

## Max Bill

Museum Marta Herford (ed.)

No Beginning, No End
New edition, Paperback, 200 pages,
215 ills, 20 × 29 cm
978-3-85881-578-1 English / German
sFr. 49.00 | € 48.00 | £ 40.00 | $ 55.00
February 2018

**The new edition of this authoritative and much sought-after monograph displays Max Bill's wide-ranging work and sets him in context with his contemporaries**

## Sonja Sekula & Friends

Kunstmuseum Luzern (ed.)

Paperback, 160 pages, 100 ills,
24 × 32.5 cm
978-3-85881-512-5 English / German
sFr. 49.00 | € 38.00 | £ 38.00 | $ 55.00

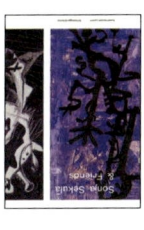

**One of Switzerland's most significant female artists and her circle of artist friends in New York**

## Bellevue

Kunstmuseum Luzern (ed.)

Robert Zünd (1827–1909)—Tobias Madörin (1965)

Paperback, 130 pages, 80 ills,
24 × 32.5 cm
978-3-85881-555-2 English / German
sFr. 49.00 | € 48.00 | £ 45.00 | $ 55.00

**A dialogue on landscape in painting and photography**

## Enraptured by Color

Laurence Schmidlin (ed.)

Printmaking in Late 19th-Century France

Paperback, 248 pages, 217 ills,
21.5 × 29 cm
978-3-85881-798-3 English / French
sFr. 49.00 | € 48.00 | £ 45.00 | $ 55.00

**Introducing color made a difference: French prints from the late 19th century**

www.scheidegger-spiess.ch

Jacques Barsac

## Charlotte Perriand
Complete Works

All volumes hardback, more than 520 pages and around 1000 ills., 23 × 30.5 cm
sFr. 120.00 | € 120.00 | £ 100.00 | $ 130.00

Volume 1: 1903–1940
978-3-85881-746-4 English

Volume 2: 1940–1955
978-3-85881-747-1 English

Volume 3: 1956–1968
978-3-85881-748-8 English

Volume 4: 1969–1999
978-3-85881-778-5 English

Fall 2018

**The definitive and lavishly illustrated four-volume monograph on French avant-garde designer Charlotte Perriand, a key protagonist of 20th-century interior design, featuring a wealth of previously unpublished designs, documents, and images**

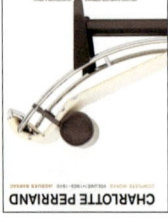

Arthur Rüegg

## Le Corbusier. Furniture and Interiors 1905–1965

Hardback, 416 pages, 867 ills., 24 × 30.5 cm
978-3-85881-728-0 English
978-3-85881-729-7 French
978-3-85881-345-9 German
sFr. 160.00 | € 160.00 | £ 120.00 | $ 180.00

**The authoritative book on Le Corbusier's work as an interior designer**

Kunsthaus Zürich (ed.)

### Dadaglobe Reconstructed

Hardback, 304 pages, 390 ills
20 × 25.5 cm
978-3-85881-775-4 English
978-3-85881-499-9 German
sFr. 59.00 | € 58.00 | £ 40.00 | $ 59.00

**Conceived by Tristan Tzara in 1921, reconstructed by Adrian Sudhalter, and published for the first time 2016 marking the Dada centenary; the Dada-movement's vast multilingual anthology**

---

Arp Museum Bahnhof Rolandseck,
Remagen; Cabaret Voltaire, Zürich (eds)

### Genesis Dada

100 Years of Dada Zurich

Hardback, 248 pages, 166 ills, 19 × 26 cm
978-3-85881-767-9 English
978-3-85881-492-0 German
sFr. 39.00 | € 38.00 | £ 30.00 | $ 45.00

**Dada's big bang in Zurich 1916: the full story**

---

Ralf Burmeister, Michaela Oberhofer,
Esther Tisa Francini (eds)

### Dada Africa

Dialogue with the Other

Hardback, 244 pages, 241 ills, 23 × 28 cm
978-3-85881-779-2 English
978-3-85881-507-1 German
sFr. 39.00 | € 38.00 | £ 30.00 | $ 40.00

**The largely unknown story of how the Dada movement explored and was inspired by art from Africa, Asia, and Oceania**

---

Museum Rietberg, Zurich (ed.)

### African Masters

Art from the Ivory Coast

Hardback, 240 pages, 304 ills
24.5 × 28.5 cm
978-3-85881-761-7 English
978-3-85881-427-2 German
sFr. 39.00 | € 38.00 | £ 25.00 | $ 39.00

**A groundbreaking overview of traditional and contemporary art from the Ivory Coast**

Peter Zumthor, Mari Lending

# A Feeling of History

Paperback, approx. 80 pages, 14 ills
11 × 19.5 cm
978-3-85881-805-8 English
978-3-85881-558-3 German
sFr. 39.00 | € 38.00 | £ 35.00 | $ 39.00
**March 2018**

Peter Zumthor reflects in conversation with Mari Lending on time and history's reverberations in his work, and how history has informed his attempts to emotional reconstruction of space

Thomas Durisch (ed.)

# Peter Zumthor 1985–2013

Buildings and Projects

5 vols, hardback in slipcase, 856 pages in total, 761 ills, 24 × 30 cm
978-3-85881-723-5 English
978-3-85881-304-6 German
sFr. 250.00 | € 250.00 | £ 180.00 | $ 250.00

"Each volume is a delight to hold and page through, and a model of Swiss design from the gray silk covers to the crisp typography and spacious layouts. Rarely has haptic architecture been better expressed in print."
*The Architect's Newspaper*

Olivier Cinqualbre, Frédéric Migayrou (eds)

# Le Corbusier—The Measures of Man

Hardback, 256 pages, 444 ills, 24 × 30 cm
978-3-85881-768-6 English
978-3-85881-469-2 German
sFr. 49.00 | € 48.00 | £ 35.00 | $ 49.00

The human proportion and how the human body should be housed: an entirely new exploration of Le Corbusier's work in architecture and art

www.scheidegger-spiess.ch

Milena Oehy

## Mexican Graphic Art

Paperback, 320 pages, 466 ills
17 × 23.5 cm
978-3-85881-799-0 English
978-3-85881-554-5 German
sFr. 39.00 | € 38.00 | £ 35.00 | $ 39.00

**Everyday reality and revolutionary departure reflected in late 19th- and 20th-century Mexican graphic art**

---

Heinz Nigg (ed.)

## Rebel Video

The Video Movement of the 1970s and 1980s. London Basel Bern Lausanne Zurich

Paperback, 396 pages, 288 ills
10.5 × 19 cm
978-3-85881-801-0 English
978-3-85881-556-9 German
sFr. 39.00 | € 38.00 | £ 35.00 | $ 45.00

**Media activism in the analog age: a unique testimonial of the video movement in Switzerland and the UK of the 1970s and 1980s and its lasting influence**

---

Kashef Chowdhury

## Dhaka

Memories of Lost

Hardback, 56 pages, 26 duotone illustrations, 23 × 32 cm
978-3-85881-787-7 English
sFr. 39.00 | € 38.00 | £ 35.00 | $ 39.00

**A personal photographic tribute by Dhaka-based architect Kashef Chowdhury to his native city**

---

Nadine Olonetzky (ed.)

## Haiti

The Perpetual Liberation

4-part set in slipcase, paperback, 628 pages in total, 143 ills, 11 × 16.5 cm
978-3-85881-515-6
English / German / Creole
sFr. 39.00 | € 38.00 | £ 28.00 | $ 39.00

**Heaven and hell on Earth: Thomas Kern's unique and striking portrait of Haiti**

Madeleine Schuppli, Aargauer Kunsthaus,
Aarau (eds)

## Swiss Pop Art
Forms and Tendencies of Pop Art in
Switzerland 1962–1972

Hardback (flexicover), 552 pages, 317 ills
20 × 29 cm
978-3-85881-536-1
English / French / German
sFr. 69.00 | € 68.00 | £ 60.00 | $ 75.00

**The definitive survey of Pop Art in
Switzerland in the 1960s and 1970s**

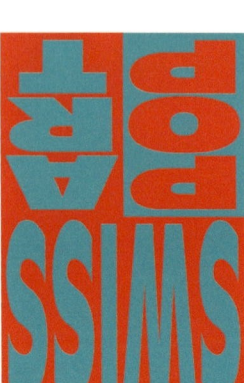

Torsten Otte

## Salvador Dalí & Andy Warhol
Encounters in New York and Beyond

Hardback, 416 pages, 57 ills, 17 × 24 cm
978-3-85881-774-7 English
sFr. 49.00 | € 48.00 | £ 35.00 | $ 49.00

**The first-ever comparative study on
two of the 20th century's most
significant—and notorious—artists**

Jeannette Fischer, Marina Abramović

## Psychoanalyst meets Marina Abramović
Jeannette Fischer meets Artist

Paperback, approx. 168 pages, 31 ills
11 × 16,7 cm
978-3-85881-794-5 English
978-3-85881-546-0 German
sFr. 19.00 | € 19.00 | £ 18.00 | $ 20.00
February 2018

**A unique insight into the relation-
ship between Marina Abramović's
biography and artistic work, offering
an understanding of the underlying
structures and dynamics of her
extraordinary performances**

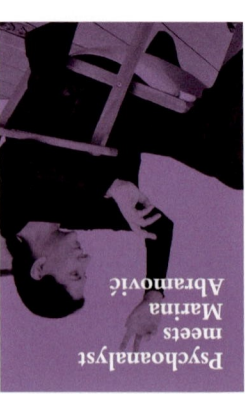

Kunsthaus Zürich (ed.)

## Alberto Giacometti—
## Beyond Bronze
Masterworks in Plaster and Other Materials

Hardback, 240 pages, 260 ills, 22 × 27 cm
978-3-85881-785-3 English
978-3-85881-786-0 French
978-3-85881-525-5 German
sFr. 59.00 | € 58.00 | £ 40.00 | $ 59.00

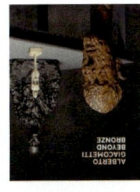

**Plaster, plasticine, marble, wood: a new perspective on Giacometti's approach to his artistic media.**

---

Ernst Scheidegger

## Alberto Giacometti
Traces of a Friendship

Hardback, 248 pages, 249 ills, 26 × 27 cm
978-3-85881-349-7 English / German
sFr. 49.00 | € 48.00 | £ 45.00 | $ 65.00

**Ernst Scheidegger's classic homage to Alberto Giacometti in a completely revised new edition, including more than sixty previously unpublished color images.**

---

Beat Stutzer

## Giovanni Segantini

Hardback, 208 pages, 141 ills, 25 × 30 cm
978-3-85881-783-9 English
978-3-85881-522-4 German
978-3-85881-784-6 Italian
sFr. 49.00 | € 48.00 | £ 35.00 | $ 49.00

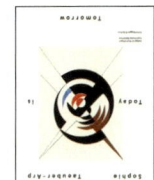

**The most comprehensive survey to date of Giovanni Segantini's painting.**

---

Aargauer Kunsthaus, Aarau; Kunsthalle Bielefeld (eds)

## Sophie Taeuber-Arp—Today Is Tomorrow

Hardback, 288 pages, 437 ills, 24 × 31 cm
978-3-85881-757-0 English
978-3-85881-432-6 German
sFr. 59.00 | € 58.00 | £ 45.00 | $ 65.00

**The authoritative monograph on this uniquely versatile artist of the early avant-garde.**

---

Scheidegger & Spiess
Art | Photography | Architecture

# Scheidegger & Spiess

**Art | Photography | Architecture**

NEW AND SELECTED TITLES 2017/18

Military base in the Negev

Bedouin settlement

Left and right page: The Mishkan Museum of Art, by architect Shmuel Bickels, built in 1938 at Kibbutz Ein Harod
Previous page: Al-Auja, a Palestinian town located 10 kilometers north of Jericho in Occupied West Bank

Greenhouse tent

Irrigation channel bringing water from the Auja spring to Bedouin villages in Occupied West Bank

This page: Sea of Galilee
Left page: Dead Sea factory, terminal for potash extraction

Nature reserve at Lake Hula, established in the 1950s in an effort to save the Hula marsh and its rich fauna and flora

# Architecture

| | | |
|---|---|---|
| 1 | Dead Sea Islands<br>Arnaud Baudouin / Yann Junod | 120 |
| 2 | The Jordan River Hydropower Station<br>Anton Rosenberg | 124 |
| 3 | A House for the Levant Water Commission<br>Xavier Barreca | 128 |
| 4 | Sorting Center in Jericho, Palestine<br>Quentin Menu | 132 |
| 5 | Makhtesh Hakatan Center<br>Martin Handley | 136 |
| 6 | From Waste to Educational Center<br>Maïlys Marty | 140 |
| 7 | The Auja Water Collection<br>Tania Depallens | 144 |
| 8 | Center for Sustainable Desert Construction<br>Marlon Biétry / Nicola Schürch | 148 |
| 9 | Thai Shed<br>Victoria Bodevin / Sophie Würzer | 152 |
| 10 | Bedouin Heritage Center<br>Marie-Pauline Cryonnet | 156 |
| 11 | Landscaped Infrastructures for Bedouin Housing<br>Félix Chase | 160 |
| 12 | Rahat Women's Garden<br>Juliette Lucarain / Laura Stoll | 164 |
| 13 | Nazareth and Nazareth Illit Linear Center<br>Florian Papp | 168 |
| 14 | Daycare and Educational Center, Karmiel<br>Stéphanie Amstutz | 172 |
| 15 | Mount Hiriya Train Station<br>Laure Péquinot | 176 |
| 16 | Food Park for a Metropolitan Area<br>Jonas Inhelder | 180 |
| 17 | Tel Aviv Hashalom Bridge Station<br>Alessandra Patarot | 184 |
| 18 | A *Kibbutz* in Tel Aviv<br>Alois Rosenfeld | 188 |

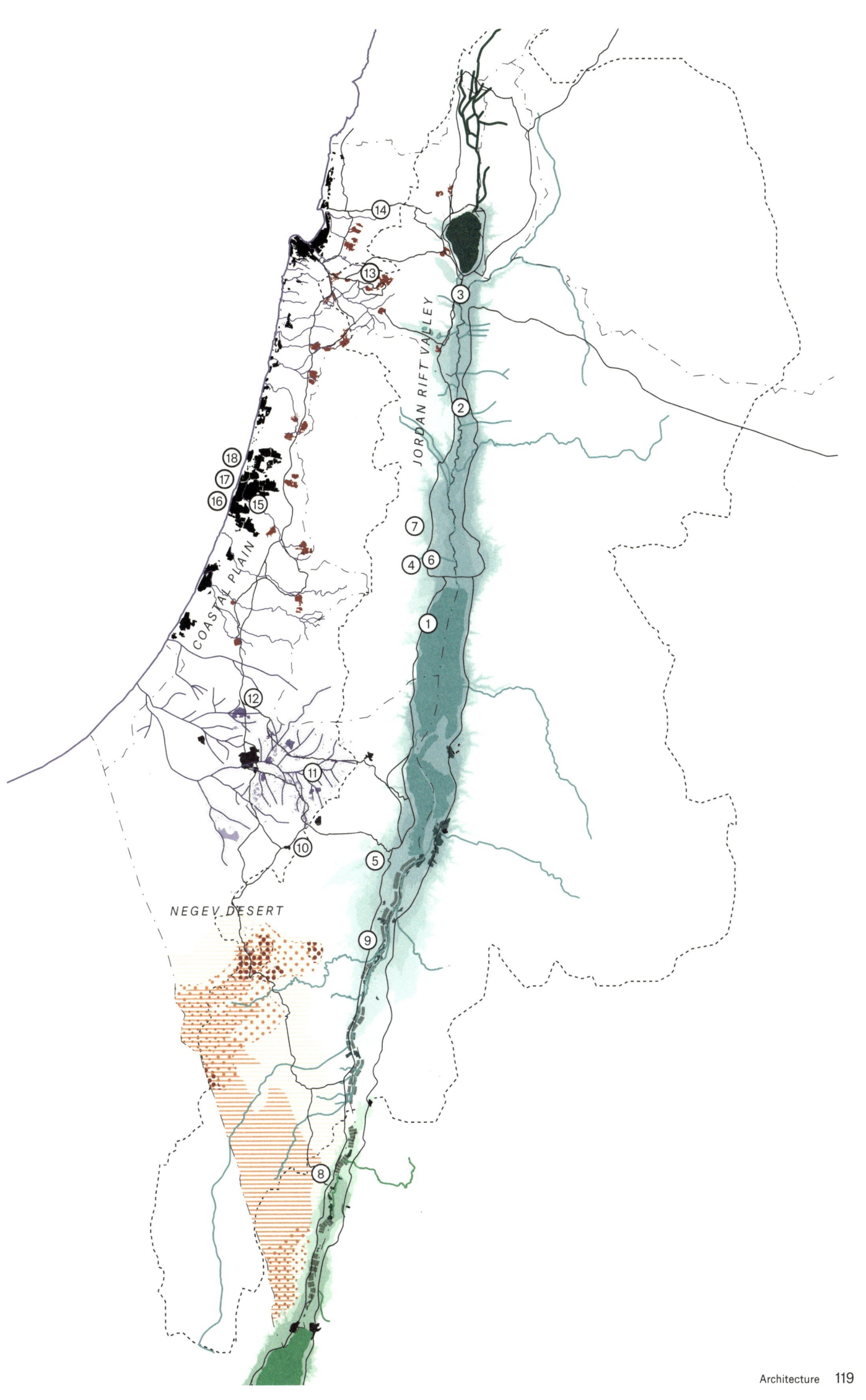

# 1 Dead Sea Islands

The Dead Sea is historically a point of intense settlement, commerce, and a major transport route. Located on the border between Israel, Palestine, and Jordan, it is symbolic of all the tensions in the region, be they political, economic, or environmental.

The Dead Sea's waters, once used as means of transportation (as shown by evidence of ancient harbors along its shores) find their value today in a unique chemical composition. The Dead Sea chemical industry, located on artificial evaporation ponds at the south of the sea where it spreads on both the Israeli and Jordanian sides, produces a significant amount of minerals such as potash and salt. The high density of minerals in the water and the presence of thermal springs along its steep shores also allowed the Dead Sea to become a privileged wellness and health destination. The uniqueness of the sea and its proximity to main urban centers (one hour from Jerusalem and Amman, two hours from Tel Aviv) make it today Israel's third-most popular destination among foreign and domestic tourists, with an average of 6,000 visitors a day. Along with the tourism industry, fertile ground and the presence of fresh water springs make agriculture an important economical resource in the area.

However, since the 1970s and the diversion of the Jordan River by Israel and Jordan, the natural and economical ecosystems of the Dead Sea basin have been seriously damaged and are today under constant threat. With its level lowering by more than one meter per year, the Dead Sea sees its shores' livelihood slowly dying. Along with the recession of the shoreline —reaching locally up to two kilometers—the formation of a sinkhole strip has begun to pull the old shore away from the sea.

The project "Dead Sea Islands" proposes an infrastructure aiming at regenerating the shores of the sea by *re*creating a safe access to the water, a bridge between existing touristic attractions and the resources they depend on. The project turns a natural and economical disaster into an opportunity. It activates and gives life to a new, isolated territory: the stretch of land revealed by the shrinkage of the sea. In some areas, vast surfaces given up by the sea get colonized by small trees, and in others, sinkholes filled up with spring water turn into multicolor pools. These natural features are made accessible and become an attraction in and of themselves.

Three different locations around the sea have been carefully chosen for their pre-existing touristic activities, their proximity to infrastructure and access to water, and the presence of natural reserves. The infrastructure intensifies the activity of each site and reveals and makes use of their specific natural qualities.

The project is located on Israeli territory on the site of Ein Gedi. It is the main touristic settlement along the Dead Sea (after Ein Bokek, located on the evaporation pounds in the south) and offers a wide range of attractions, spas, and a natural reserve, Ein Gedi's natural park being Israel's third-most visited attraction. Yet Ein Gedi is suffering heavily from the consequences of the Dead Sea's fast retreat. Indeed, infrastructures and services have been destroyed or abandoned in recent years as a result of sinkhole formations.

Beginning at Ein Gedi Spa, located four kilometers south of the settlement, the project is conceived as a series of piers reaching out toward the shrinking sea. A path takes the visitors on a journey to "Ein Gedi's Dead Sea Island," on the other side of the sinkhole strip, where the vast and flat landscape is colonized by a date tree grove. The plantation is the entrance to the "island," a link to the ground and a site for campers to set up tents. A rail system allowing for transport of the dates continues down to the sea and can be used by those who came for a beer at the seaside instead of a hike.

In the distance, a lighthouse indicates the access to the water. The tower, meeting point of the earthly and marine structures, adapts to the changing level of the sea and gives access to the floating beach. For those who are curious, the path continues all the way to Ein Gedi, with different attractions along the way, including a bird-watching platform, the sinkholes park, and a slide tower. At the extremity of the path, Ein Gedi's new gas station is the link to the road and the village as well as the starting point for hikes along the natural reserve's *wadis*.

The 5.6-kilometer infrastructure offers an expedition into an industrial and marine universe. The simple and repetitive structure of steel trusses supporting a four-meter-wide wooden deck leads visitors to wider platforms with specific views, activities, and pavilions. To bridge the sinkhole strip, the structure will require deep foundation piles reaching below the fragile geological layer, a salt layer located 15 to 20 meters below ground level. At the sea level, the water's high density of minerals will cover and protect the structure, leaving behind the white trace of its retreat.

— *Arnaud Baudouin / Yann Junod*

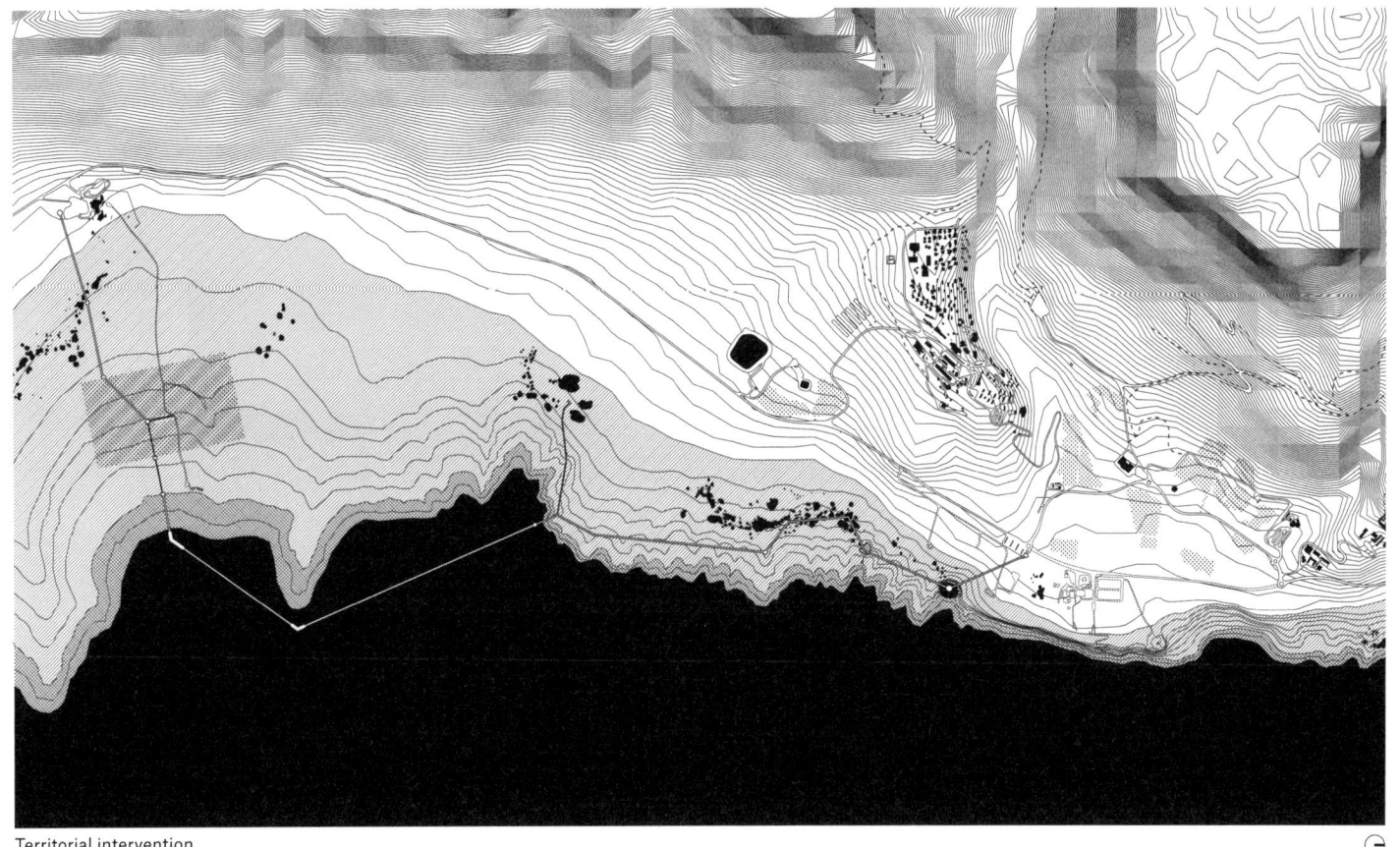
Territorial intervention

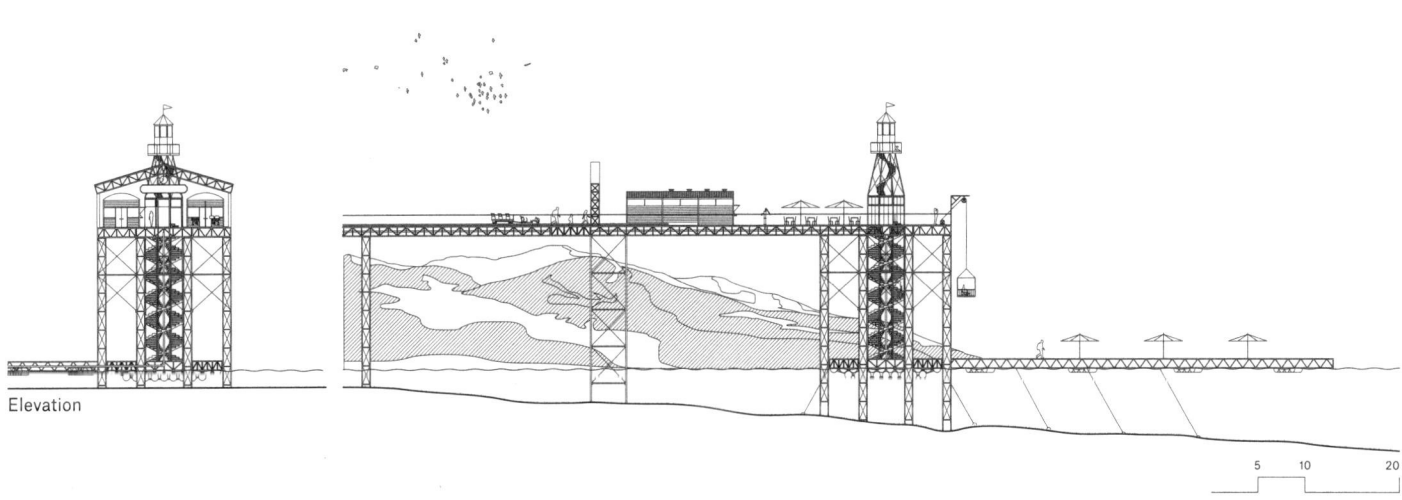
Elevation

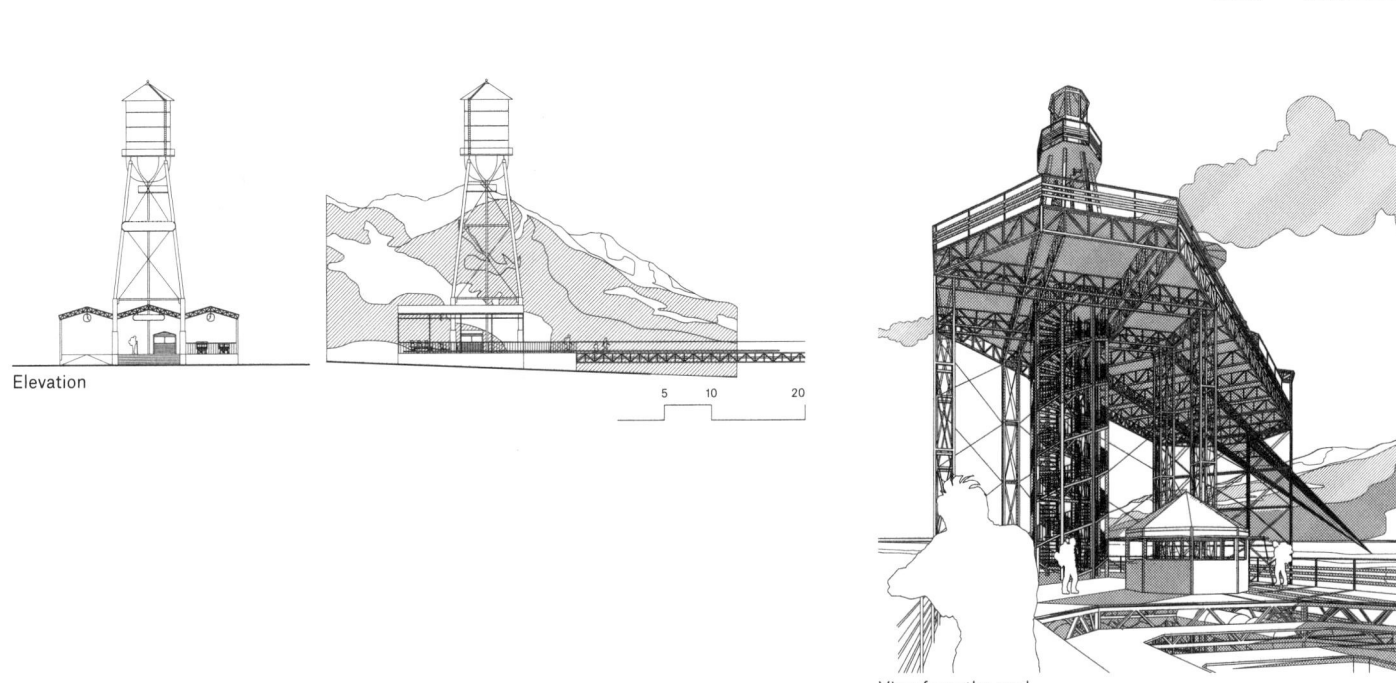
Elevation

View from the pool

Architecture: Jordan Rift Valley   121

Architecture: Jordan Rift Valley 123

# 2 The Jordan River Hydropower Station

This project is based on the assumption of the implementation of an international water accord between the countries of the Jordan River catchment area. In case of such an agreement, the Jordan River water flow could be increased up to five times. The Jordan River Hydropower Station presents some of the benefits of rehabilitating the river, one of which could be the production of sustainable energy. The West Bank is almost completely dependent on Israeli energy produced by coal and gas. The power plant could produce sustainable energy amounting to 10 percent of the West Bank energy needs.

The site for this project has been chosen to best suit the demands of a hydropower plant. Site characteristics include a high sloping river and steep riverbed walls. The site was found close to the Israeli settlement Shadmot Mehola and the Jordanian village of Salkihat w Hajijah. The building proposed is not only a power plant; it has two other main functions, a river/border crossing, and recreational areas along the shores of the new lake.

The top level is the border crossing, used mainly by cars. This is the system with the highest speed and demand for efficiency. The shape of the road is determined by the surrounding topography. The road cuts through the landscape to combine an efficient international path but also to minimize the visual impact it has on the environment.

Eight meters below is the pedestrian level. This becomes an extension of the park along the river and lake. The pedestrian level and park are connected to small roads and hiking paths. On this level there are benches, plantings, viewpoints to the overflow channels, a fish stair, a small café, restrooms, an entrance to the power station, and an access road to the turbine hall. Here the visitor can rest after a hike along the lake, walk up to the turbine hall, and see the heart of the dam. The visitor can also see to the other side of the border.

In the turbine hall all the apparatus is housed. The ceiling height allows for the turbines to be lifted up by a winch in case of maintenance. The large windows of the monitoring hall allow the space to be light and visible to the observers at the pedestrian level. The light is also practical in case of technical work. Below the monitoring level is the turbine level. This is where the water is led through the power sta-tion to create the energy. The turbines are accessible from above through service hatches for maintenance.

This building shows the potential of a land not used due to political obstructions. The open sightlines across the border aim at demonstrating the connections between the peoples. The transparency of the turbine hall and the open overflow channels display the power of providing energy and create curiosity for technical innovation. The glazed monitoring hall symbolizes the core of the valuable cooperation that provides the people with sustainable energy.

— *Anton Rosenberg*

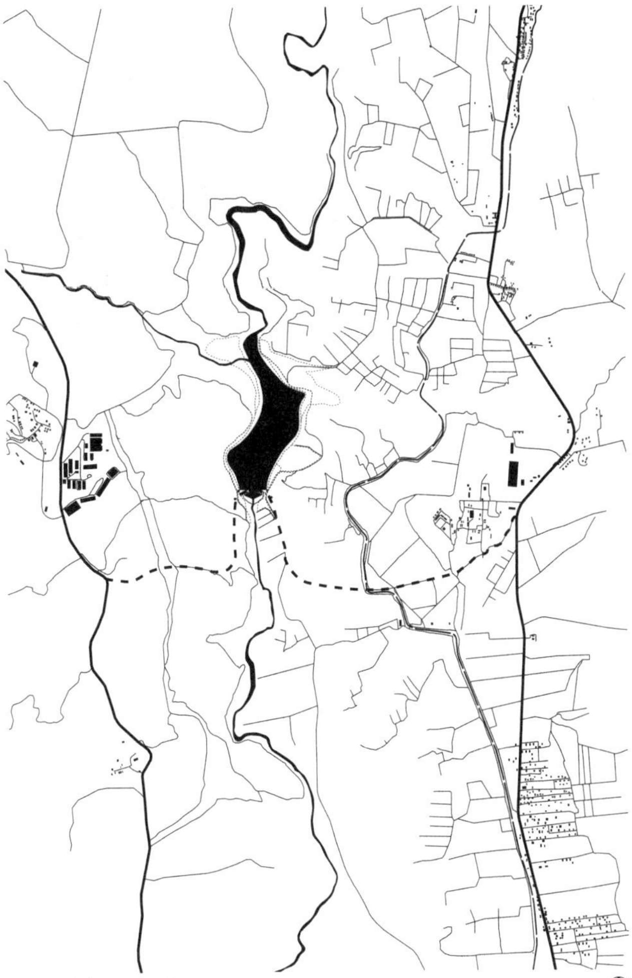

Territorial intervention

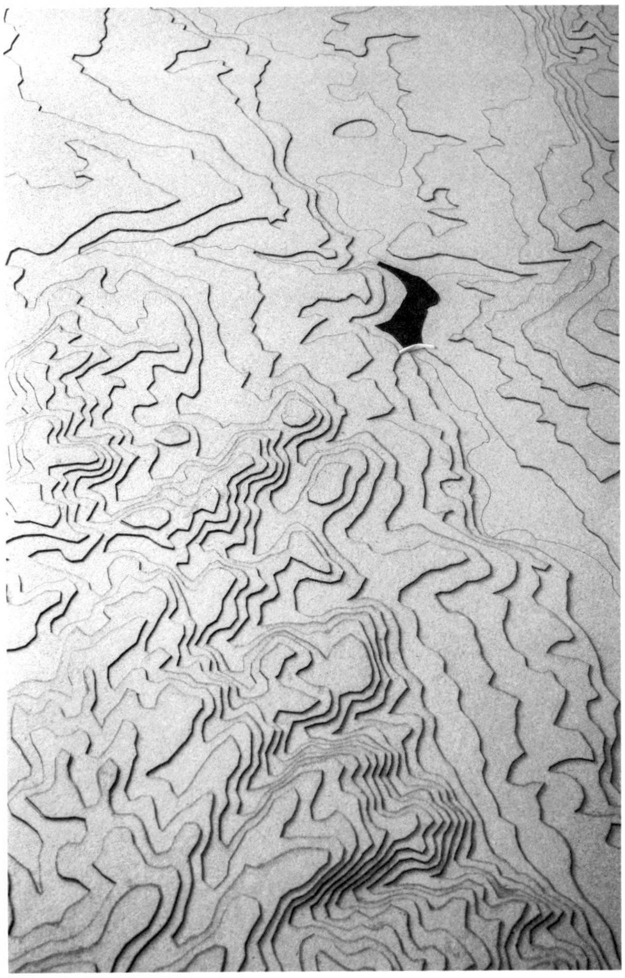

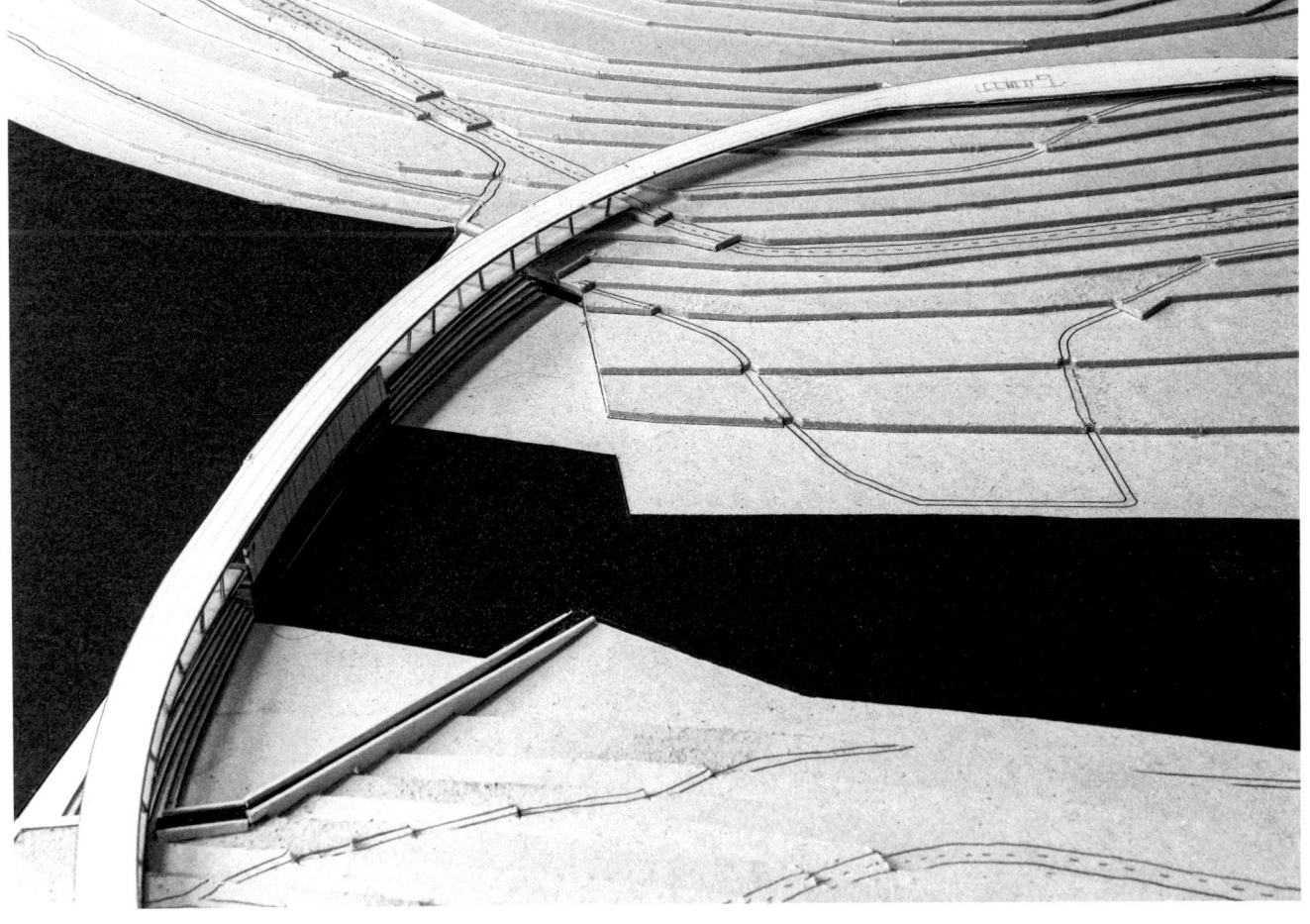

Architecture: Jordan Rift Valley

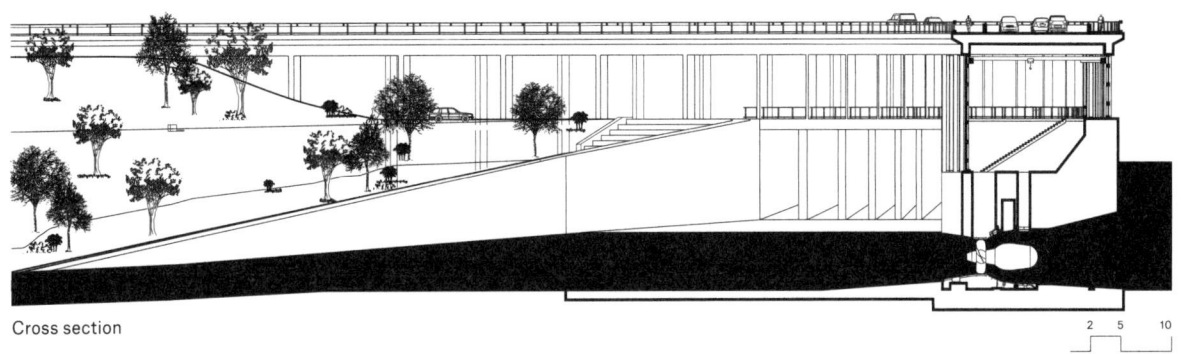
Cross section

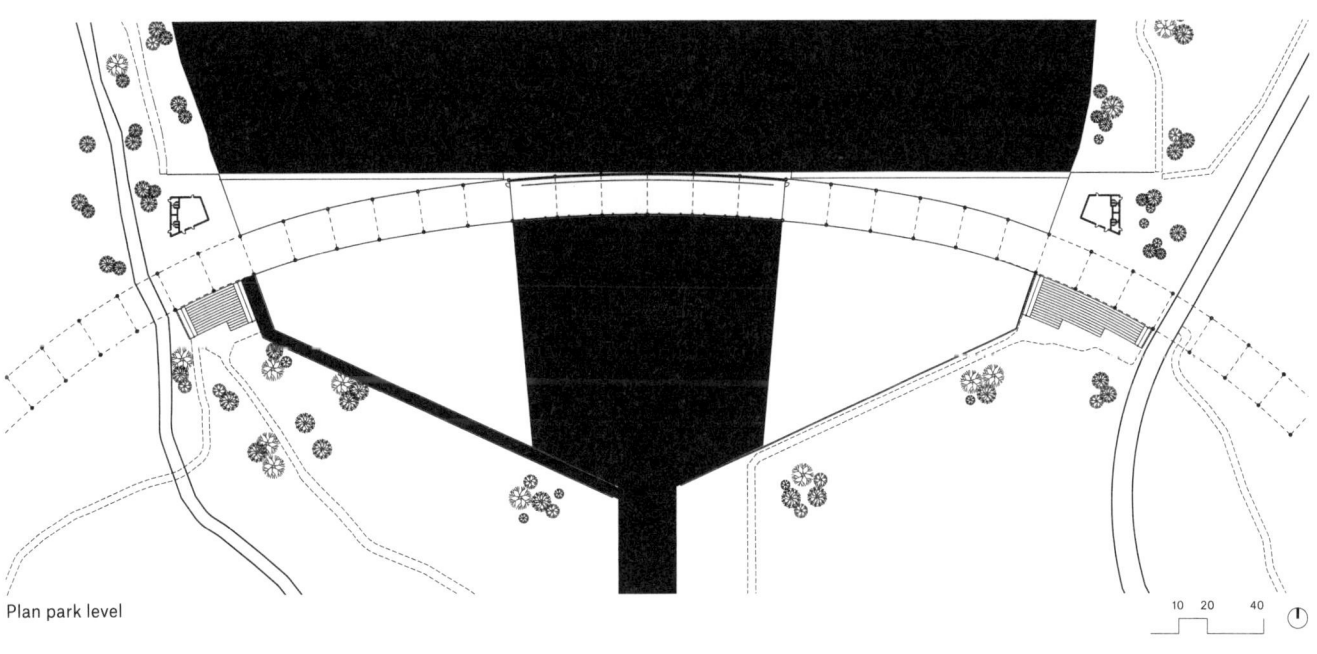
Plan park level

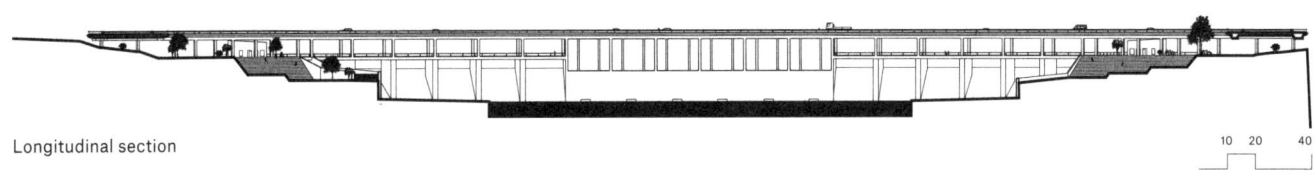
Longitudinal section

Architecture: Jordan Rift Valley 127

# 3  A House for the Levant Water Commission

The Levant is a region of great water stress, a situation that has often led countries to engage in wars to ensure their sufficiency in water resources. If these countries would engage in multinational agreements, the region could persist peacefully. The same goes for the survival of the Dead Sea, which is constantly decreasing because of the excessive use of its tributary rivers. One emblematic location of the importance of restoring the balance of hydraulic circulation is the confluence of the Yarmouk into the Jordan River; the two rivers are almost entirely drained by Israel and Jordan today.

This confluence is the site of a proposed Jordan River Peace Park, to be established by Israel and Jordan together as the first peace park in the Middle East. This park will be located on both national territories and would abolish the border at this location. This is the place where an institution in charge of the peaceful management of water in the Levant could be established as a sign of goodwill on the part of the two most concerned countries.

Located in the Jordan River Peace Park, the proposed project aims to establish the Levant Water Commission, whose role is to manage the rightful division of water resources among the Levant countries of Lebanon, Syria, Jordan, Israel, and Palestine. The Levant Water Commission will be coupled with a Visitor Center of the Jordan River Peace Park. The proposed project involves the refurbishment of an abandoned hydroelectric power plant to become the Visitor Center and the Assembly Hall of the Levant Water Commission. To complement this institution, a building containing offices for the members of the commission will be added.

The new building is embedded into the existing dam in order to highlight the hydroelectric power plant commissioned by Pinhas Rutenberg and designed by German architect Erich Mendelsohn in the early 1930s. The dam's arc-shaped form reveals the traces of the man-made riverbank, designed to withstand flows coming from the power plant. The "Naharayim" plant supplied much of the energy that was consumed in Palestine until Israel's War of Independence in 1948, when it was destroyed and the site abandoned.

With the accessible roof of the new building, the dam that was separating the Jordan River from the streams of water released by the power station becomes the access point to what is called the "Power Island" of the Jordan River Peace Park. In the design of the Peace Park project it is planned to restore a dam that used to form a lake that provided water for the power plant. The water of this recreated artificial lake will then pass through the power plant before reaching the Jordan downstream, as it was when the plant operated.

The power plant is accessible by two roads. Public access will be through the northern road. From here, people enter the Visitor Center where they will find an information desk, a cloakroom, and exhibitions. The helicoidal staircase in the power station connects to the new extension. There is also an employee entrance from the south at the other end of the building, located in a small pavilion accessible by a footbridge. Downstairs, visitors will find the public restaurant, which is separated from the offices, all of which face the power station. The central wall pierces the roof and becomes a bench for the visitors on the roof. There is a skylight along this bench that brings light to the corridor and to the offices.

For the choice of the building material, it is crucial to look at the context. In ancient times, for important buildings, people in the Northern Jordan Valley used a volcanic black basalt stone. The structure of the building would then be constructed with concrete using local aggregates of black stone. As for the façades, they would be entirely glazed to allow light to penetrate as much as possible into the embedded building. The project results from the conversion of an abandoned heritage building into a regional institution while respecting the integrity of the infrastructure.

— *Xavier Barreca*

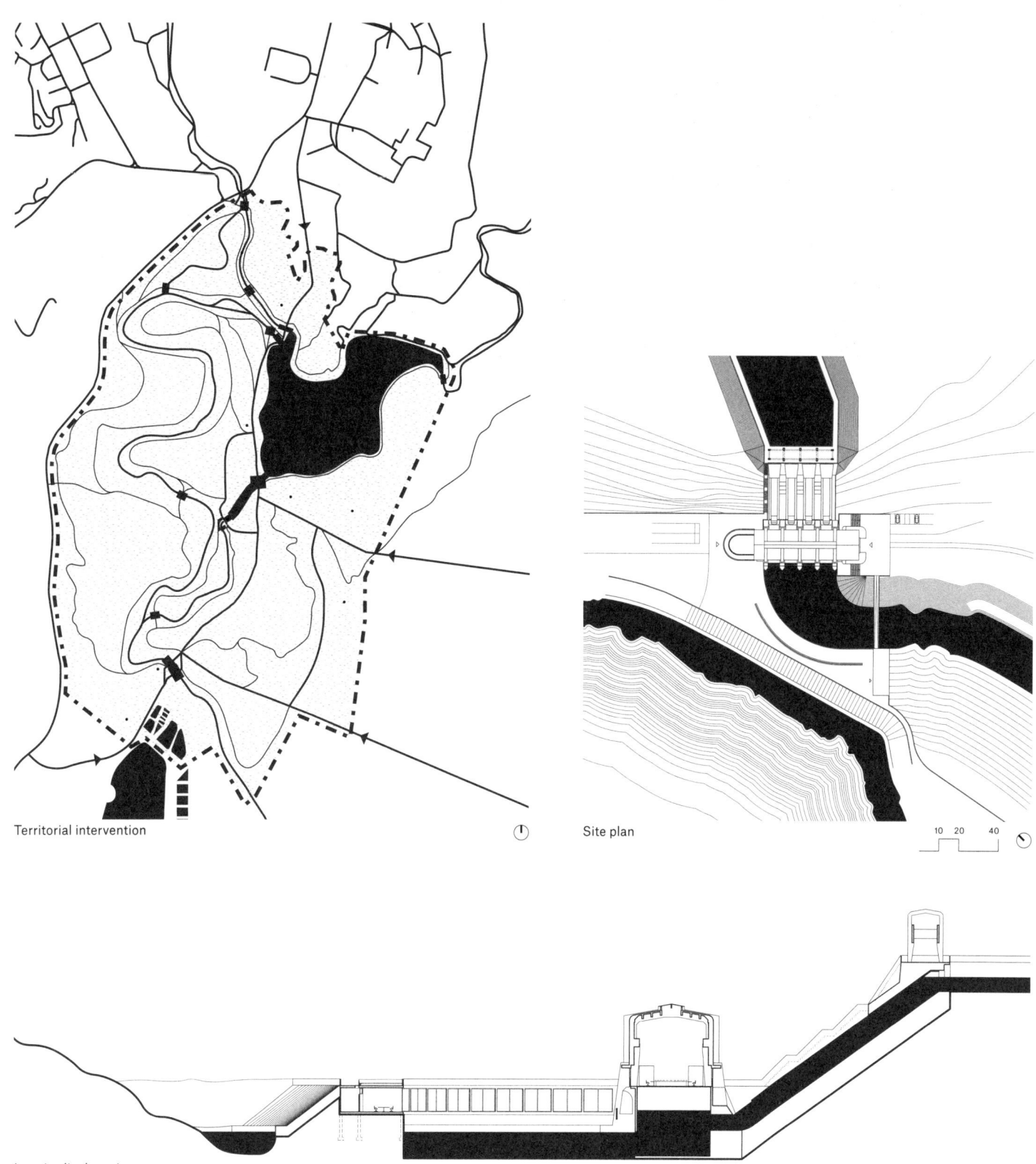

Territorial intervention

Site plan

Longitudinal section

Architecture: Jordan Rift Valley

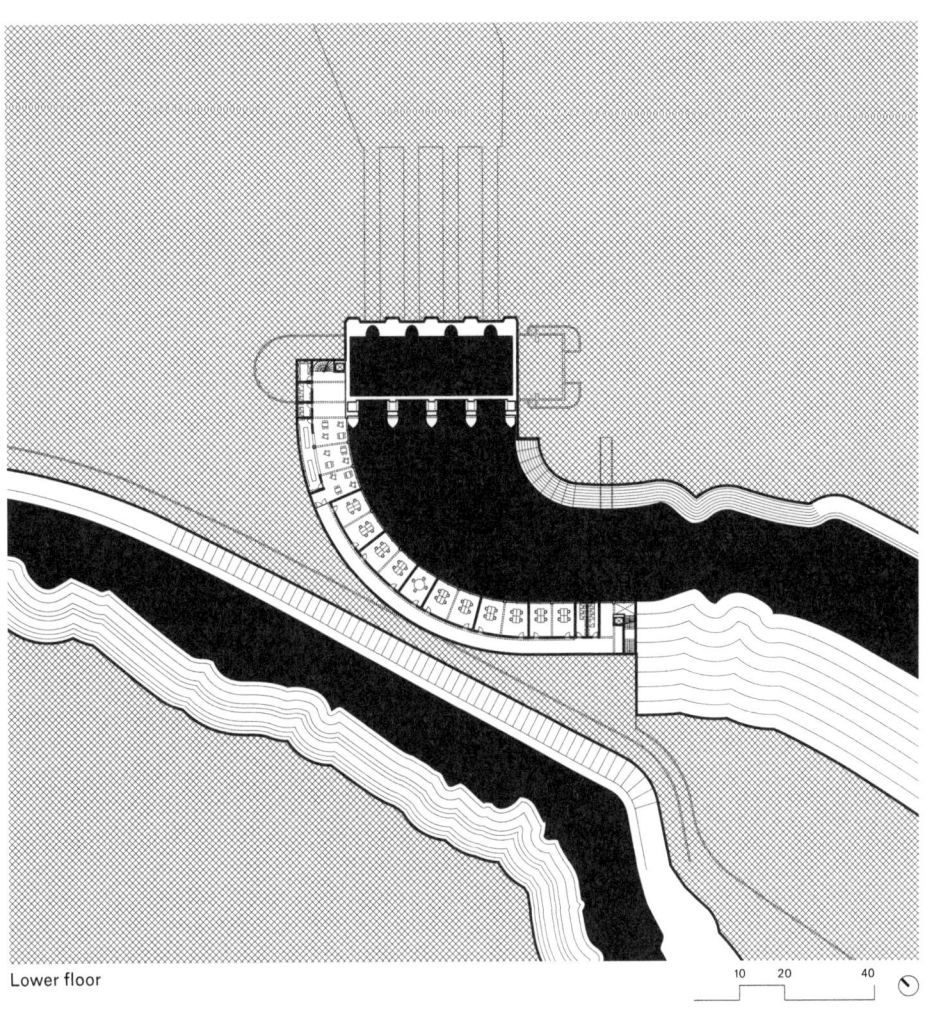
Lower floor

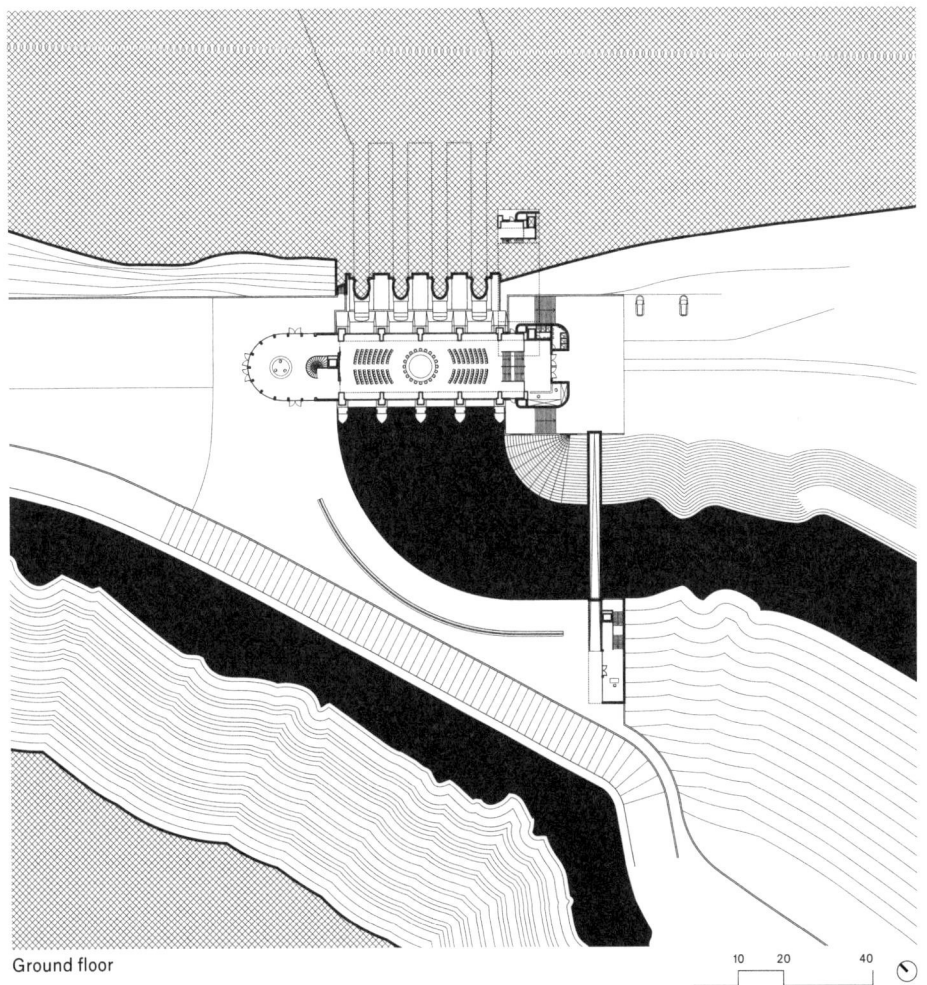
Ground floor

131

# 4 Sorting Center in Jericho, Palestine

Antoine Lavoisier wrote, "Nothing is lost, nothing is created, everything is transformed" (Traité élémentaire de chimie, 1789). While in nature everything is integrated into an endless cycle where nothing is wasted, human activities currently produce large amounts of discarded matter. This research project aims to embrace our consumerist attitude and find a solution to integrate the natural recycling system into our way of life.

Waste presents a serious problem in Palestine where it has become a threat to the environment and public health. The city of Jericho's main landfill was expanded in a move to manage waste over the next 10 years, yet 15 percent of the trash ends up in the streets due to a lack of coherent organization and local infrastructure. The question at stake is: How to organize a system that combines both the creation of profit in relation to solid waste management and of awareness raising of recycling practices among Jericho's residents?

The project begins with the establishment of a collecting strategy: splitting the recycling part into 3 programs scattered on the east/west main axis of the city. Firstly, a compost/biogas center has to be constructed as an extension of the old landfill on the west side of the city that takes care of 60 percent of the actual waste production. Secondly, a pedagogical workshop and a second-hand shop—called Waste to Resource Educational Center—is placed on agricultural land next to the refugee camp Aqabat Jabr for inhabitants of the Jericho district. Thirdly, a sorting complex is established at the city center making a link between an industrial factory and an open public space.

The sorting process promotes the city's economic development by using steel from the local factory and creating between 15 to 25 working places. It's also an opportunity for a future commerce of recycled raw material, especially for the construction industry of the Jordan Valley.

A pedestrian connection through the Wadi Quelt is proposed. This ephemeral river normally full of trash needs to be cleaned and celebrated as a symbol of the merger between humans and nature. The building sits in the riverbed, facing toward the city, and marks the end of the pedestrian walk.

This gesture defines the main space and the entrance point for the building. It is articulated by three curved terraces for a double use. When the *wadi* becomes a river (2 to 6 weeks per year) it is used as a water pond to regulate the stream and the water flow in the canal penetrating the sorting center. During the rest of the year it serves as a recreational public space that can be used as an amphitheater.

Access to the building is via a covered street at the bottom of the façade linked to a floor overhanging the engine room, which contains all the offices and public programs. On the lower floor the sorting process engages with gravity, taking benefit of the slopes to create a rational organization. A second perpendicular and more functional axis makes the link with neighboring roads. The building uses this axis to also create a linear pedestrian bridge on the roof of the factory connecting the two separated neighborhoods.

The consideration of work conditions is a central aspect when discussing social/environmental issues. The main goal is therefore to create the best atmosphere according to the climate of Jericho. A double-skin façade with perforated metal openings regulates light and creates a natural dual-aspect ventilation.

The internal skin intensifies the programmatic difference between lower and upper floors, between visitors and workers. The alternation of colored polycarbonate panels and standard windows defines some specific views to the surrounding nature, staging the link between the building and the environment of Jericho.

— *Quentin Menu*

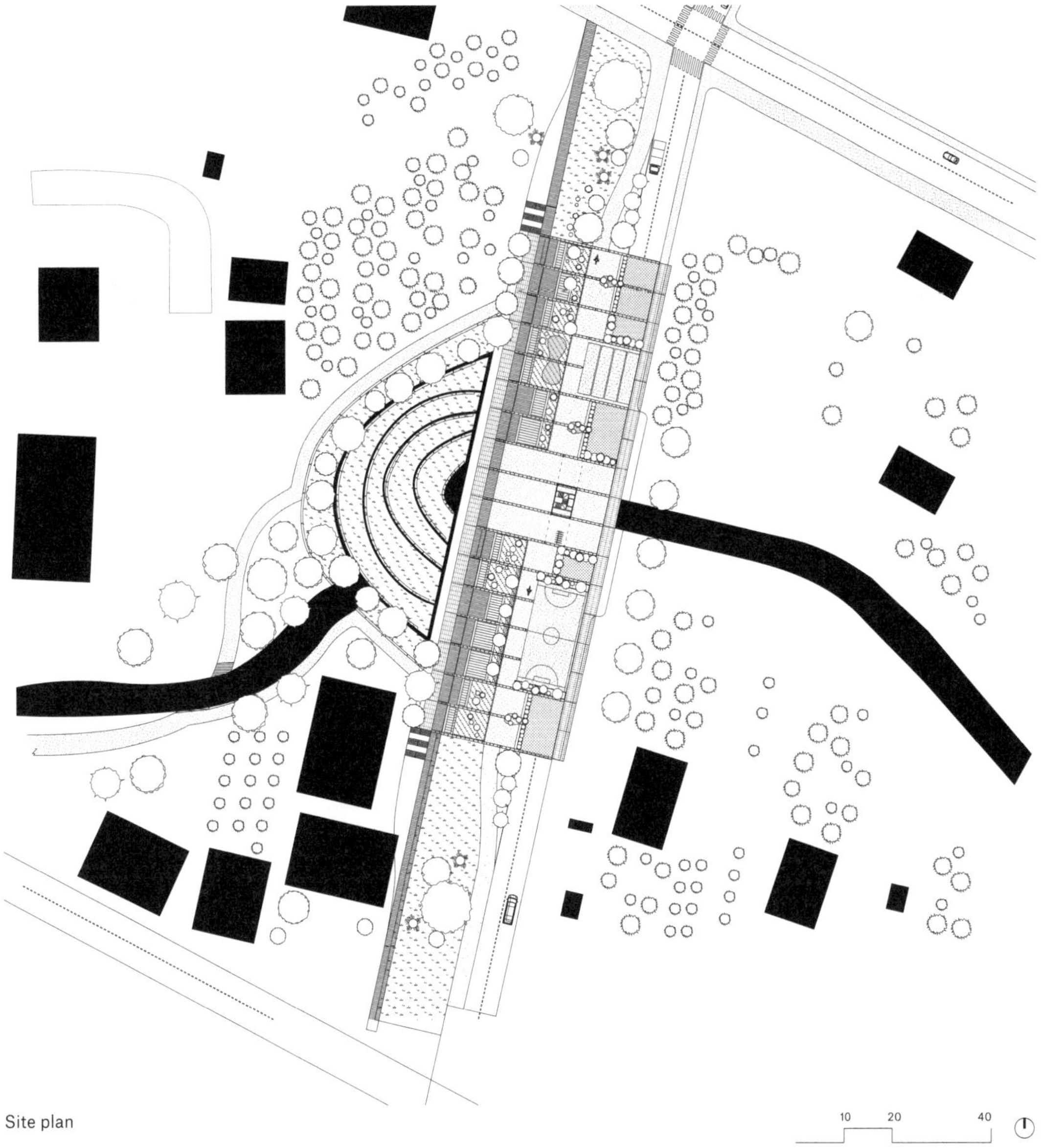

Site plan

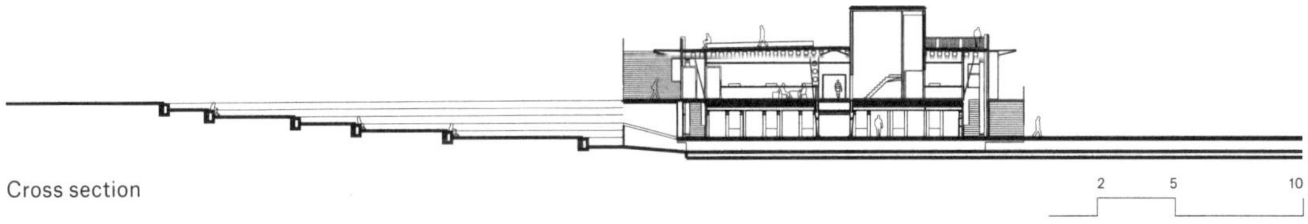

Cross section

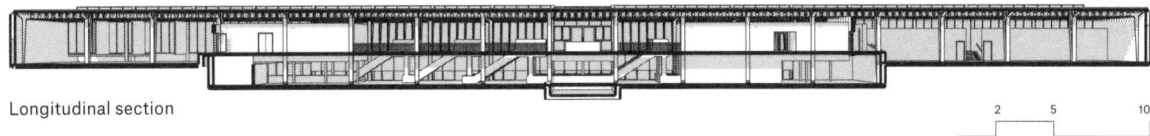
Longitudinal section

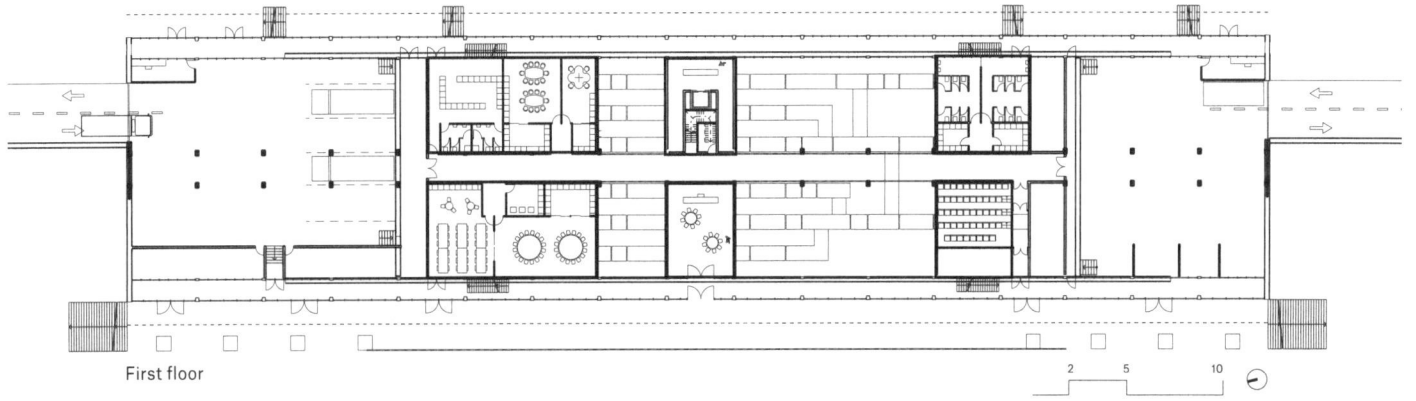
First floor

# 5  Makhtesh Hakatan Dam

The need to achieve energy security through the use of renewable resources is one of the main challenges Israel needs to tackle. Furthermore, the shrinking of the Dead Sea is causing economical and ecological problems such as the development of sinkholes along its coast. This has prompted several projects of pipelines linking the Dead Sea to the Red Sea or the Mediterranean. Water scarcity caused by increasing desertification is another serious concern in the region.

In response to these challenges, the proposed Makhtesh Hakatan Dam would enclose a naturally formed crater ten kilometers southwest of the Dead Sea. It would be fed by deviating the current pipeline project without the use of any additional energy. The two billion cubic meter reservoir will be the largest grid energy storage of the country. It will feed a 350 megawatt power plant, which could be used in times of peak demand.

Moreover, the lake will offer new opportunities for the tourism industry, which is already shifting toward the southern part of the Dead Sea because of the absence of sinkholes. In this sense, the resort culminating at the top of the dam represents the first gesture in what could become a much larger leisure landscape surrounding the lake.

This crowning location offers exceptional views over the Arava Valley and the newly created lake. All the hotel rooms take advantage of this by facing both ways. The bedrooms look toward the vast openness of the valley while the living spaces are oriented toward the lively esplanade and have the lake as a backdrop. The esplanade, which stretches over 700 meters, offers the guests and tourists an outdoor walkway from which to appreciate the lake. As well as being a public place to wander and rest beside the water, it also acts as a primary circulation for the resort. The public amenities, such as restaurants, the hotel lobby, the spa, and the tourist information and marina center, are on the same level as the esplanade, whereas the rooms are elevated by two meters for privacy. An indoor passage for the guests and service personnel, opened toward the Arava, will run through the entire complex.

The spa, located on the southern end, houses a variety of services as well as a collection of pools with different temperatures, salinity, and atmospheres. For instance, the most southern one leads you into the pipeline arrival space from where you can witness the power, sound, and scale of this infrastructure. The spa also expands outdoors onto the west face of the dam. As the lake descends and rises, it reveals a landscape of retention pools of different salinities.

At the other end of the dam, the tourist information and marina center provides guests and travellers with information about the crater and seasonal activities. It also acts as one of the three marinas surrounding the lake offering boat accessibility.

For structural reasons, the dam will have a stepped concrete facing, which has the added benefit of allowing an easy access to the retention pools and to the lake. The pitched frames will also be in concrete, whereas the fill in between will be earth colored to respond to the surrounding landscape. Natural materials found abundantly around the crater, such as clay and limestone, will be used to create warm indoor spaces.

— *Martin Handley*

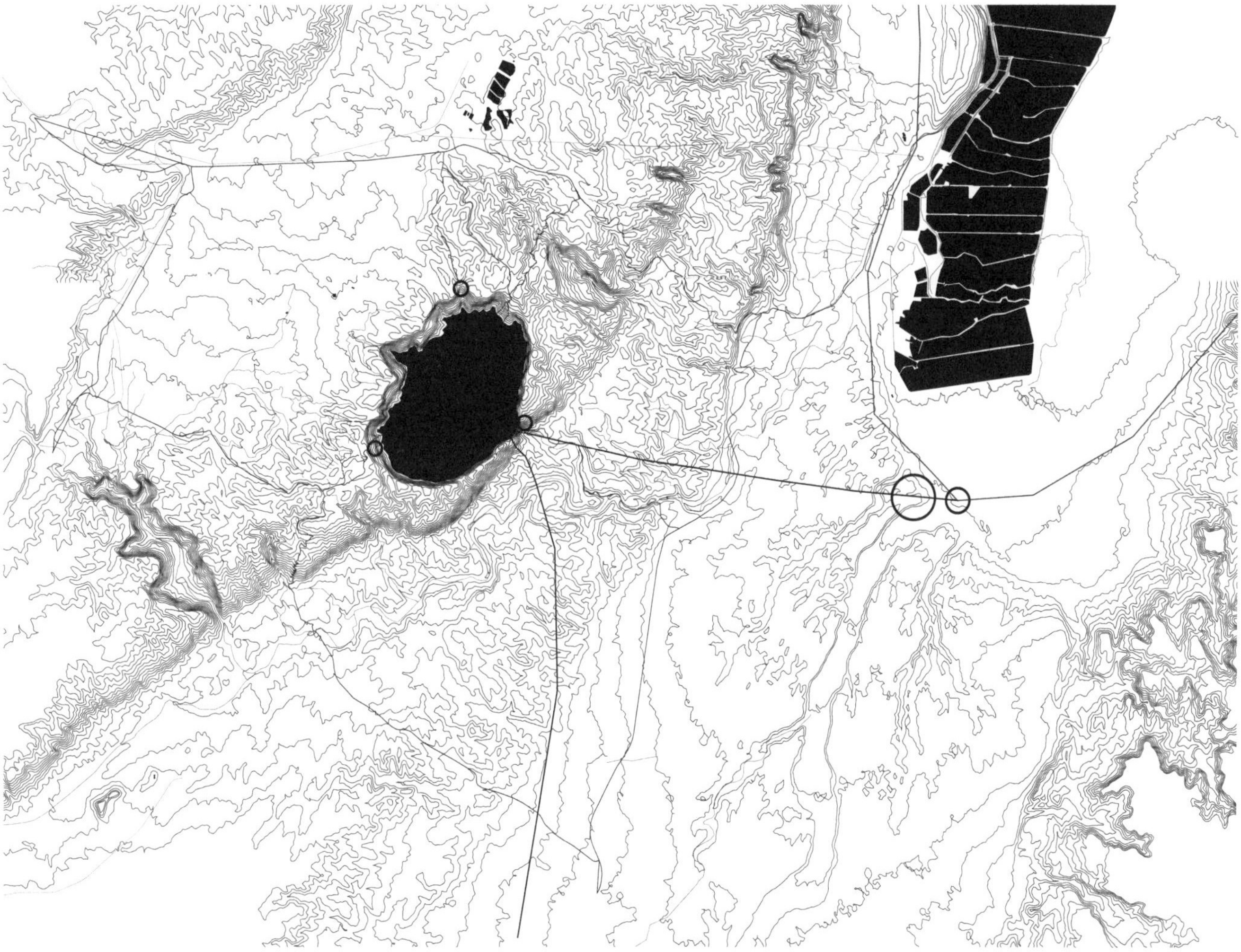

Territorial intervention

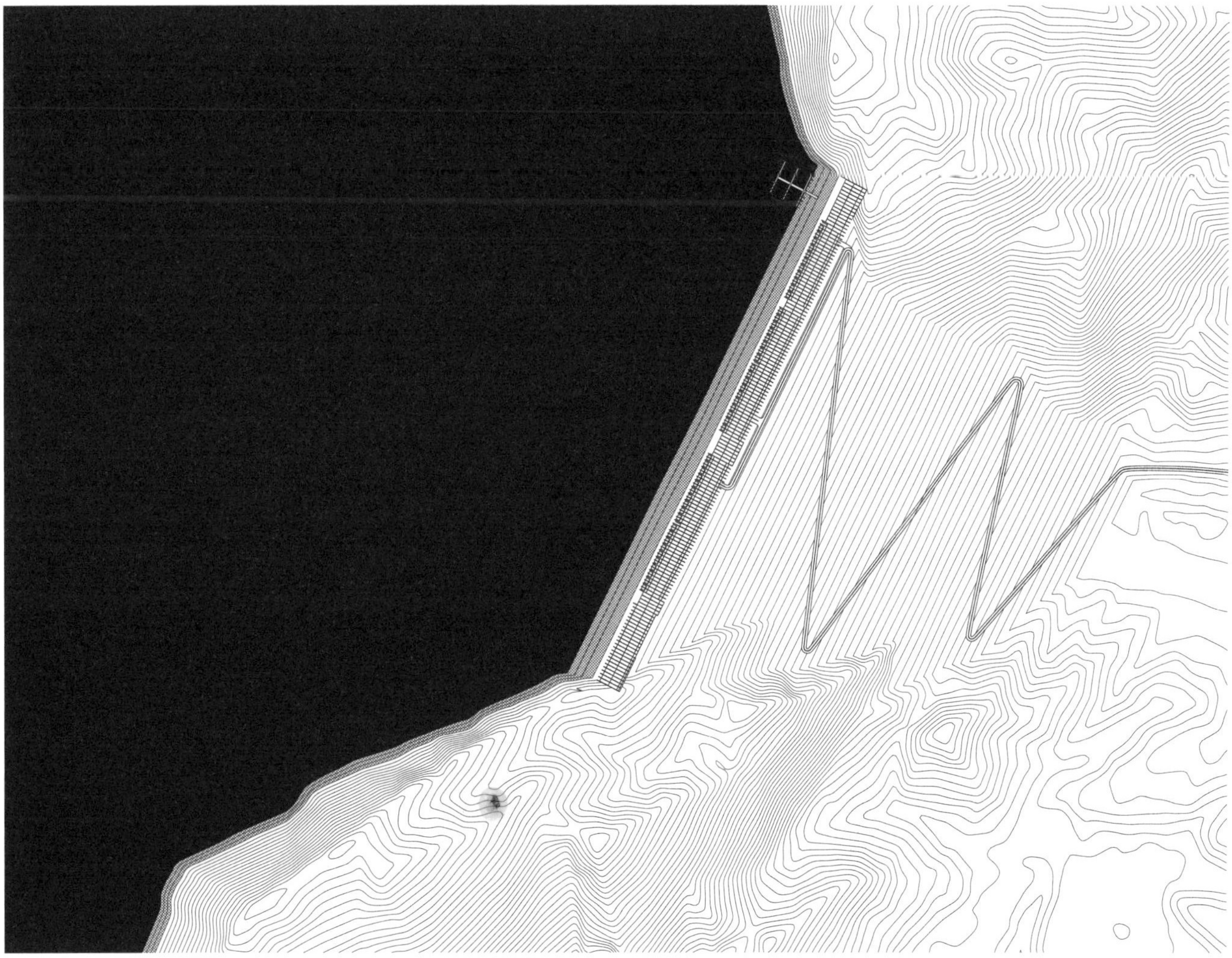

Site plan

Architecture: Jordan Rift Valley

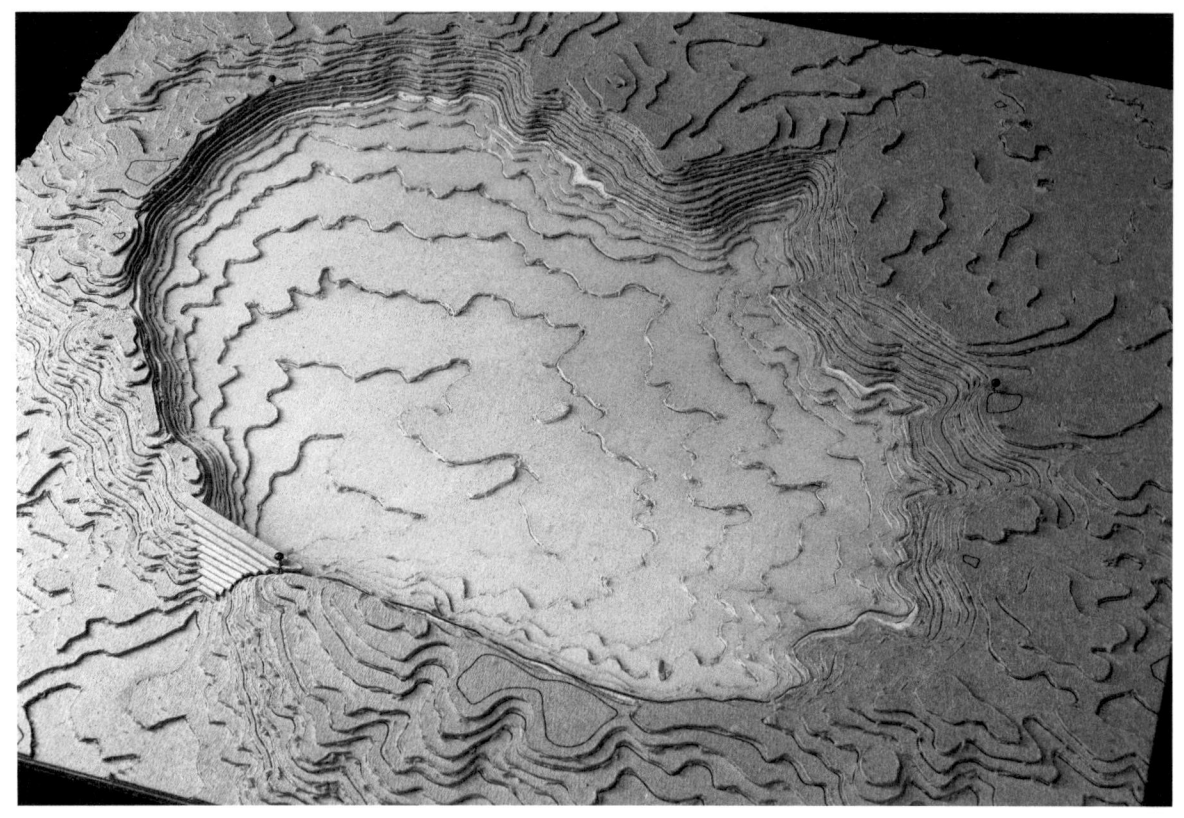

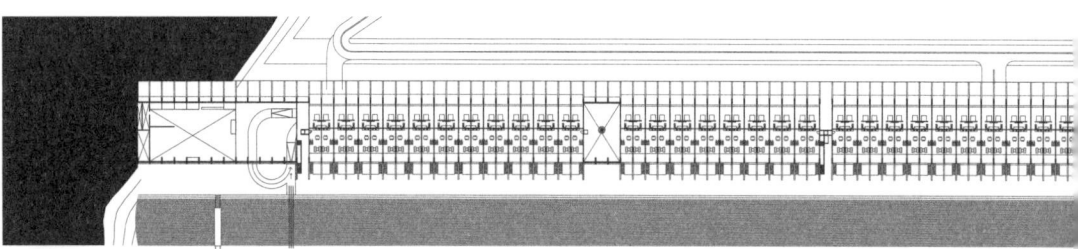
First floor

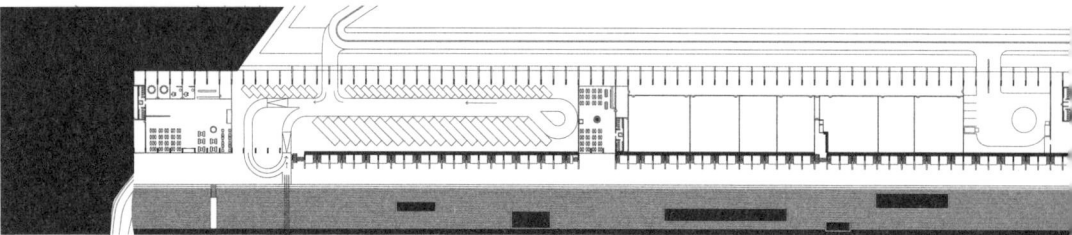
Ground floor

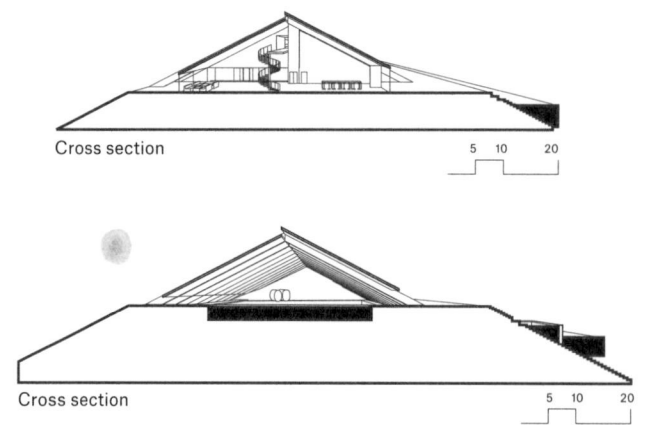
Cross section    5  10    20

Cross section    5  10    20

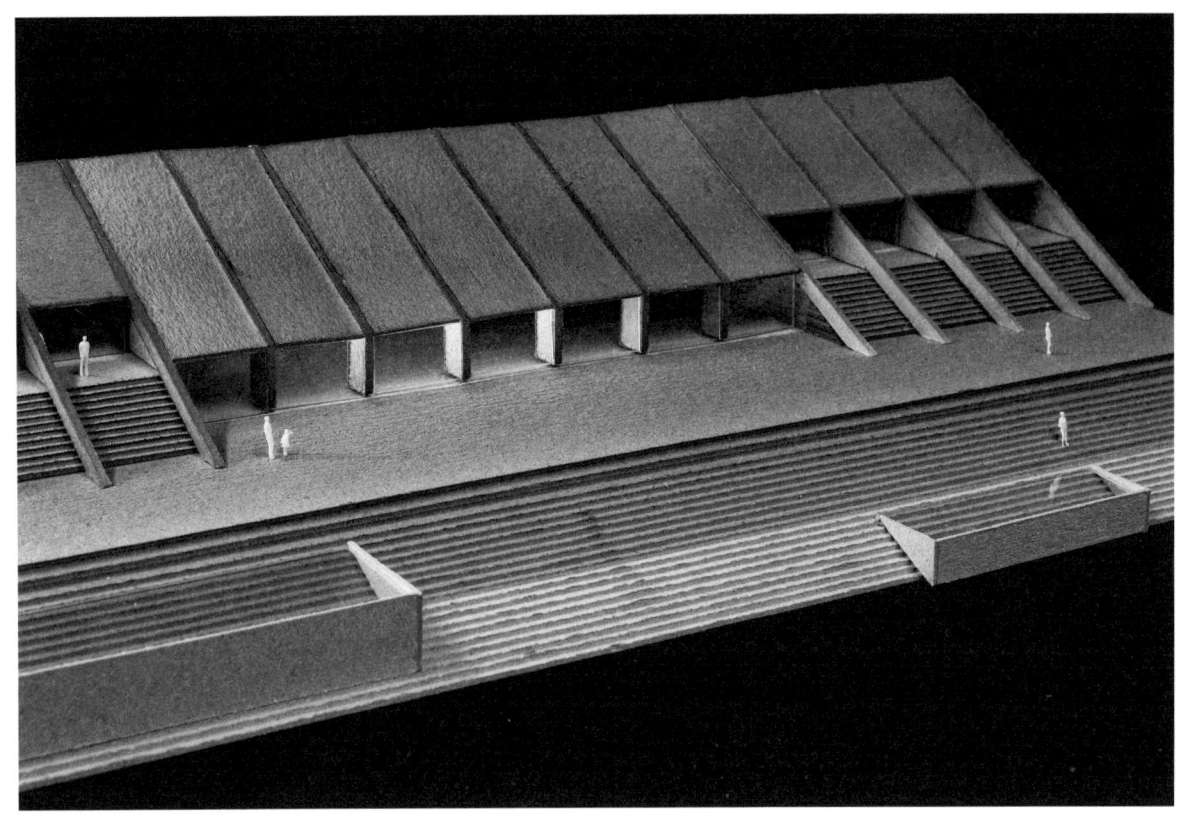

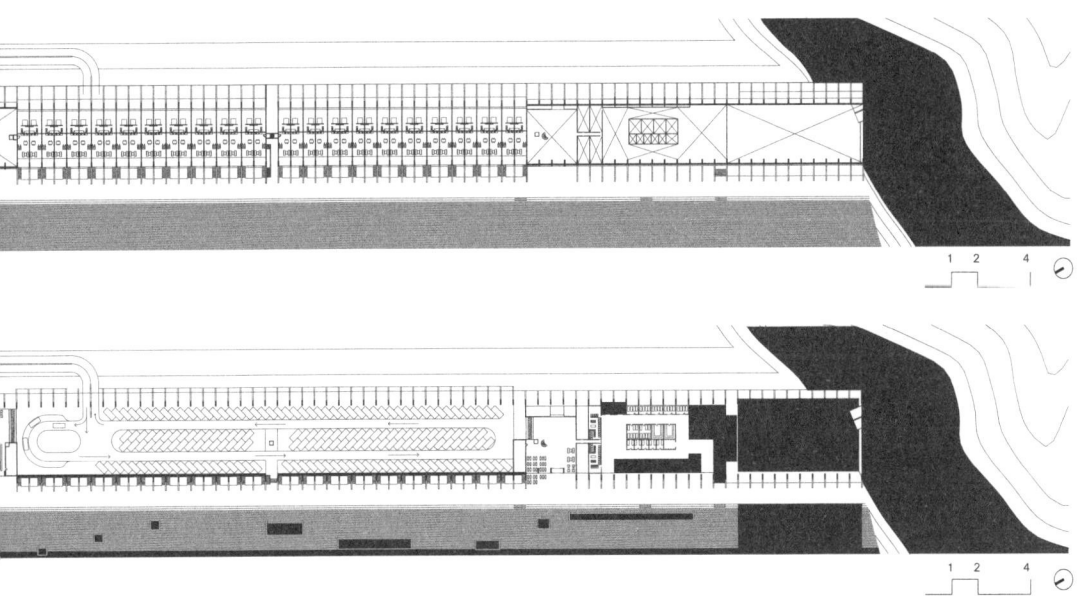

Architecture: Jordan Rift Valley

# 6  From Waste to Educational Center

The area of Jericho has a solid-waste problem: Every piece of collected waste is dumped in a landfill. To make matters worse, 16.5 percent of the trash ends up in the streets and in the natural surroundings of the city. Improving the waste situation means sorting the different types of garbage in order to reduce the quantity of non-recyclable trash going in the landfill. To address this issue, awareness by the area's inhabitants needs to be raised. This project uses an educational center to bring about this public awareness and to encourage consciousness of proper waste disposal.

The site is located on the road linking Jerusalem to Jericho, with a refugee camp on one side and a big luxury hotel and aquapark on the other side. Aqbat Jaber Refugee camp is one of the 59 Palestinian refugee camps handled by UNRAW, the UN Relief and Work Agency. The camp is situated three kilometers south of Jericho in Zone A of the West Bank, which is under full Palestinian authority. The camp is considered temporary by the refugees although they have been living there for almost 70 years, since 1948. There are 9,082 inhabitants in the camp, mostly coming from north of Haifa, and they all hope they will be able to go back to their land soon. This mindset inhibits the social-connections process between the refugees and the inhabitants of Jericho. The new educational center creates an open area where everyone benefits from shared access to the educational garden. This addresses the missing social coherence and the lack of public space in the neighborhood.

The educational center creates a new landmark. The shape of the building as an extruded catenary arch is borrowed from the omnipresent greenhouses in the region. There is no separation between the different parts of the program, except for the changes of level, creating four sub-spaces: the café faces the main road, and next to it sits the classroom that is directly connected by an entrance to the garden. The workshop is situated between the classroom and the shop. The programs and services that need to be enclosed are situated in boxes.

The relation of the building to the road network is important due to the public character of the program. Therefore, a new road crosses the site to create the main access to the building and the park. The public can also reach the site via footpaths, which create a subdivision of the garden. The main footpath bisects the building and allows a connection between the mosque and the houses on the other side of the site.

The compost cycle is implemented in the center's program through a compost area, cultivation fields, and the café space. The other highlighted area is for larger, bulky waste, with electronic devices and old pieces of furniture being repaired in the workshop and then sold in the second-hand shop. The aim is to make people understand how unused items can be a source of income.

The compost pits are situated at the southeast end of the site to avoid odor. They are placed in the shadow to keep the compost wet and to allow decomposition of the organic matter. The footpaths delimit zones in the garden: The outer ring is a public space and acts as a buffer zone between the garden and the surroundings. A small fence prevents uncontrolled access to the areas for animals and people. Inside this ring are three zones. The first one close to the building has vegetables and some fruit trees, which need care and watering every day. The second zone has orchards that need less care and attention. The third zone placed the furthest away from the building hosts field crops.

— *Maïlys Marty*

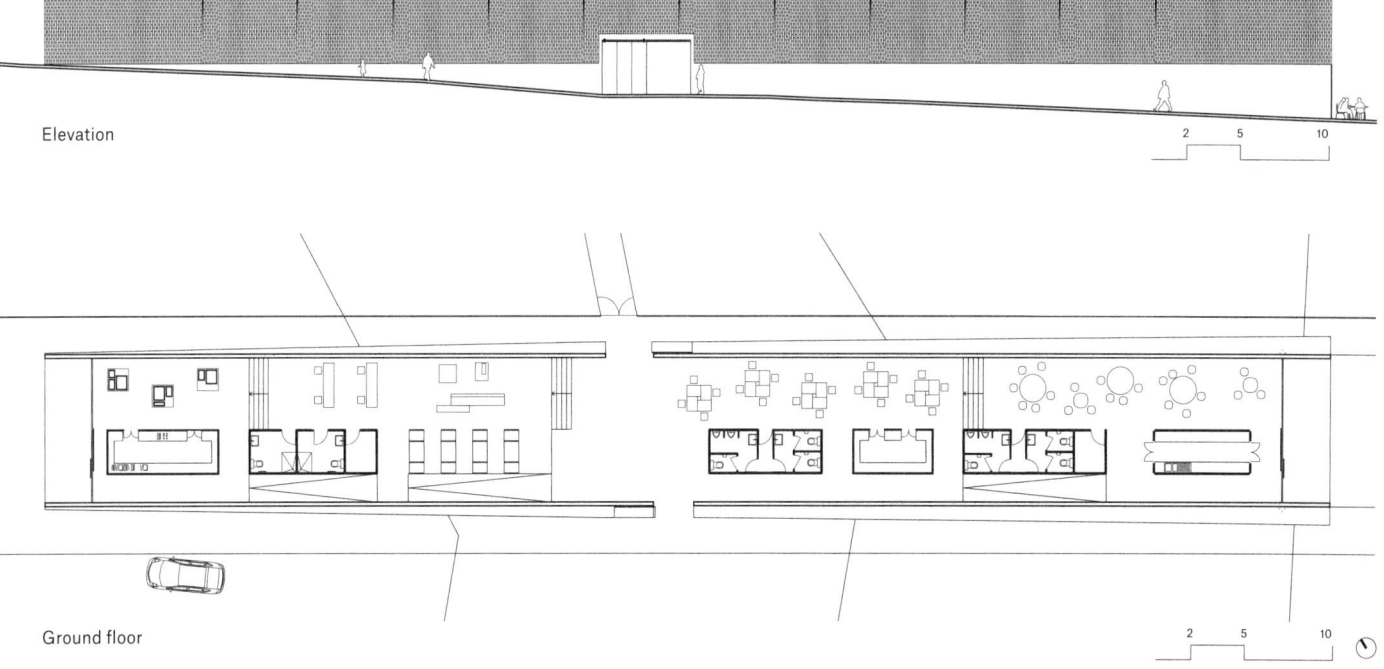

Site plan

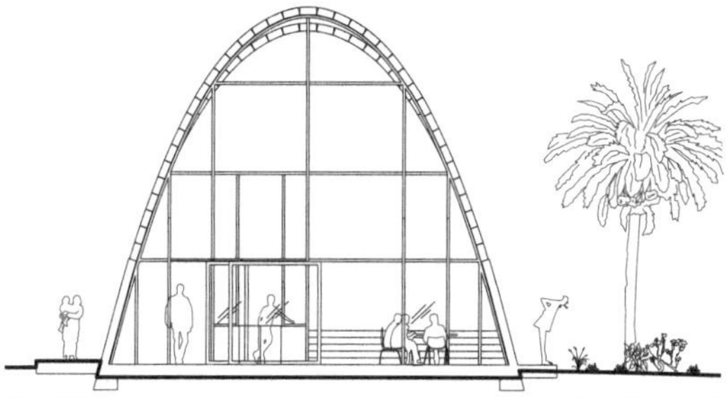

Elevation

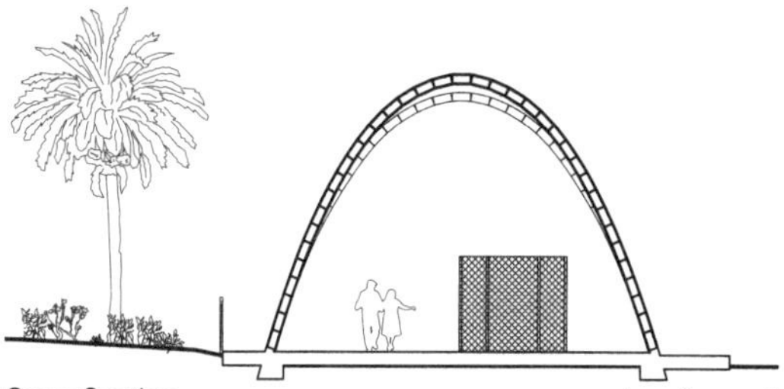

Cross Section

Elevation

Ground floor

Architecture: Jordan Rift Valley

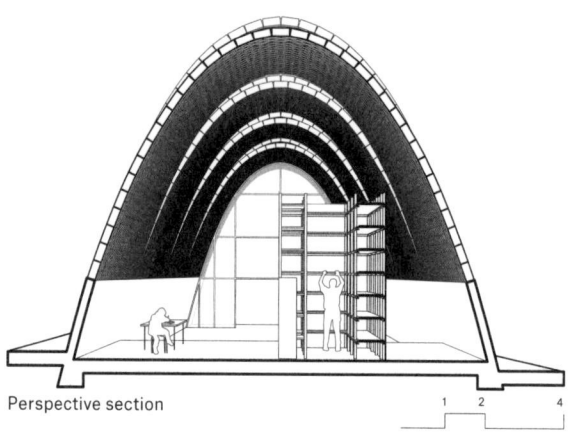
Perspective section

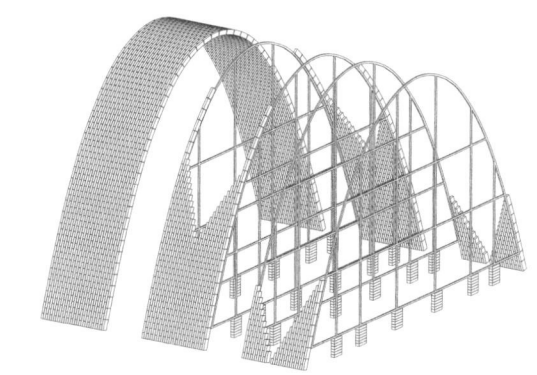
Construction process

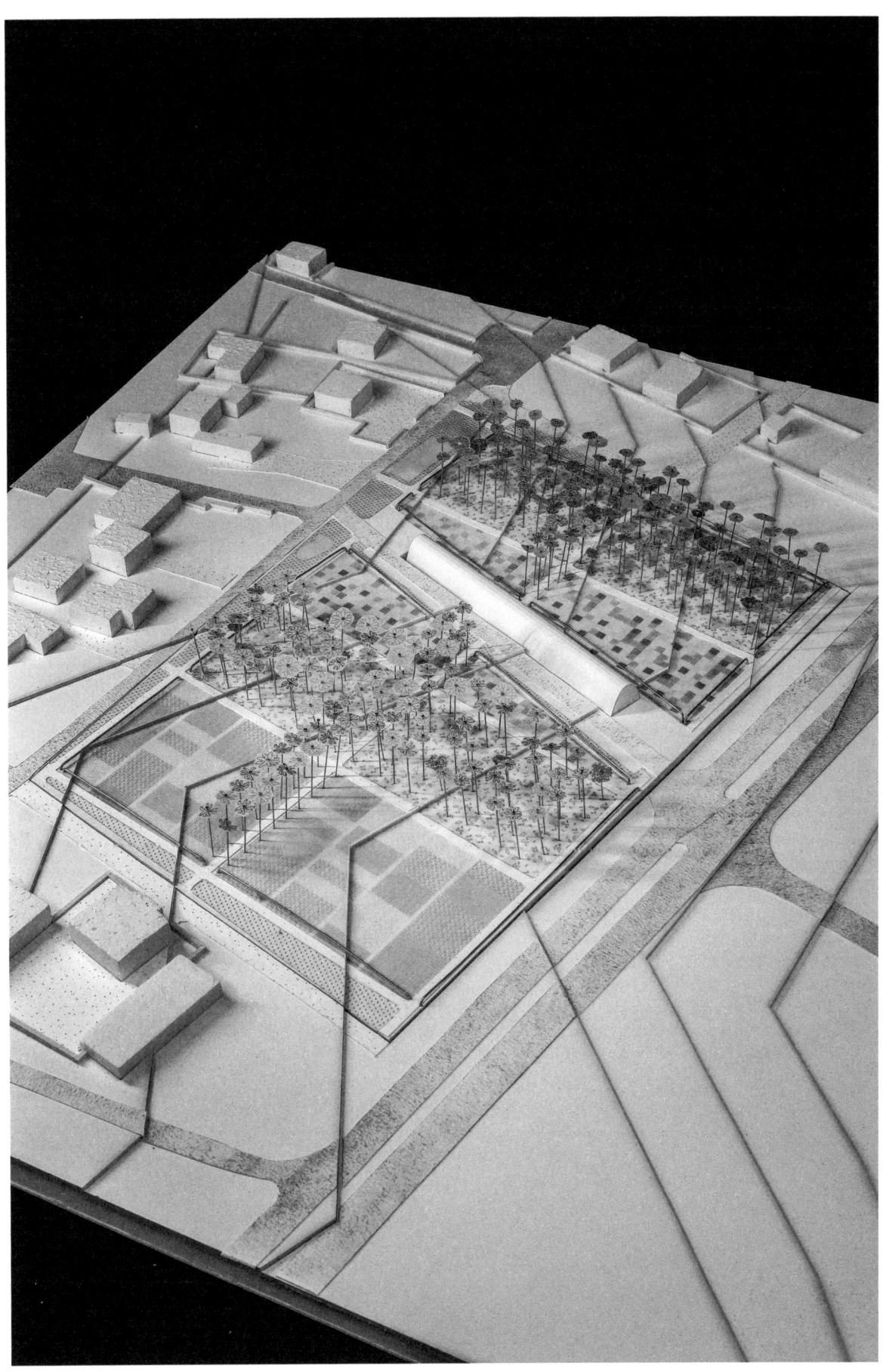

Architecture: Jordan Rift Valley

# 7  The Auja Waters Collection

The Auja Valley is situated in the West Bank near the Jordan Valley, north of the old city of Jericho. It gets its name from the Auja *wadi*, a temporary stream that used to be one of the most important in the region but has seen its flux decreased. When water runs into the *wadi*, local people enjoy being by the river. The Auja Valley is a popular hiking path and attracts tourists. It has been increasingly important in Palestine to preserve open spaces for leisure and recreation following the Six Day War of 1967.

Access to water in the region has grown problematic, with restrictions to Area C and the Jordan River. Bedouin communities on the site were gradually forced to settle and are currently off the grid. In this context the following architectural interventions seek to evolve with social, cultural, and environmental considerations.

The project aims at strengthening the water system of the Auja region. It looks at its water as a connecting element and a cultural landscape with regard to the territorial constitution of the "Dead Sea Catchment Basin." For decades, underground water sources have been endangered by overexploitation in the West Bank. In arid regions infrastructures that do not overstress water sources have been developed for centuries. Some examples are the qanats in Persian countries, *baolis* in India, or *aflaj* in Oman.

On the present site a canal was built for agriculture irrigation and livestock. It takes its water from the Auja *wadi*, whose source comes from runoff water and two springs, Ein Samia and Ein Auja. The proposed project attempts to work with this structure as a cultural element of the local landscape and strengthens the sense of belonging and identity for the inhabitants.

The canal becomes a public infrastructure along which three interventions tackle the water catchment problem. These interventions magnify the experiential potential of water's presence or absence for people. One could think of them as oases where senses are heightened. In 2011, a loss of 60 percent of water was estimated in the canal. The canal is rebuilt into precast concrete pieces and lined in the ground at its largest part. Its cross-section is a parabolic shape that gives stability against seepage, has no sharp edges that might crack, and prevents livestock from going through or inside. The parabola becomes an inspiration for the interventions' structures. They are mostly made in concrete in order to be understood as an extension of the canal.

The first intervention is situated at the beginning of the canal and is a bathing spot. Many inhabitants bathe in the *wadi* next to the Ein Auja spring nearby but also use the canal. The formalization of a specific spot for bathing prevents the misuse of the canal. It invites tourists hiking in the Auja Valley to use it for refreshment and then to continue further along the canal to the second and third interventions. It is designed in three parts, a desanding place, a sitting pool, and a swimming pool. They are protected from the nearby road by a wall creating a threshold. The canal fills first the desanding spot and subsequently the two other pools via communicating vessels. Since water does not run all year round, the water can be retrieved and reused by means of a well pump, and the sitting pool can be used as a picnic spot when there is no water present.

The second intervention is next to Ras Ein Al-Auja, the Bedouin settlement. The canal is redirected to provide access to water. An aqueduct is built to elevate the canal, as was the case in the Roman period when water was brought to Jericho. Gravity lets water flow to a series of reservoirs on three different levels. The first one collects the untreated water while the second filters and the third holds the clean water that can be retrieved with a well pump. The elevated arched structure supports both water and a path on the side for public access and as part of the hiking trail. It provides shade thanks to a light wooden structure whose spans are covered by pieces of fabric.

The third intervention is a public reservoir covered by a green roof, situated in the middle of Al-Auja where the canal starts to split into many arms, feeding private ponds for agriculture. Water is fed to the reservoir by a secondary arm through a gate valve. It runs along a slope surrounded by two terraces of date groves, which are watered by the canal. The water reaching the reservoir cascades through a small channel into the center of the basin. This feature is meant as a way to signal to the population when the *wadi* contains water. The reservoir basin is carved into the ground and stairs invite people to sit and enjoy the fresh atmosphere. When empty, the reservoir can be used for public events. The surrounding green area is turned into a park with acacias, tamaris, date, and palm trees along the small paths.

— *Tania Depallens*

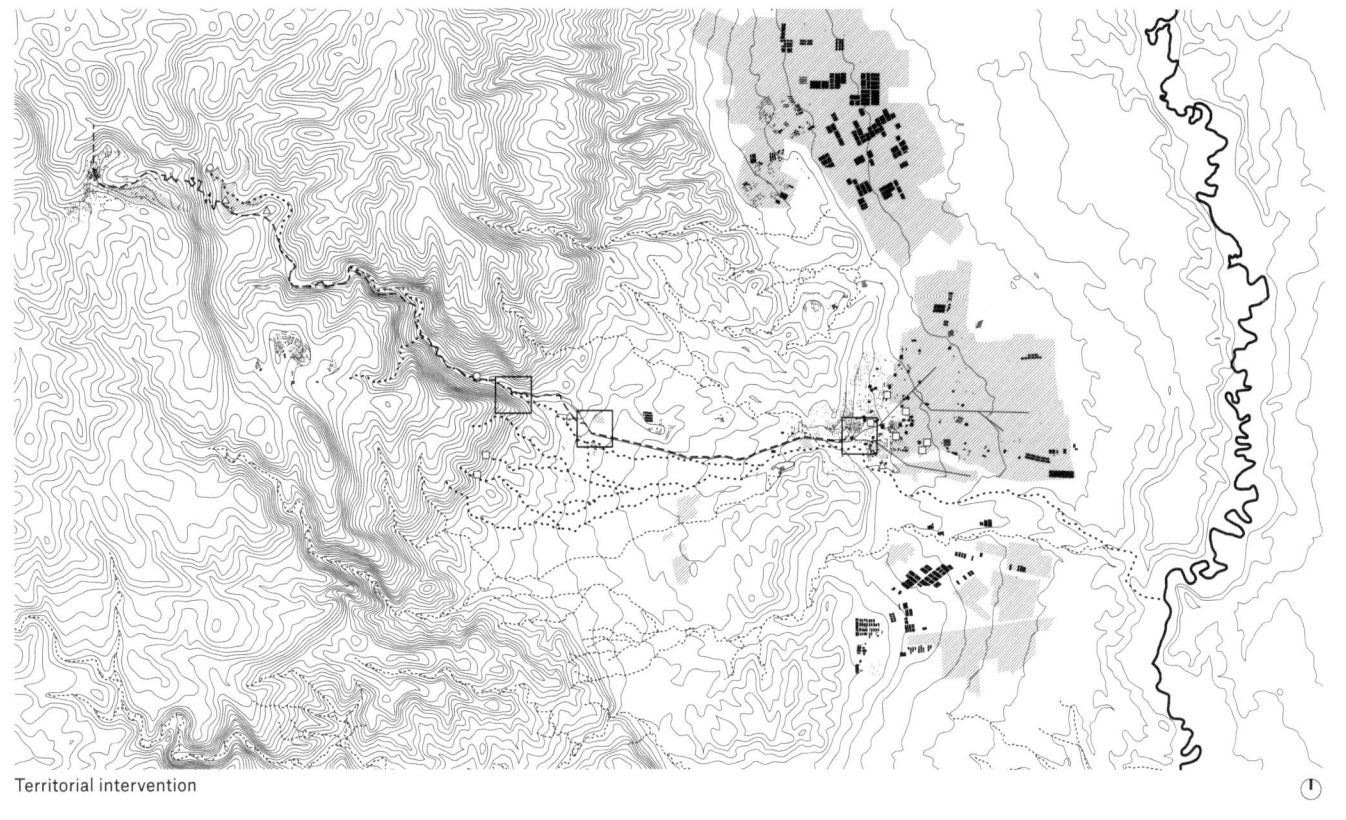
Territorial intervention

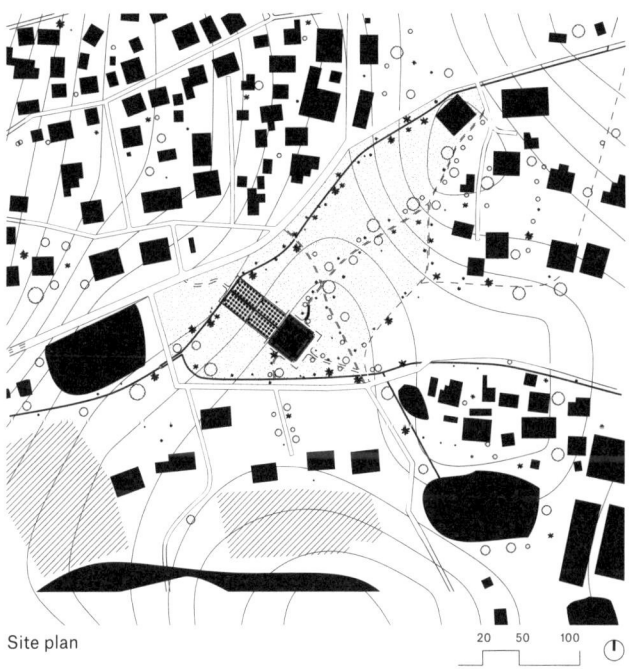
Site plan

Site plan

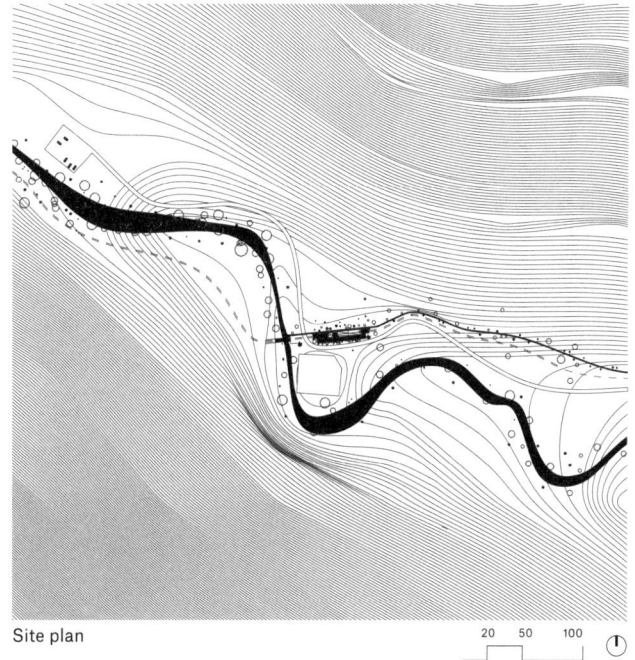
Site plan

Architecture: Jordan Rift Valley 145

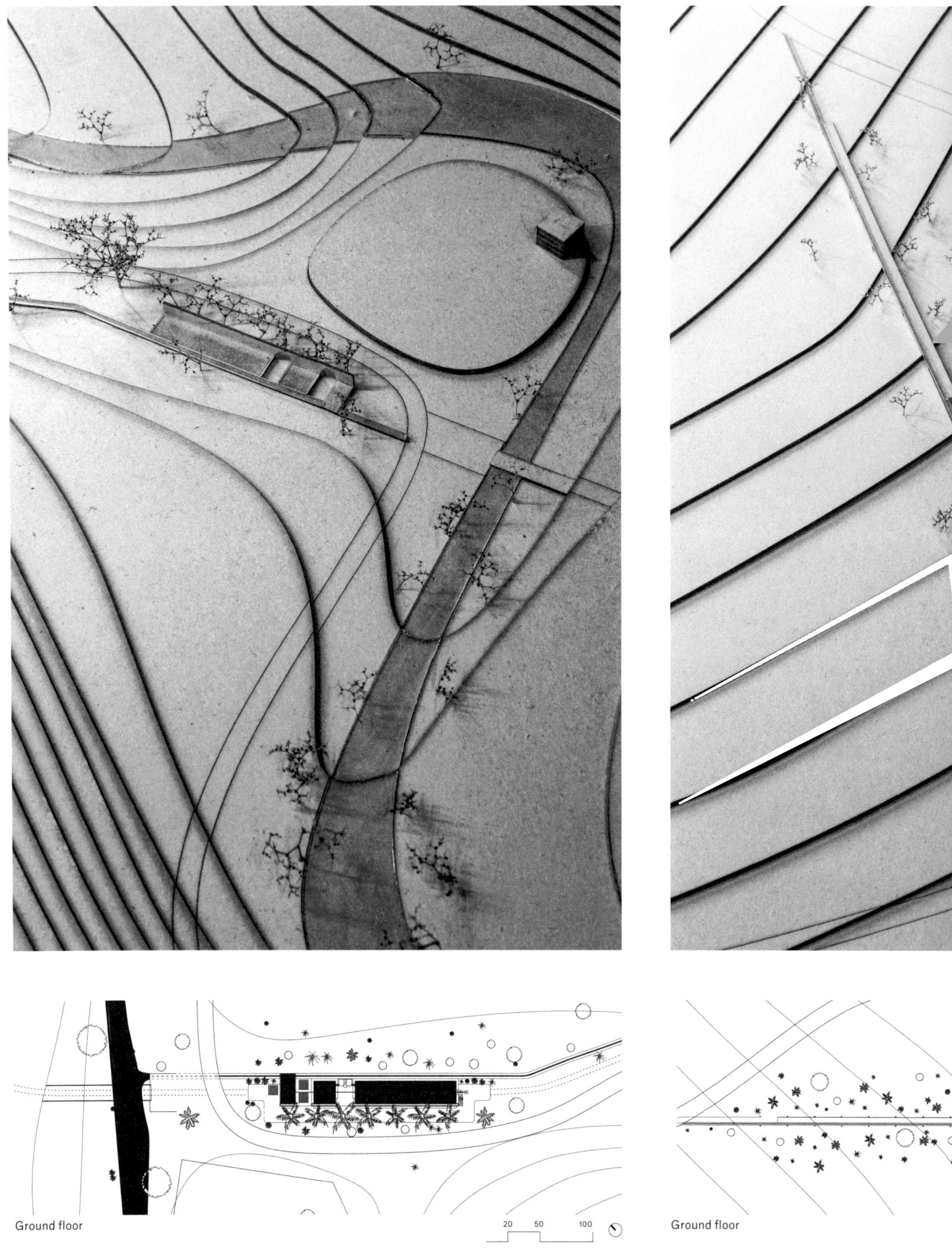

Ground floor

Ground floor

146

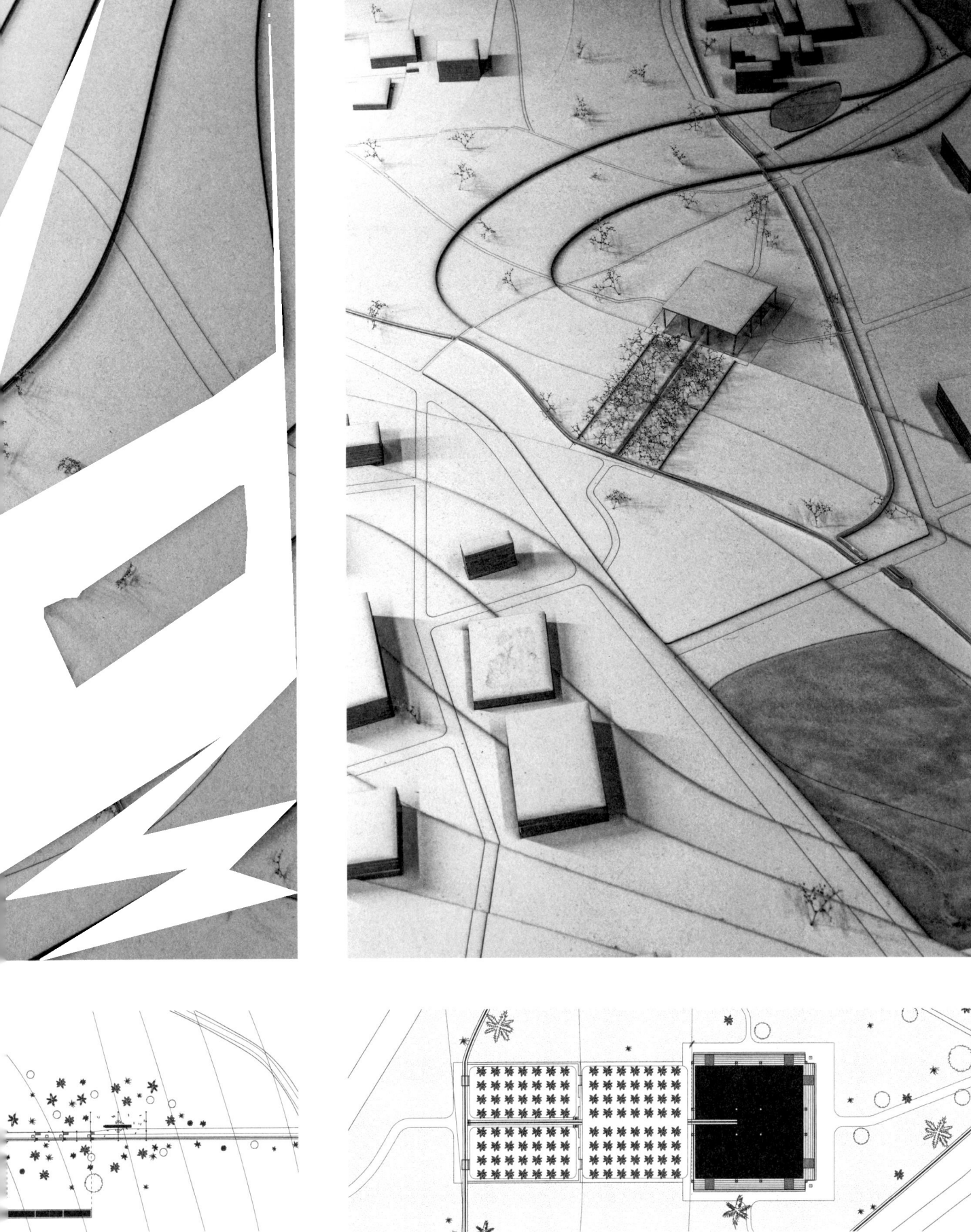

Ground floor

Architecture: Jordan Rift Valley 147

# 8 Center for Sustainable Desert Construction

According to U.N. sources the world is facing severe desertification. At present, drylands account for 40 percent of the earth's land mass and more than one-third of its population. As this surface is steadily increasing, more and more people will live in arid regions and will be affected. In Israel the desert represents 60 percent of the territory, but only 8 percent of the population lives in the Negev and Arava regions. As the population continues to grow, space will become rarer and more expensive around the urban centers in the coastal plane, and more people will spread into the Negev.

Nowadays most of the buildings in the region are made of concrete, often prefabricated, and the construction is done fast and cheaply. Usually little or no insulation is put in place, the buildings are equipped with countless AC's and other equipment to create comfortable living conditions in a region where the temperature can reach up to 50° C in summer. While neighboring countries like Jordan and Egypt have centuries of heritage of construction in desert conditions, there is a lack of appropriate knowledge in Israel. In fact there is nearly no traditional desert architecture in the country due to its short modern history and the background of most of its inhabitants.

Only a few people are looking to improve the situation and to find a more appropriate architecture; some of these people live in Kibbutz Lotan, a small village in the Arava Valley. It's a green oasis of a progressively thinking community that is trying to overcome its original military barracks architecture. With self-taught construction techniques, water recycling, and a lot of enthusiasm, its inhabitants try to make their world a better place. The Center for Creative Ecology, a kibbutz institution, offers workshops and study programs about mud building, recycling, and permaculture. Earth as a building material has a special focus, most of the time in the form of adobe bricks or plaster to cover straw houses and requiring labor-intensive handwork. Unfortunately, most constructions, for example the eco-domes, temporary living units for the students, show a rather clumsy integration of equipment and services.

The project proposes to build a center for sustainable desert construction, giving the kibbutz and its institute room to develop their ideas and visions further. The building is erected in compressed-earth bricks, an easily accessible and economic solution that provides excellent properties for the hot local climate. With its thermic inertia and hydrodynamic properties the earth can compensate for the extreme temperature differences and creates a comfortable indoor climate.

The building is an articulation between the residential and the industrial part of the kibbutz, offering its inhabitants shade for their everyday walk to work. It provides a roof for a path to the south and three major programs to the north, a public part on the west side, an educational part in the center, and the factory and storage spaces on the east side of the building. The long and slender building is oriented east-west. The structure is organized on a grid of four identical vaults, one continuous over the whole length to cover the path and the others varying with double and triple spans, depending on the programmatic needs.

A raw earth brick press produces bricks of 29 x 14 x 6.5 centimeter in size, the module for the entire construction. The semi-industrial process of hydraulic pressing allows for the production of strong and consistent bricks. They are assembled to form the vaults and walls with the help of wooden formwork, which is reused phase by phase until reaching the full length of the building. The phased construction enables the press to first produce the building material for its own shelter and then for the other programs. The structural walls are pierced by concrete elements to create transversal apertures while stabilizing the openings in the structural brickwork.

To respond to the hot desert climate the building has a ventilated second skin wrapping around the structure to prevent its overheating. The skin consists of a perforated assembly of earth bricks held in place by a substructure of bricks lying on top of the vault. A passive air-cooling system of earth-air heat exchangers helps to temper the fresh air during hot summer days and cold winter nights. From the air intake at the west façade, the air goes through four tubes and is distributed into the spaces through the nonstructural intermediate walls.

The project is to initiate the development of a more conscious architecture in the desert while assuring the future development of the kibbutz. The building should itself be a functioning prototype while at the same time functioning as a breeding ground for new ideas and concepts. The project intends to help the Negev and other arid regions around the world find better and more sustainable solutions for the increased construction activity and future climatic challenges.

— *Marlon Biétry / Nicola Schürch*

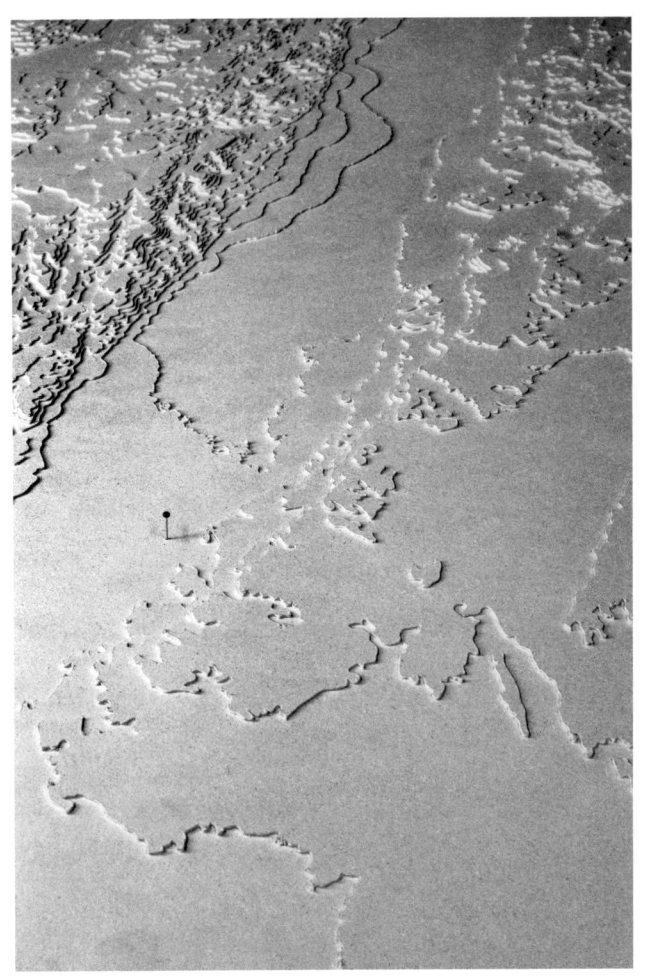

Site plan

20 50 100

Architecture: Negev Desert

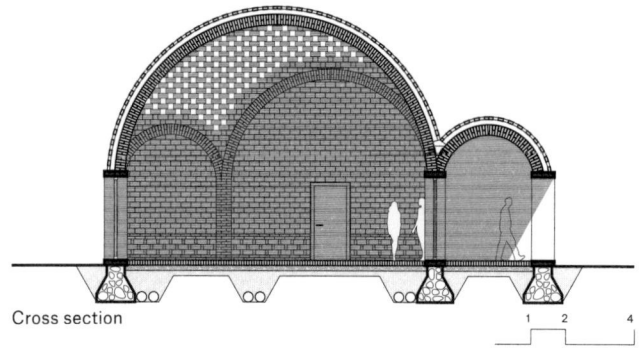
Cross section

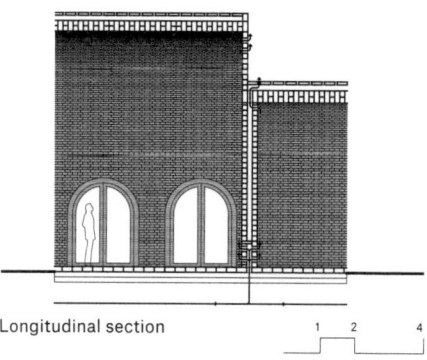
Longitudinal section

Elevation

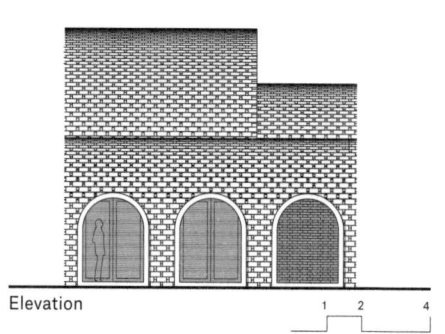
Elevation

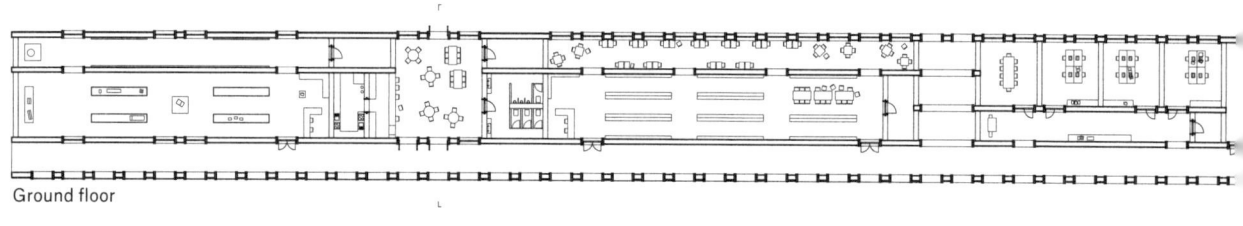
Ground floor

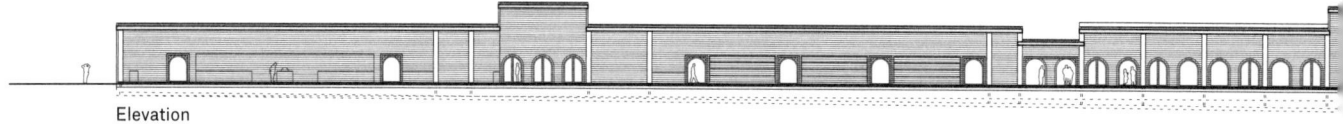
Elevation

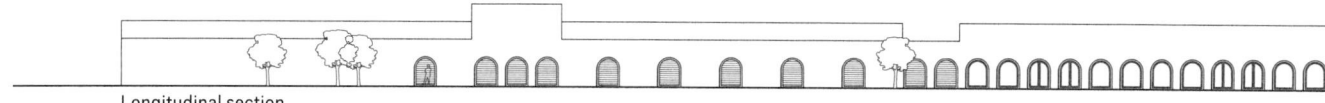
Longitudinal section

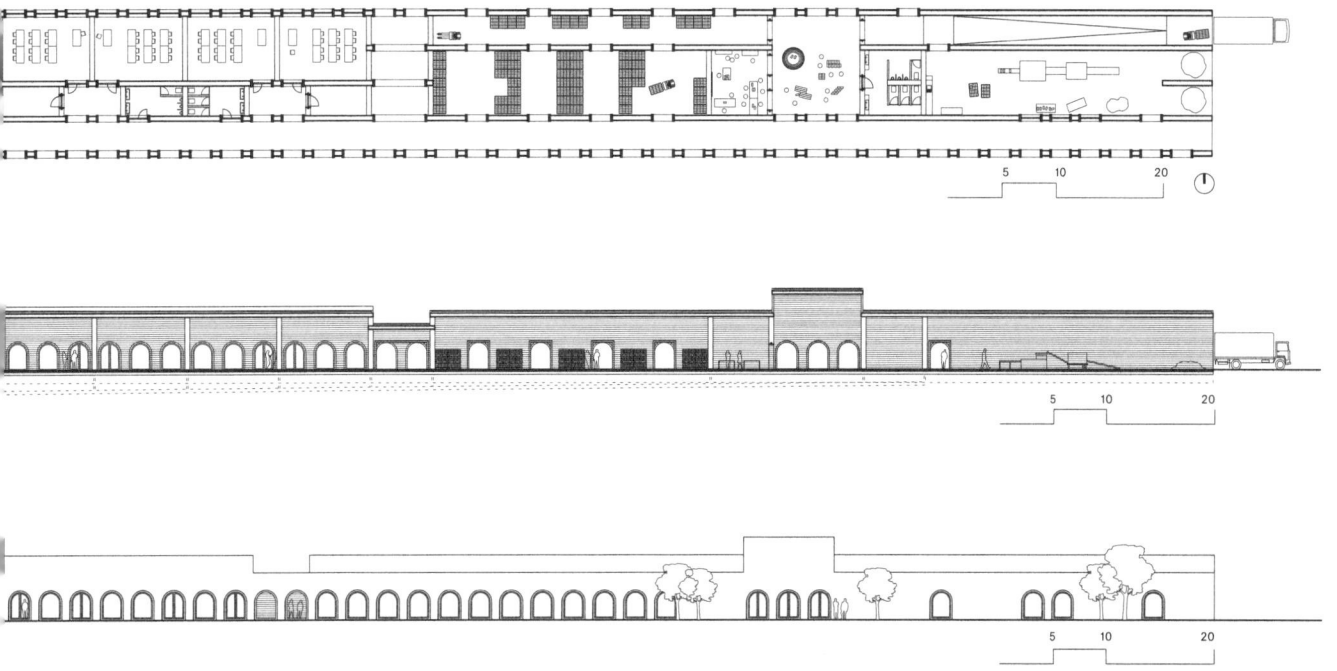

Architecture: Negev Desert

# 9  Thai Shed

Since the state was established by and for Jews, Israel's migration policies have focused almost exclusively on Jewish immigrants and their integration. However, due to the decline in the number of Jewish migrants, along with the increasing number of labor migrants and asylum seekers in recent years, Israel now faces major challenges in terms of migration management.

The agriculture sector employs 22,000 migrant laborers mainly from Thailand, accounting for 30 percent of the national labor force in this sector. Bilateral agreements with Thailand signed in 2011 have facilitated recruitment procedures without enhancing the living and working conditions of the migrant workers.

Intensive agricultural work is undertaken in the southern part of the country in the Arava Valley. This area is below sea level, and the climate is extremely hot and dry. Due to the harshness of the working conditions, Thai workers have been recruited in huge numbers since the 1990s. Most Thai workers are "kept out of sight," living in the backyard work sheds of their employers. These agriculture settlements, in particular the *moshavim*, were designed at the outset for permanent workers, based on the organizational plan of an orthogonal military camp.

In Ein Yahav, one of the oldest *moshavim* in this region, the neighborhood units are all arranged around a square, centralizing the main activities and facilities of the secular *moshav*, all reserved for Israelis. In fact, nothing is dedicated to the Thai workers, in an area where they outnumber the nationals. The necessity of providing the Thai workers with a structure that acknowledges their presence is urgent; they need a common space to share their own culture and rituals.

Since all community facilities are centralized, the proposed structure is also proposed to be located within the 's center, in order for the Thai workers to gain the recognition they deserve. The center of the *moshav* is organized into different activity zones with a large public square in the middle. An empty plot on one side of the square offers the opportunity for erecting a building dedicated to/for the Thai workers.

In the popular mind, the word "Thailand" is synonymous with "temples" of almost fairy-tale appearance. Whether set in the luxuriant greenery of a remote village or confined by the development of the city, these temples (or more properly, monastery compounds) are expressions of the vitality of the Buddhist faith in Thailand.

Common to all temples, whether simple or grand, is a basic traditional layout. Separating temple grounds from the secular areas are an outer and an inner wall. Between these walls are housed buildings that form the "everyday" side of a wat. The inner wall of a temple encloses at least one rectangular wooden gathering hall or chapel, *viharn*, with an entrance facing east, for ordination based on a proportion of 1:5.

The proposal provides the Thais' with a shelter. In essence, the project is a reinterpretation of a monastery compound with various degrees of privacy, offering a communal shared space with a kitchen separated by an internal courtyard from the chapel. Exterior sounds are muffled by the dense interior vegetation. Stretching ahead, the passerelles that link these two programs are sunlit interior salas covered with vegetation. The sunlight filters through the vegetation in contrast to the cool concrete floors where the visitors may sit and contemplate. The entrance to the gathering place for the faithful faces east. The chapel's interior is cool, and light from the outside filters dimly through windows on the lateral walls.

The ground level is kept clear in order to maintain a space continuity with the existing plaza and provide a public shaded area. The exterior façade of the building has no openings to prevent Israelis from feeling observed from above. Furthermore, the height of the building does not compete with the surroundings nor does its aesthetic. The use of a load-bearing, prefabricated concrete structure coupled with the metallic language provides a reinterpretation of the surrounding materially and typologies: concrete (mainly prefabricated) of the bunker housing and the metallic frames of the working sheds where the Thais live. Finally, the wooden fit-outs and the elevation of the first floor echo those of traditional Thai dwellings.

— *Victoria Bodevin / Sophie Würzer*

Site plan

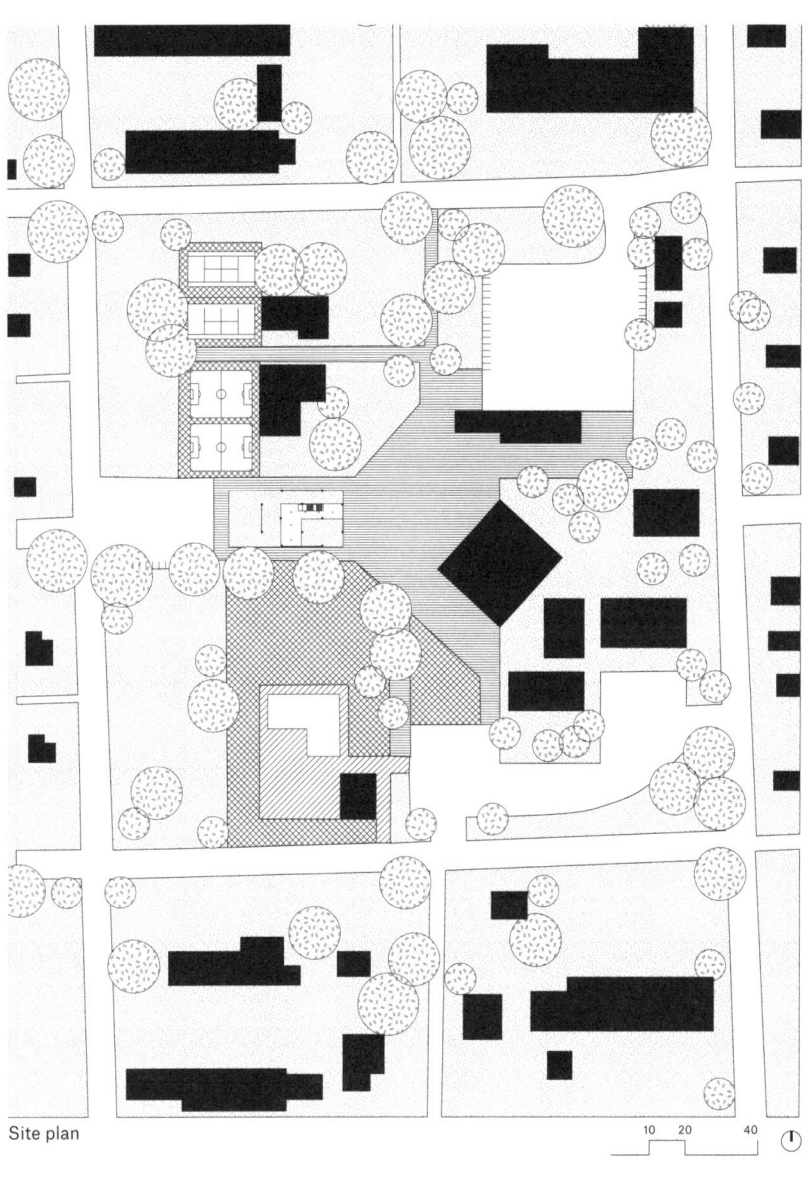

Architecture: Negev Desert 153

Students visualizations: Internal courtyard, temple, and communal space

First floor

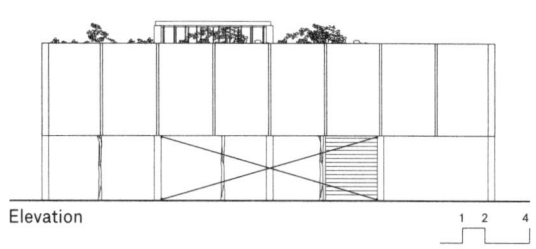

Elevation

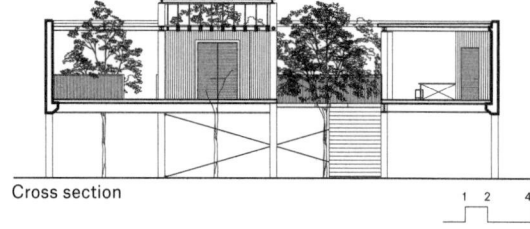

Cross section

154

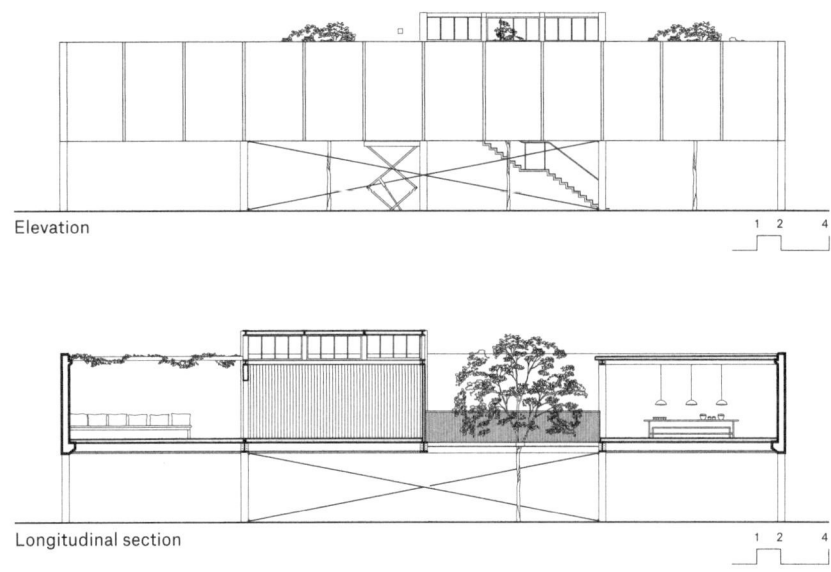

Elevation

Longitudinal section

Architecture: Negev Desert

# 10  Bedouin Heritage Center

If at first sight the Negev appears like a hostile and empty territory; by looking closer one discovers that it is home to many ecosystems. On Road 204, between Sde Boqer and Dimona, the city of Yeruham, surrounded by *wadis*, seems to resist well the harsh desert conditions. Low-level vegetation flourishes embracing the town of 10,000 and structuring the landscape in a unique way.

Based on the Negev constitution, the project highlights the "Bedouin heritage ecology" and develops a runoff agriculture in order to grow medicinal plants. A system of terraces is built in the *wadis* in order to store the runoff rain in the soil.

The project focuses on the development of a local know-how into a sustainable industry of medicinal plants. It has the ambition of combining tradition, technology, and education in order to improve the local conditions of both Bedouins and Israelis. Situated at the entrance of Yeruham, the building places itself at the crossroads of the main cities of the Negev but also in between a manmade park, the Bedouin village of Rahme, and the Jewish town. This in-between condition is still readable as one gets closer. The intervention reveals itself as a transition from fields to factory as the building is implemented in the continuity of the existing industry and faces the terraced plantations.

The linear structure of the terrace walls is applied to the building and organizes the program along a gradient of publicness. The scale is given by the diverse programs, which include an apothecary, a café, an auditorium, a factory, and a storage facility. The diversity of the activities suggests a fragmented architecture. The image of a hangar is used but broken down into the repetition of industrial flat roofs. The walls are made of rammed earth, which guarantee a dry and cool atmosphere inside while the overhanging steel roofs provide shaded outdoor spaces and keep the walls cool. These two languages give the building a vernacular touch while recalling its industrial function.

The metal framework sits lightly on the thick walls and separates the roofs from the rammed earth. Clearstorey windows are introduced to provide light to the different functions. Blocks of services form a backbone along the south-east façade and close the system. On the other side the architecture opens itself to the landscape. The transparent façade is set back, revealing the fingers as of a comb and allowing the design of outdoor spaces in shaded conditions. Local plants in front of the building make a gentle connection with those growing in the *wadi*.

— *Marie-Pauline Cryonnet*

Site plan

Architecture: Negev Desert

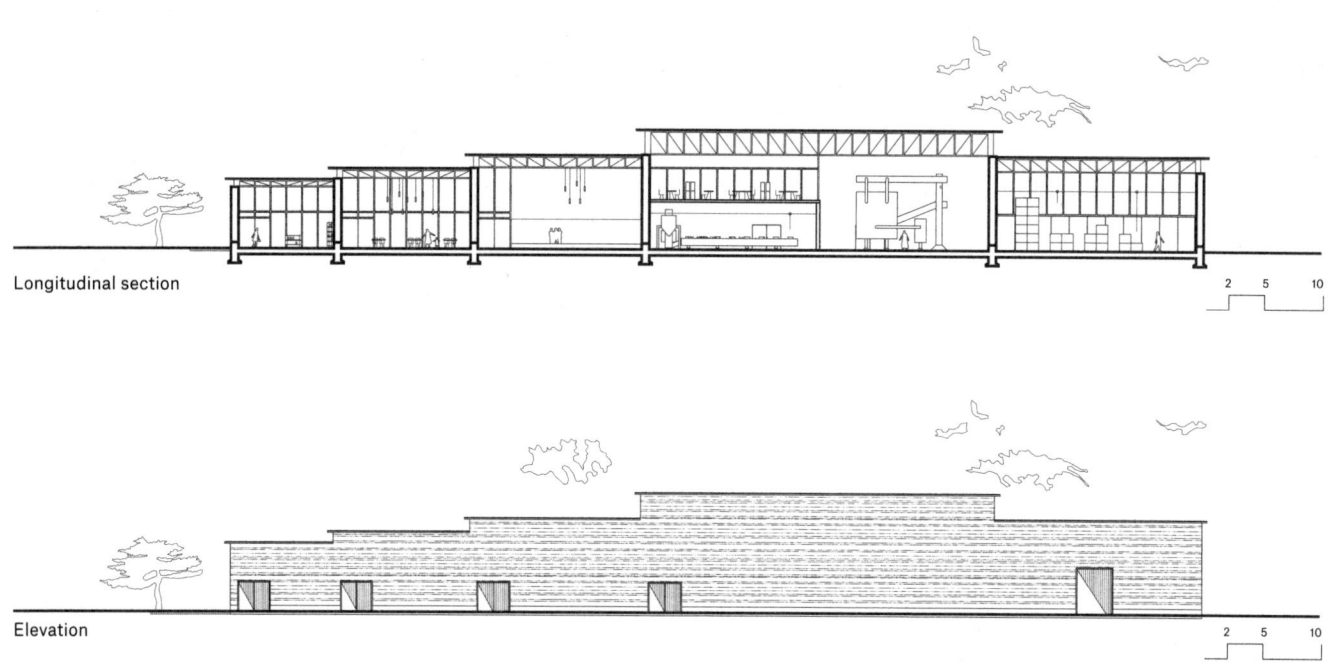

Longitudinal section

Elevation

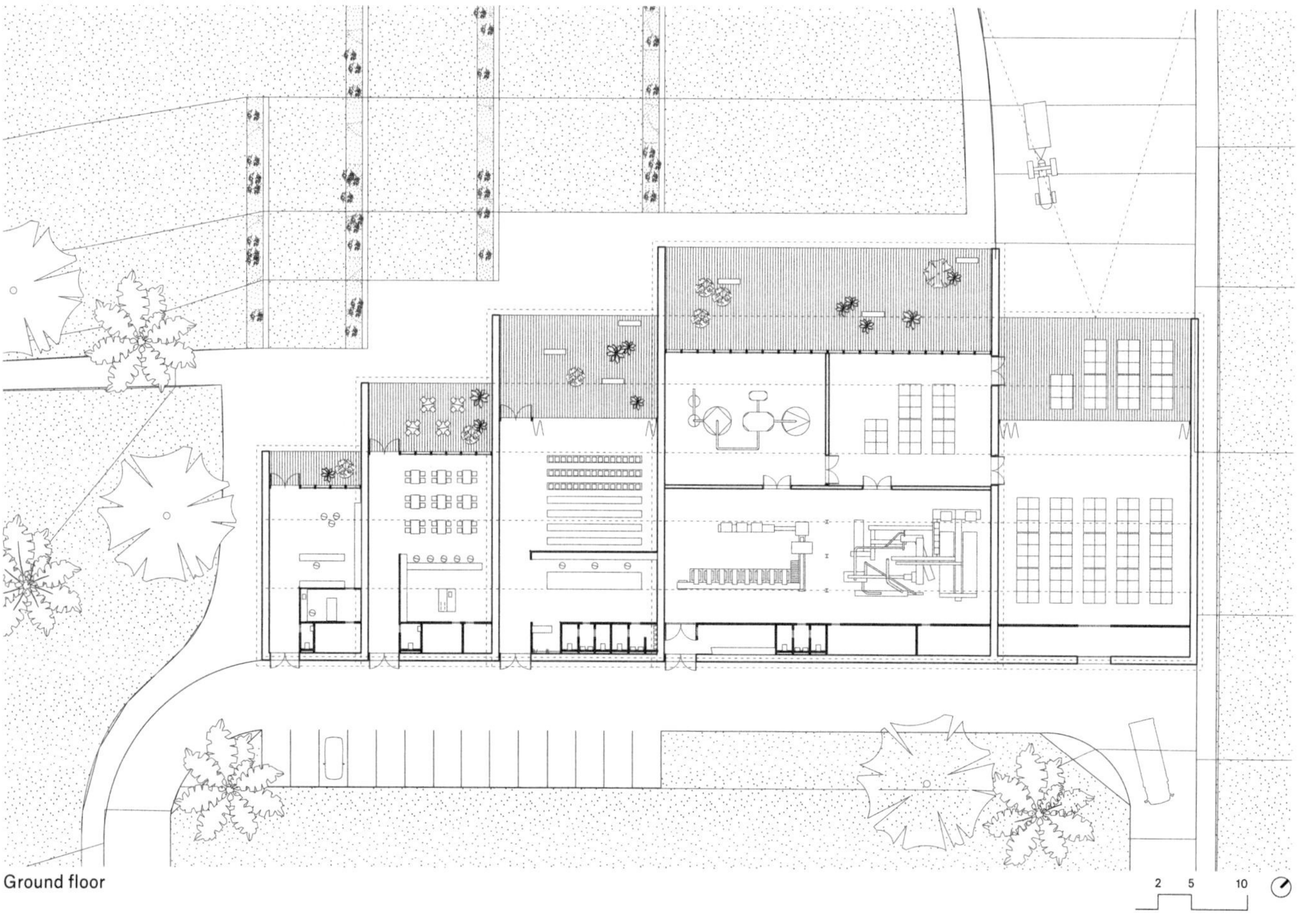

Ground floor

# 11 Landscaped Infrastructures for Bedouin Housing

In the loessal plain of the northern Negev, the Bedouin population used to develop their ancestral knowledge of agriculture and animal husbandry with their semi-nomadic lifestyle. This knowledge and lifestyle helped them to live for many centuries in this territory.

Nowadays the Bedouin community of Israel is no longer nomadic, mainly due to political forces. In fact, the Bedouin population underwent a settlement phase that had begun under the Ottoman and British Mandate eras. The permanent settlement policy of Bedouins was reinforced at the creation of the State of Israel in 1948 and it is still actively pursued.

The Bedouins are now mainly dispersed in conglomerates of permanent villages in the loessal plain, where they try to maintain their traditions. Most of these Bedouin villages are not recognized by the State of Israel because they are the fruit of a sporadic expansion due to the high birth rate of the Bedouin population, which doubles every fifteen years. Israel's government tried in the last decades to contain the expansion by building relocation towns for Bedouins and forced them to adopt an urban lifestyle, which was in conflict with their traditions. The Bedouin population faces a dilemma, to either settle in urban centers or lead a life in the hills under precarious conditions.

The purpose of the project is to provide a territorial structure that accomodates the Bedouin lifestyle. The prerequisite is to allow the Bedouins to be nomadic again within specific designed locations.

A new image for the Bedouin village needs to be found, and this prototypical image tries to transform the cultural Bedouin heritage into a spatial capital that can become a common value for the country in the form of agricultural landscapes.

The designed proposition is to build first, at the bottom of a valley, an underground dam—a concrete wall that goes deep enough to go through the pervious stratum, the sedimentary stratum, and reach an impervious stratum, the clay or bedrock stratum.

This dam will act like a seal and create an artificial aquifer. The underground dam will be completed at the surface by an embankment dam that retains the water from flash floods. This embankment dam will be made of rocks, soil, and sand found on site. With this system, the water is retained and forced to infiltrate slowly into the sedimentary stratum. The water is then filtered by the sediments and stored in the ground, protected from evaporation, and can be collected by means of a well.

This main embankment dam will be completed by a series of smaller embankment dams in the upper part of the valley that will help the water infiltration process upstream. These embankment dams host service spaces and a well for the Bedouin camp. Between each of these embankment dams, the land can be cultivated by a Bedouin family, which represents on average 24 people.

The service spaces comprise the water closets, rooms for compost, rooms for greywater sand filters, bathrooms, and changing rooms. These spaces don't have roofs but will feature instead fabric awnings that are employed during the day to protect from the sun and folded during the night to allow the spaces underneath to cool down. The well works with an electric pump powered by solar panels to collect the underground water.

— *Félix Chase*

Territorial intervention

Architecture: Negev Desert

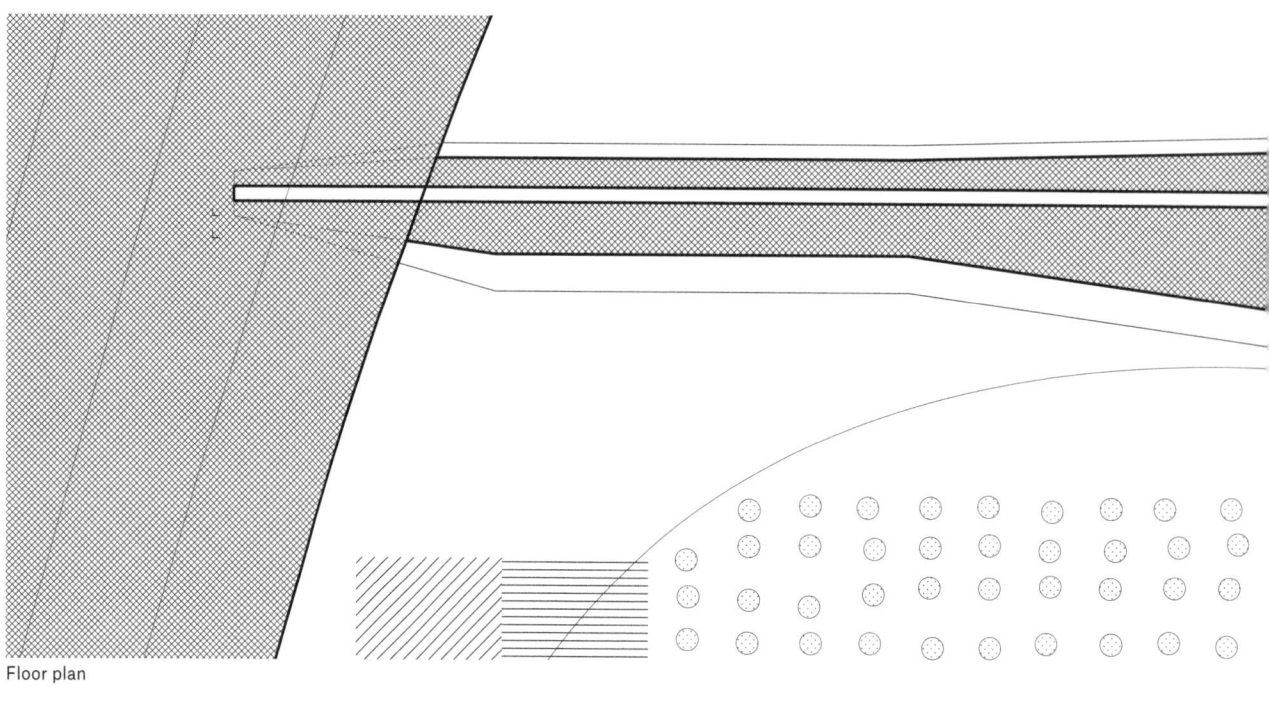
Floor plan

Longitudinal section

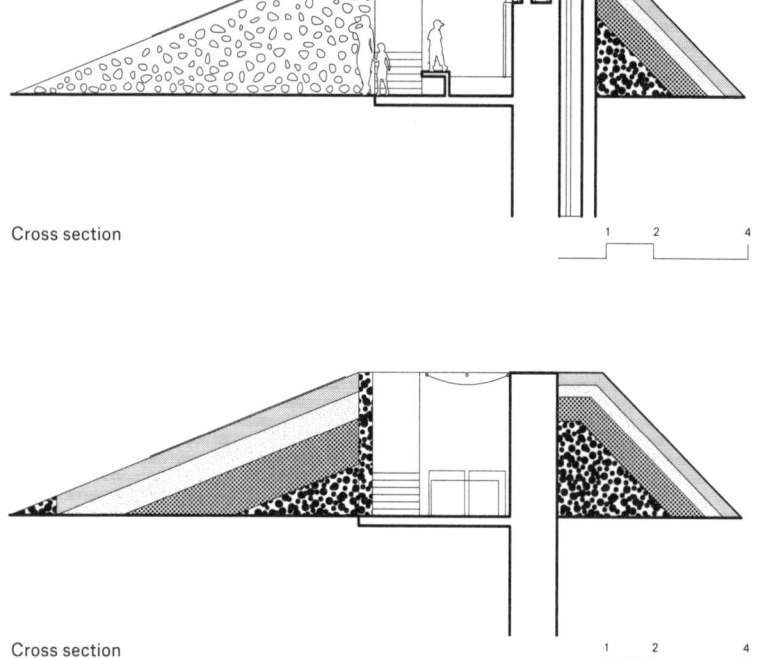
Cross section  | 1  2  4

Cross section  | 1  2  4

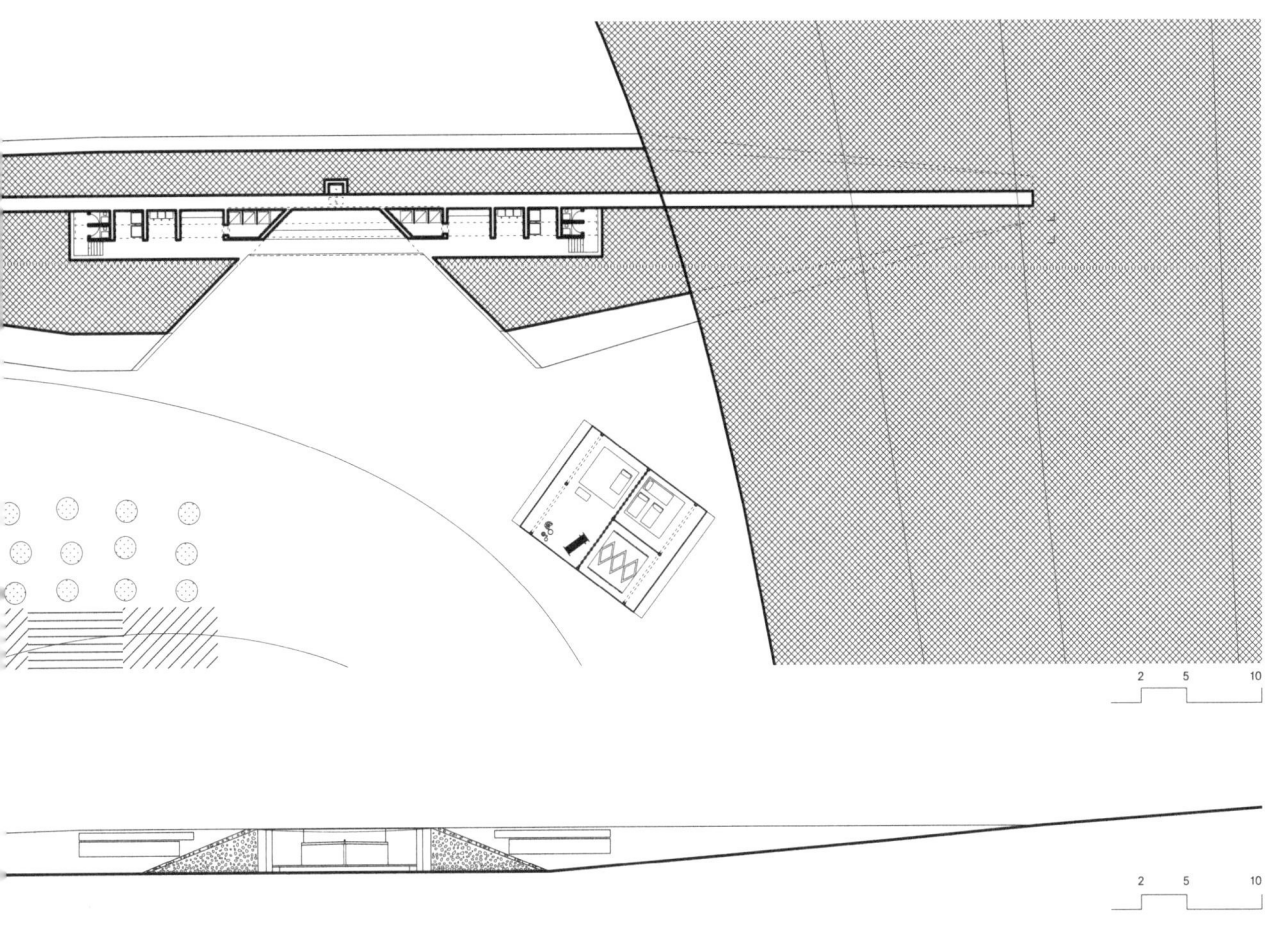

Architecture: Negev Desert 163

# 12  Rahat Women's Garden

In the mid 1960s, the Israeli government tightened its control on the northern Negev, which led to the construction of a new township for the Bedouin community, as well as a relocation master plan. In consequence, the Bedouin lifestyle shifted from a nomadic one organized around tents to an urban one.

This new kind of urbanism was implemented based on the Bedouin way of life and respecting the following principles: rejection of collective housing, neighborhoods organized by tribes, and a plot big enough to build a son's house on the father's plot. But even with these principles in place, the concentration of Bedouins in a dense urban setting still raises many social issues: high birth and unemployment rates, social violence, low education levels, health issues due to a lack of physical activities, and Bedouin women's isolation at home with their children.

Traditionally, Bedouin women can't interact with men outside the family cluster. The new proximity between tribes in an urban context therefore disconnects them from the public sphere. In the villages, Bedouin women used to play an active role, both inside and outside the tents. They would generally meet at the well, where they could freely talk, smoke, gossip, or dance. But in Bedouin townships, spaces like this do not exist anymore. This Women's Garden project aims at a reinterpretation of the well—a place where women can gather in the public sphere.

Rahat is the largest relocation town in the northern Negev, and it is organized by tribes' neighborhoods along two main roads. The public facilities are in-between spaces among residential areas. Public amenities dedicated to the entire city, like city hall, markets, or community centers are located at the crossing point of the two main roads.

The project aims to be both a green space for the entire city and a place for women. Leisure, physical activities, praying, and child day-care are part of this garden for women. Both enclosure and permeability characterize the place. Women can come during the day, with or without children, to spend time outside their houses.

A clear geometry is given to the garden by recessing the plot boundary. Taking the idea of an enclosed garden, *hortus conclusus*, it creates an inside, a place for women only, and an outside, a green strip that narrows and widens, bringing nature to the city center and offering a place for leisure. The enclosure should be visually permeable and establish a relation to the city. The idea of the latticework window openings called *moucharabieh* from the Islamic tradition is reinterpreted to guarantee this permeability. Plants ensure the principle of "seeing without being seen." Women can get close to the wall from inside and have a glimpse on what happens outside, but outside, blocked by the bushes surrounding the wall, no one can get close enough to peek inside.

Different programs are arranged in three different buildings, each with a dedicated outside space. Atmosphere and relation of the building to its direct outside space and to the perimeter wall respond to each program.

The access to the garden is announced by a public space oriented to the city amenities. The entrance building is a nursery where women can go through and drop off their kids before entering the garden. The façade facing the garden is more open than the one facing the street, and the programs' organization depend on this difference of openness. Finally, an orchard is dedicated to children's play. Having children part of the garden is important as it is also for them an opportunity to see their mothers acting freely.

A concrete path leads the women to the main space: a sunken plaza, which marks the threshold of the rest of the garden. At the center, the presence of water is an analogy to the traditional well. The plaza is characterized by concrete floor and high trees and is used for gatherings and social exchange. It can be used also by the two programs linked to it: the café-library and the dance area. Dance is a physical activity rooted in old tradition, and the café provides a place to relax.

These two functions are linked with a pergola in order to provide shade to the café terrace. Both parts are organized the same way: a front open space oriented to the plaza, and more closed space at the back with services along the exterior wall. A less organized space surrounds the plaza, acting as a buffer zone. Here women can gather informally and find shaded areas where trees are more densely planted. Crossing this part of the garden they reach the praying room.

The praying room is used during the different prayer times of the day or for any moment of contemplation. The Qibla wall is oriented perpendicular to Mecca, giving the praying room its orientation. The entrance is lateral and located at the back of the building. A first space is used as a foyer, separated from the main room with a curtain. A water basin is there for ablution rituals. The garden of the praying room is densely planted.

To create unity, the same construction and materiality are used for the whole compound wall and the three buildings. The skeletons are prefabricated concrete pieces, based on a 3x3-meter frame. They are covered by alveolate concrete slabs. Emphasis is put on the simplicity and rapidity of construction and on using local materials at low cost. The façade's pattern depends on the permeability required and is inspired by traditional Bedouin embroidery.

— *Juliette Lucarain / Laura Stoll*

Site plan

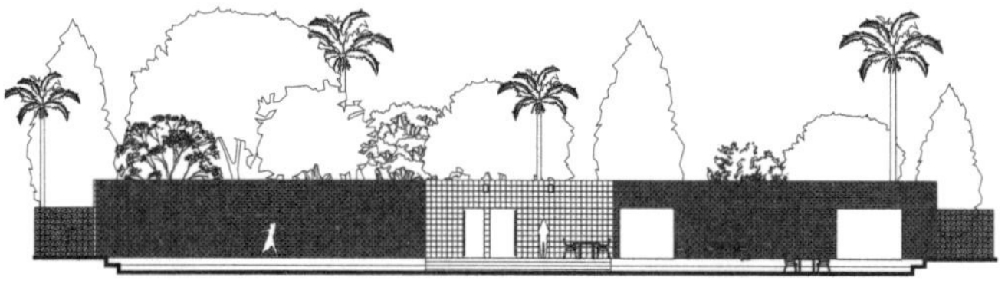

| Elevation | Elevation |
| Cross section | Cross section |
| Ground floor | Ground floor |

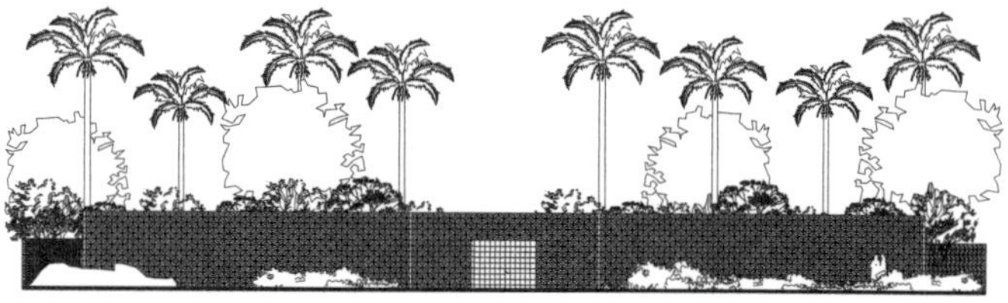

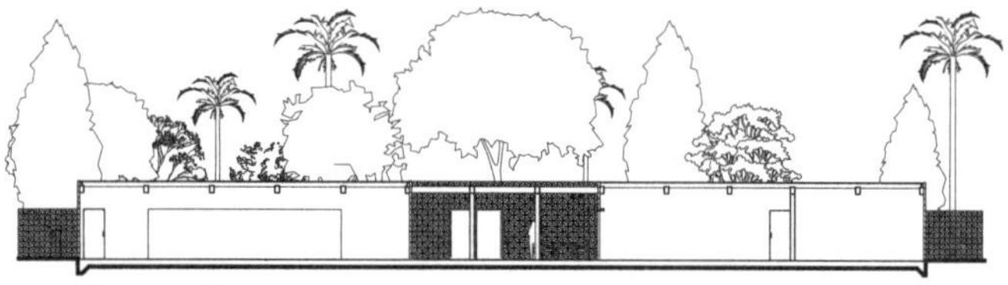

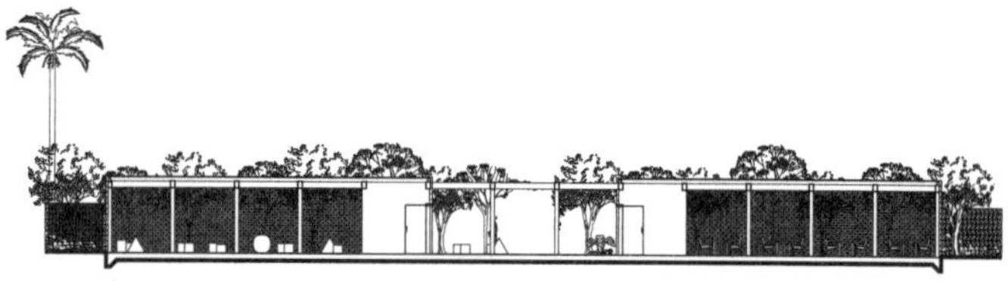

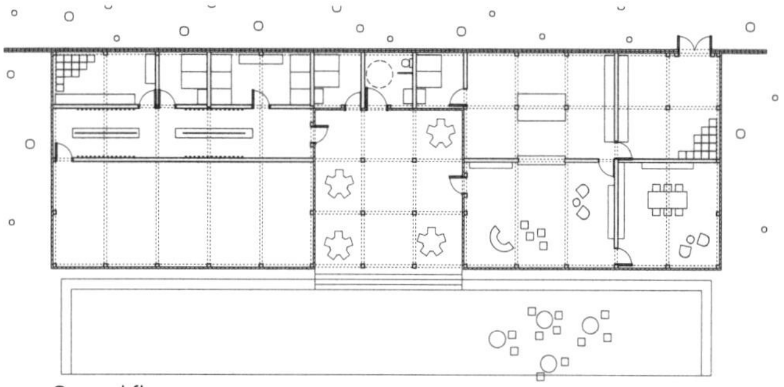

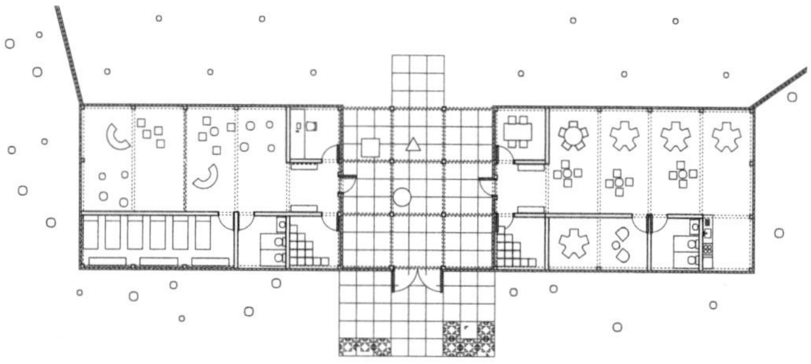

166

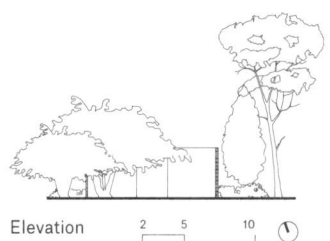
Elevation  2  5  10

Cross section

Facade mock-up

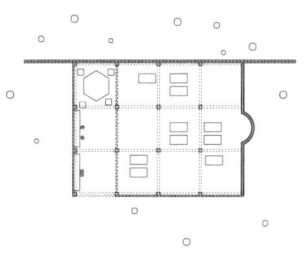
Ground floor

Architecture: Negev Desert

# 13  Nazareth and Nazareth Illit Linear Center

Israel has become a highly urbanized country. Early urbanization was driven by agriculture and was then dominated by the development of a network of middle-sized cities, called development towns. These cities often were added to the preexisting network of historic Arabic towns. One of these, Nazareth, is located in the northern part of the country. It borders Nazareth Illit, an Israeli development town built in 1956. The population and urbanization of the two towns are very different from one another. The administrative limit between the two cities, marked by a highway, creates a space for an attractive linear center for both sides.

Many functions activate this edge, such as government buildings, shopping malls, bars, restaurants, markets, sport facilities, education facilities, and a park. Within this central node, three major poles of attraction can be identified: one administrative and educational; one for shopping malls; and a third linked to the old town of Nazareth. However, connection between them, other than via the highway, is impossible. Thus, as an alternative to the car-oriented linear center, a proposed pedestrian path will link the different poles of attraction and will be strengthened by public programs and spaces added at critical points.

The planned concept for interventions is a sequence of roofs and trees placed at critical moments to provide sun shelter and create coherence. When relevant, the roofs will provide platforms for activities. To allow the pedestrian path to connect to the historic center, the main public program, Nazareth City Hall, will be located at the entrance round-about. A pedestrian bridge will allow people to cross the highway from the park to the city hall. This program will also include a community center and a sport center.

A series of concrete arches will act as an infrastructure for the varying programs inside, adapting itself according to its needs. Its organization is oriented to a public square that is hidden from the street, following the logic of Nazareth's other squares. Nazareth City Hall is located along the main street on the west side. The community center is placed on the opposite side, facing the mall. The sport facility terminates the building's northern side, with its interior field being a continuation of the exterior public space, thereby allowing public events to take place.

The entire building sits on a parking facility, which is accessible from the east and west sides of the building. The square will be studded with a grid of trees and will be accessible from the main street on the west side, from the neighboring mall on the east side, and from a platform where the pedestrian bridge connects to the roof park on the south side. An arch open to both the platform and the public square will offer outdoor shaded space for pedestrians.

Along the building on the street or around the courtyard, the walls will be moved back from the end of the arches to allow people to walk in a covered and shaded space. When relevant, roofing arches can adapt, by means of cuts in order to leave space for an interior courtyard in the city hall, or increases in their spans in the case of the sport field. The concrete arches will be made of a regional stone aggregate to comply with Nazareth's tradition of public buildings built out of local stone. By the same logic, the floors will be covered with local stone. The roofs are covered with mineral surfaced roofing rolls tinted in the color of the concrete. Solid walls enclosing interior spaces will be built with prefabricated concrete to allow for flexibility beneath the roof infrastructure. Through its materiality and space organization, Nazareth City Hall responds to the old town's urbanity and architecture. As a roof covering the main public building it strengthens the beginning of the pedestrian path, as a roof park promenade.

— *Florian Papp*

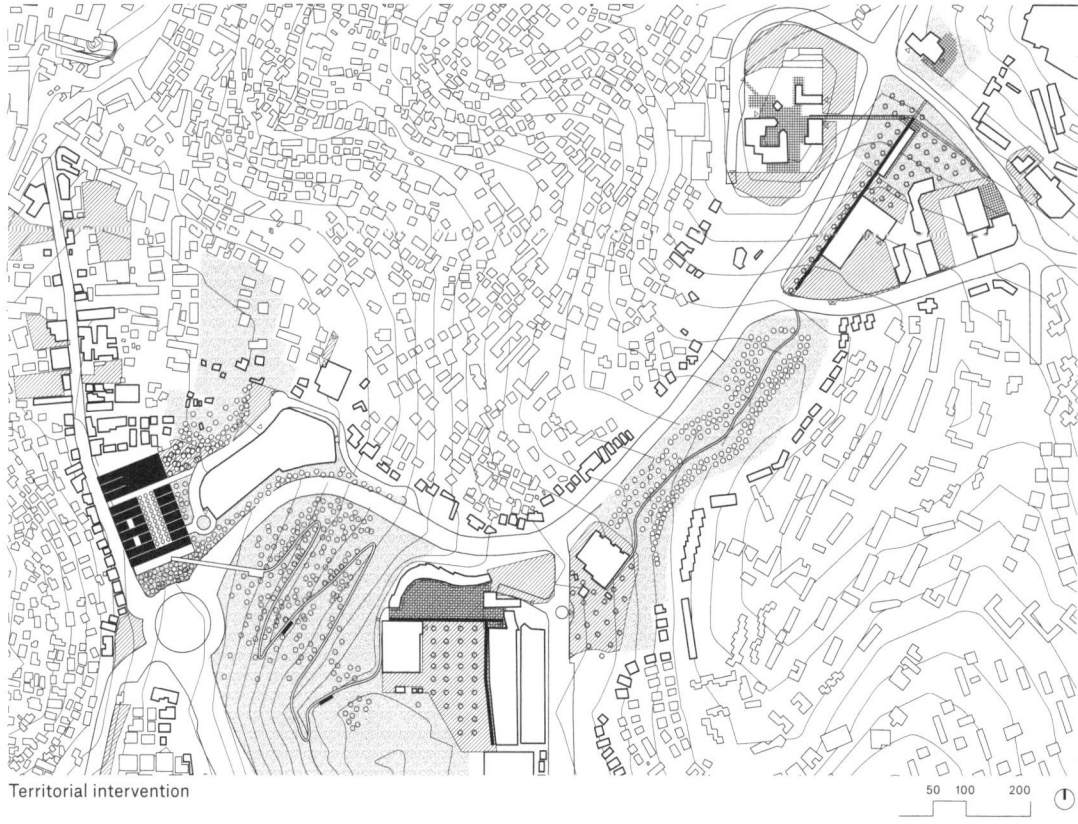

Territorial intervention

Architecture: Coastal Plain 169

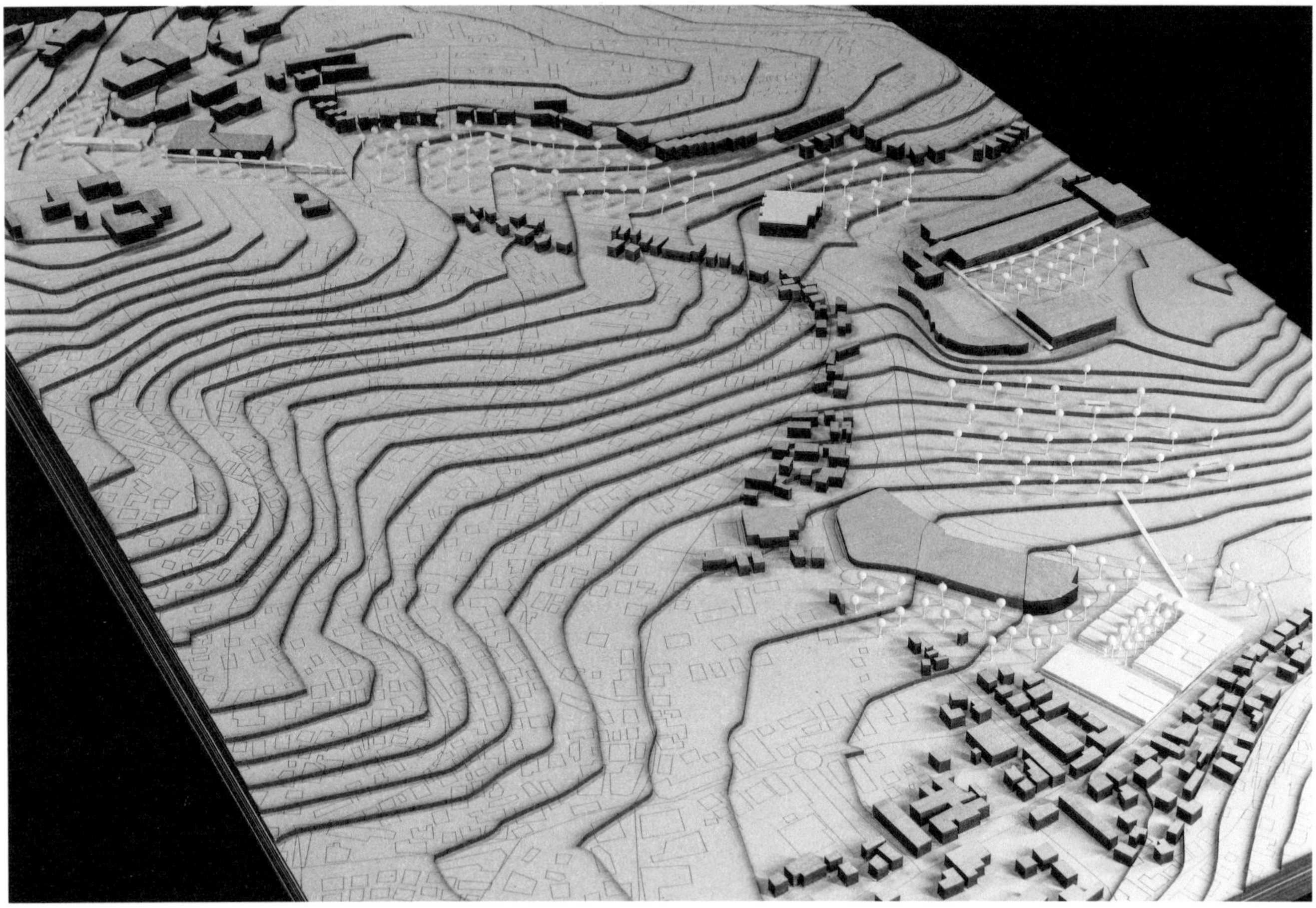

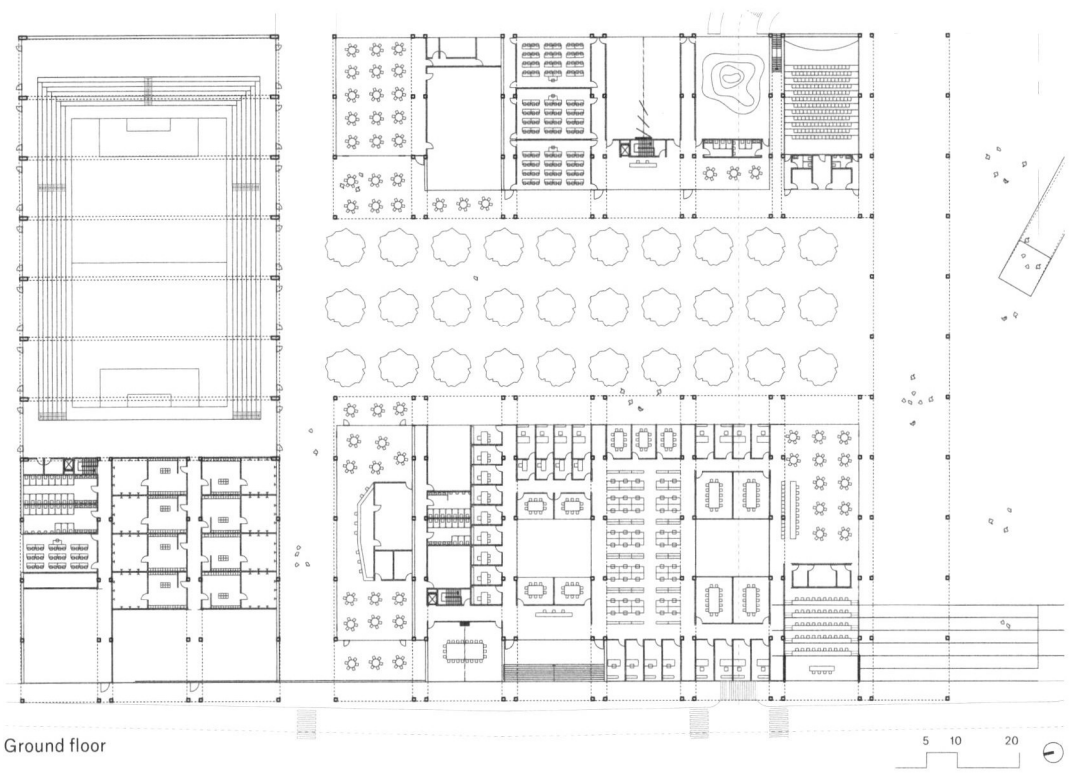

Ground floor

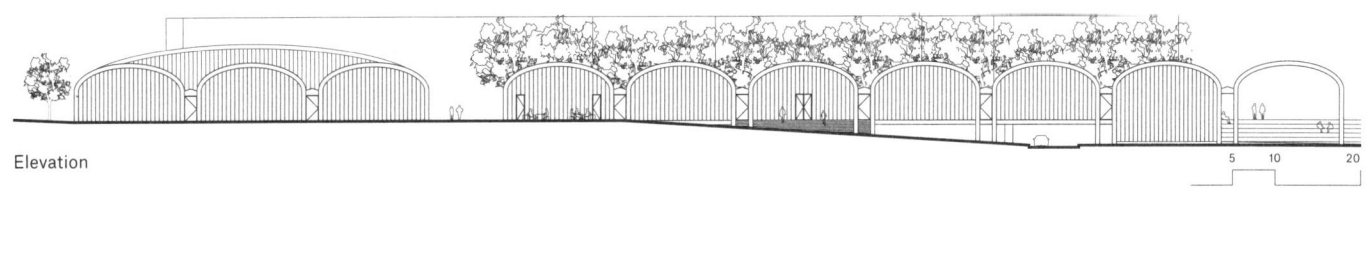

Elevation

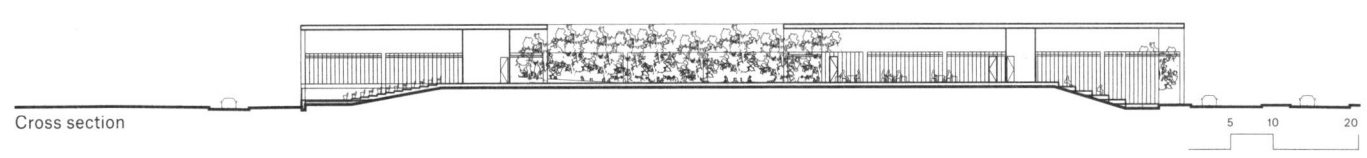

Cross section

Architecture: Coastal Plain 171

# 14 Daycare and Educational Center, Karmiel

Israel showcases a great diversity of town typologies. The heterogeneity is particularly strong in the northern part of the country, with Arab towns, Bedouin villages, Jewish private settlements, and development towns. In the Beit Kerem Valley, a road separates the city of Karmiel from its surroundings. Despite their proximity, the division between the development town—founded in 1964 to absorb new waves of immigration—and the six Arab towns around it is not only physical, but also social.

Poverty level for Arabs and for Jewish immigrants is high. Unemployment, above all for women, is especially problematic. A lack of child-care facilities and a bad transportation system prevent women from working. Food insecurity is another challenging issue, particularly for children who don't have access to lunch facilities at school and often live in families where food is scarce.

The industrial zone of the region is situated at the center of the neighboring cities. The site is neutral, as it is the common working ground for the whole population and is easily accessible from anywhere since it is directly connected to the main road. This makes the site ideal for a project aiming at connecting the children of the whole region: a day-care and after-school center. The education center is based on learning about food, and therefore includes experimental gardens. In addition, a bus pick-up system is planned, which will also enable women to reach the industrial zone.

At the edge of this industrial area begins a forest. A slope, into which the project is integrated, opens up onto a narrow and deep valley. The courtyard-shaped building, touching the ground only on its upper part, allows the project to open up onto the valley, while containing inside a common space for children of all ages and ethnicities.

The building is made of three parts: the common rooms, the gardening workshops, and the canteen. Placed on the slope at the rear and elevated over the hillside and into the tree canopy toward its front, it creates three different conditions and relations to its environment. This ascension defines different atmospheres that characterize each of the spaces in the building.

The children come in from the workshops area, with an entrance hall offering a view onto the courtyard. The workshops are the only sections touching the ground and working directly with the outside, capable of opening up completely toward the experimental gardens. From there, the inside circulation allows visitors to reach the common rooms on both sides of the building. Those are directed toward the exterior, offering a unique experience of the leafy trees. The wide corridor offers a connection with the courtyard and finishes its loop at the canteen. This generous open space allows a view toward the valley, as this part of the building reaches the top of and then goes beyond the tree canopy.

The building strengthens its connection to its environment by minimizing its impact on the existing setting. There is only minimal connection to the ground. That way, nature can flow freely and penetrate into the courtyard, translated into the man-made gardens. The numerous pillars carrying the load of the southern part reflect the foundations of the northern one, while the lateral spaces work as elevated bridges. The light structure and material of the bridges—steel—is opposed to a heavy and massive concrete structure.

Underneath the canteen, the pillars form a playground for the children. Under the trees and surrounded by the trunks, a feeling of protection gives a comforting atmosphere to the playground. The pillars echo the trunks, and together the columns allow for a multi-use and creative space for the children. The project aims at connecting children of different cultures and backgrounds with each other, while offering them a heightened relation to their environment.

— *Stéphanie Amstutz*

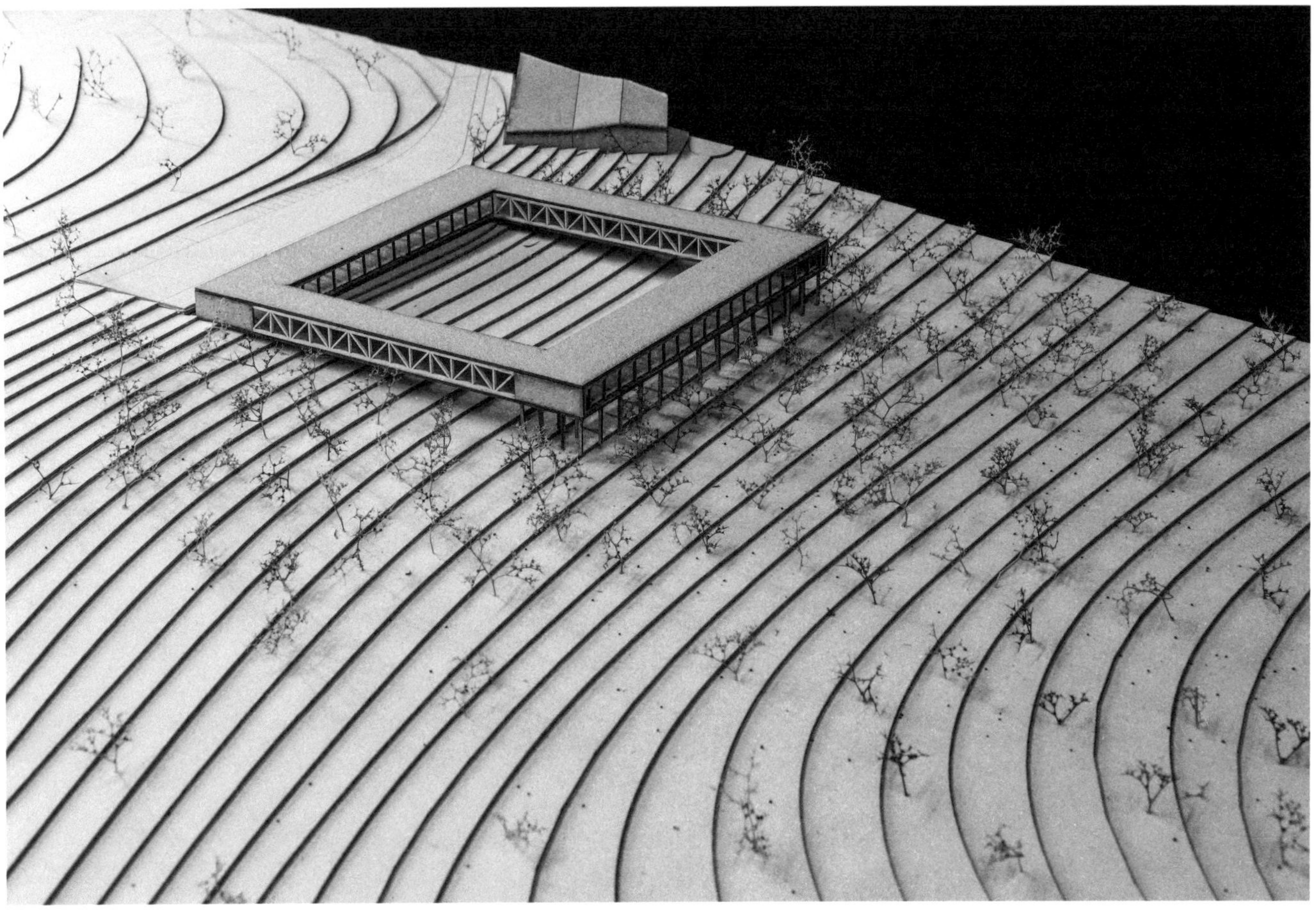

Territorial intervention

Architecture: Coastal Plain

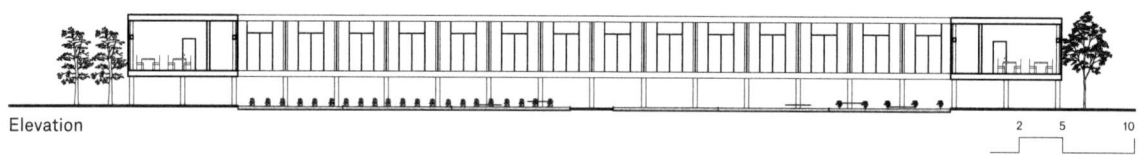
Elevation

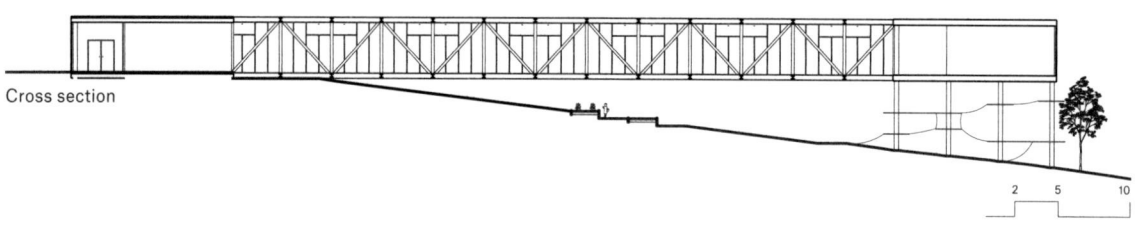
Cross section

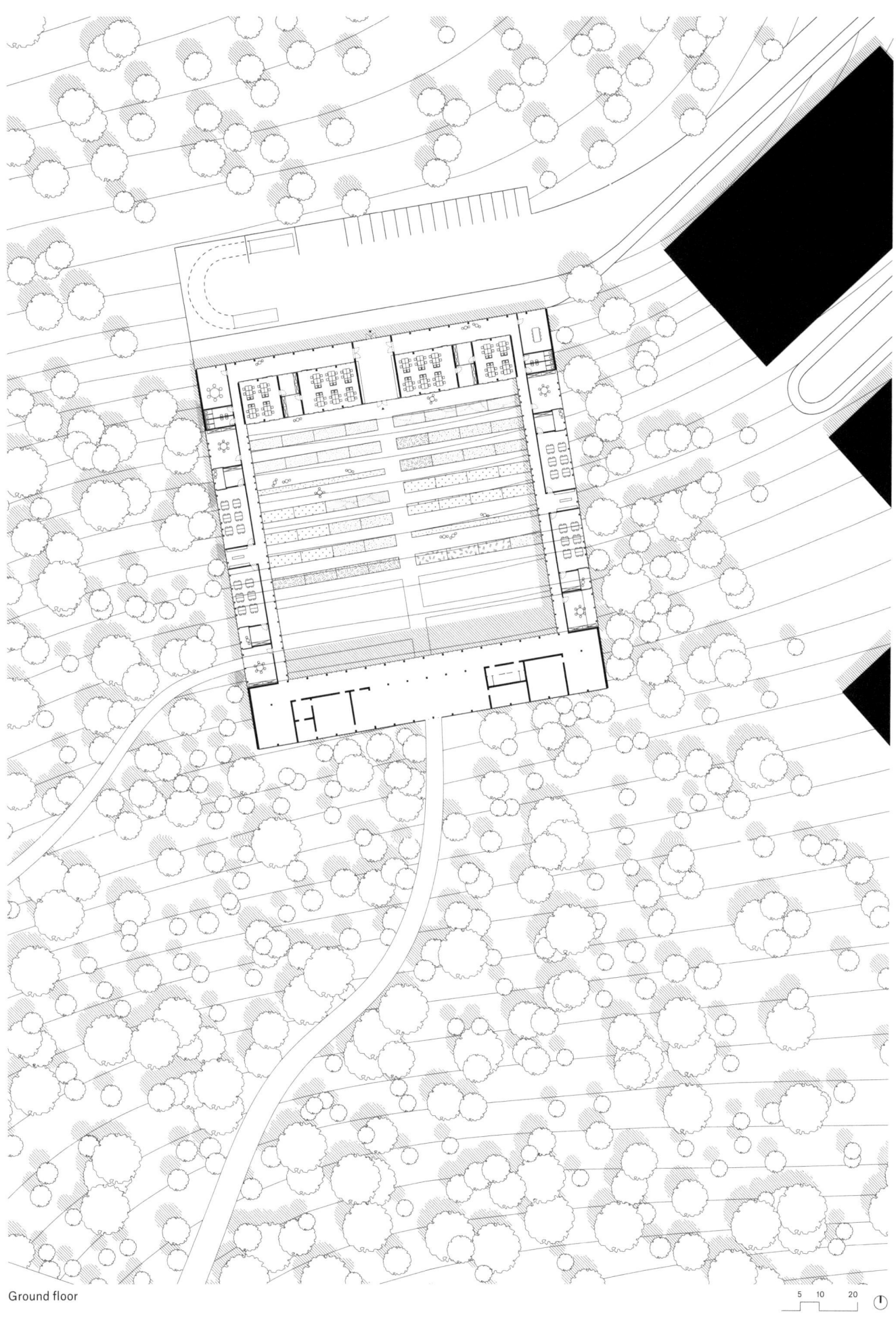

Ground floor

Architecture: Coastal Plain

# 15  Mount Hiriya Train Station

The Tel Aviv metropolitan area hosts close to 40 percent of the population of Israel and supports 50 percent of Israel's total employment. Predictions are that Israeli population will grow by roughly 4 million inhabitants by 2050, leading to an additional population of roughly 2 million in the Tel Aviv metropolitan area. Therefore, preserving quality of life will be an important challenge there, particularly concerning environmental issues and open spaces preservation.

This project aims to provide an easy escape from the noise of the city and enhance people's awareness of sustainability by improving access to a highly environmentally focused project. Ariel Sharon Park is an ongoing project that turns the Mount Hiriya landfill into a green and flourishing park. For 50 years Israel has been dumping all solid waste in these open fields, contaminating the soil and the aquifers, and releasing methane and unpleasant smells. Over time Mount Hiryia reached a height of 60 meters and a volume of 16 million cubic meters of waste. The rehabilitation of the landfill was completed under the direction of landscape architect Peter Latz in 2005. Ariel Sharon Park is expected to be completed by 2020. It was supposed to be accessible via a light railway stop, but this project was called off in 2015. The Mount Hiriya Train Station will create a new connection with the city and with the present and projected infrastructures.

The chosen site lies on the existing railway line from Tel Aviv center to Jerusalem. As with most infrastructures, this railway line creates a paradox. While infrastructures are made to link and to provide access they also divide the territory by creating borders. This particular line defines the limit between the neighborhood of Azor and Ariel Sharon Park. Mount Hiriya Train Station seeks to create a new exit, allowing people to gain access to the park and attempting to improve the link between the city and the urban void.

The station functions on three levels. The first one is the existing road coming from the Azor neighborhood and leading to Ariel Sharon Park through a steel truss bridge spanning train tracks and highway. The traffic on the present structure of the bridge is reasonably low and is shared by cars, bikes, and pedestrians. To provide all users with a pleasant and safe crossing, a new structure of steel beams and cables is balanced upon the existing structure to accommodate pedestrians on either side of the roadway. The whole skeleton of the bridge is wrapped in metal mesh.

The second level is the infrastructure corridor. It consists of a 6-lane highway split on the two sides of the train tracks. Room for a small platform of 8 meters is made by moving the rail tracks slightly apart. The existing low walls, which separate the railway system from the motorway, are raised to act as noise barriers. The bridge provides shelter on the central section of the platform to allow a dry and shaded waiting area.

The third level stands high in the sky, 30 meters above the ground, in the form of an observation platform. It proposes an unobstructed 360° view over the whole territory. This perspective gives an overall understanding of the project's immediate context and of the "green void" when entering the Tel Aviv metropolitan area.

The vertical circulation between the three floors is managed by two elements growing out of the concrete platform. The first one offers a direct link between the bridge and the platform: straight sculptural stairs perpendicular to the bridge land in the middle of the platform. This stair is wide at the bridge level to welcome the flow of people and to provide additional shelter underneath it and gets narrower as it goes down to give way to people walking along the platform.

The second link is the second vertical element, which also grants access to the third level. This circulation is built up by a concrete spine composed of two lifts and stairs. One lift stops at the bridge level, while the second one goes up to the top along with the secondary stairs starting at the bridge level.

The viewing tower gives a very pragmatic answer to the context. At the platform level where the space is limited, the footprint on the platform is limited to the two lifts. At the bridge level a 1.8-meter-wide strip circulation is added to give access to the lifts and to make room for the stairs. At the top a wide passageway is added that offers a pleasant space to stand on and enjoy the view.

Like the bridge, the concrete tower is wrapped. Here the skin is made of wooden bars. The shape of the building distorts these vertical elements. On the way up as the volume grows the beams move apart and offer a more open view to the outside. At the summit, the beams' height creates either a balustrade toward Mount Hiriya or a permeable wall.

The tower creates a landmark indicating the location of the new train station. When approaching from either Tel Aviv or Jerusalem it draws a cross in combination with the bridge, conveying the junction character of the project.

— *Laure Péquignot*

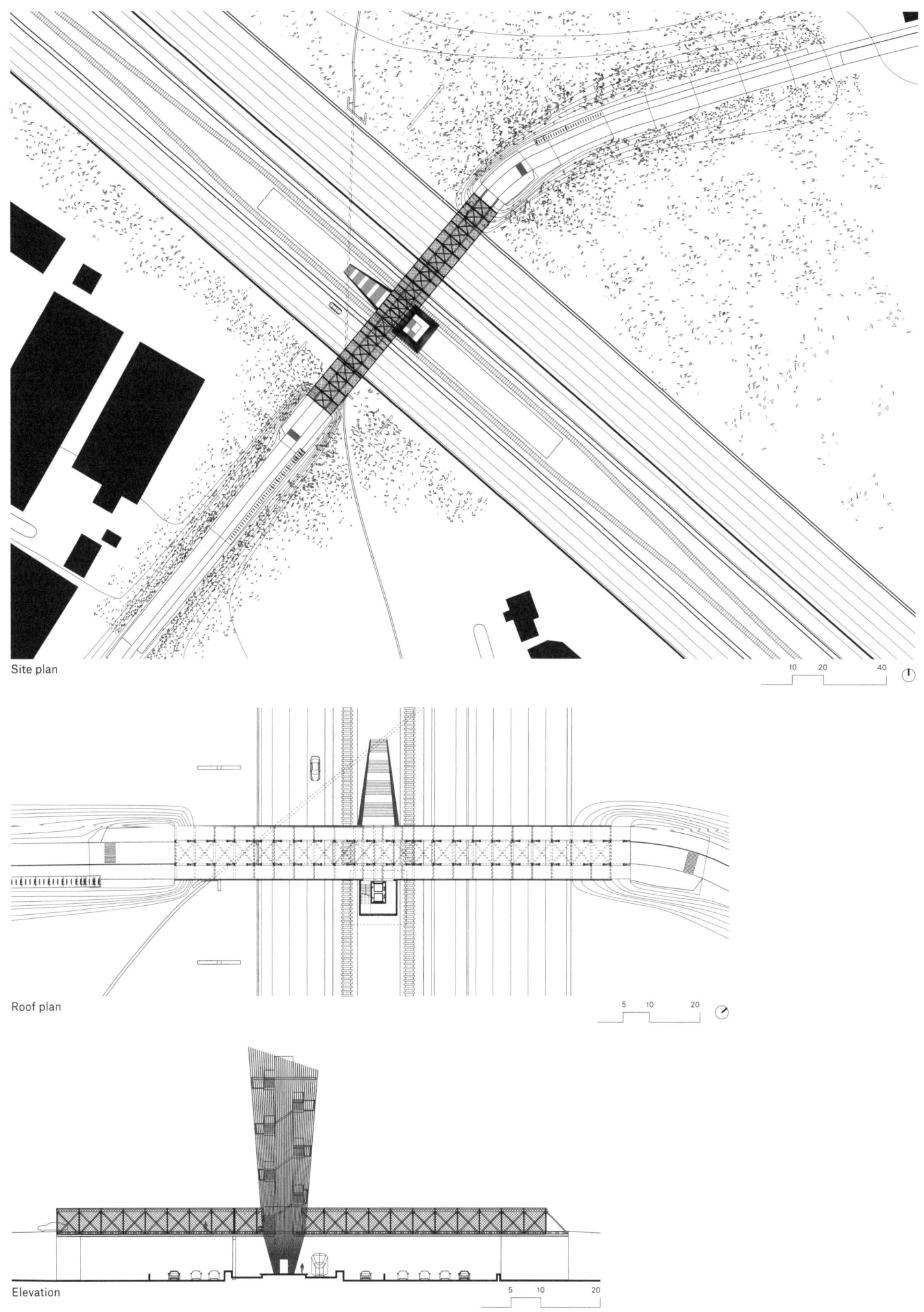

Site plan

Roof plan

Elevation

Architecture: Coastal Plain 177

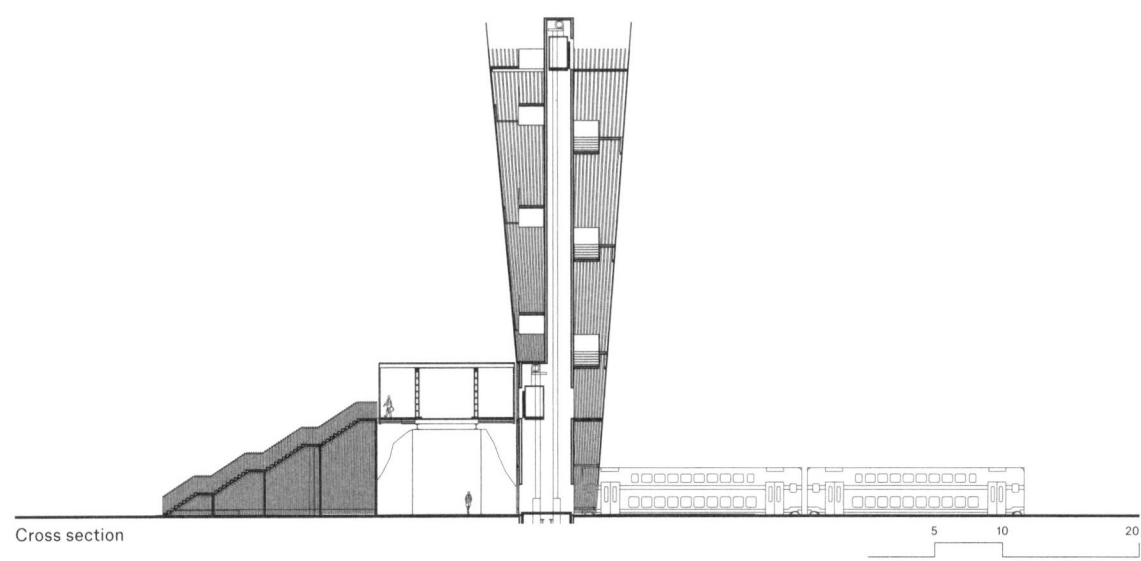

Cross section

# 16 Food Park for a Metropolitan Area

Neglected open space can be preserved by adding value to it. The present project brings food production closer to the consumer and seeks to increase awareness of agriculture in the Tel Aviv metropolitan area.

The area along the Israeli Mediterranean coastline was once an important pillar of the country's food production. Nowadays the coastline is a metropolitan area with about three million inhabitants. Due to the fast-growing population in this region, more and more agricultural land is given up to allocate housing. To guarantee a sustainable future for the region, the protection of open space is a necessity. What once has been the foreground—the open agricultural landscape—has been turned into a background without a clear identity. As long as this open space is seen only as the negative form of the built, it will be given up too easily.

It is therefore important to value the void. For metropolitan residents, agriculture usually doesn't seem to have much importance. This is true in Tel Aviv as well. The quality and origin of fruits and vegetables is less important to the city's residents than is their price. Generally, agricultural products travel a long way through several production facilities at different locations before being purchased. This proposed project, the Tel Aviv Food Park, seeks to bring consumers and producers closer together while still guaranteeing regional products of high quality. The building is located in an existing void in the urban area, at the periphery of the Tel Aviv municipality. The site is about 1,500 meters long and 300 meters wide and is currently mostly used for agriculture. The fields are surrounded by residential zones, and on the southern border they are delimited by a highway.

Israel's second-largest university, Bar Ilan University, is located right next to this area. The projected light rail system will connect the university to the city center. By this means, residents of Tel Aviv will also receive direct, fast, and convenient access to the proposed Food Park. People will come to the area to buy fresh and locally produced fruits and vegetables and also for recreation in the park portion of the project. Agriculture becomes part of their everyday lives.

The project includes a market hall and a restaurant and will substantially enlarge and enhance the already existing agricultural production. When coming to the park via the university, pedestrians can use a generous promenade that leads along fields devoted to public harvest and thence to the building. The entrance area consists of a permanent market as well as a covered area for weekly markets and food trucks.

— *Jonas Inhelder*

Site plan

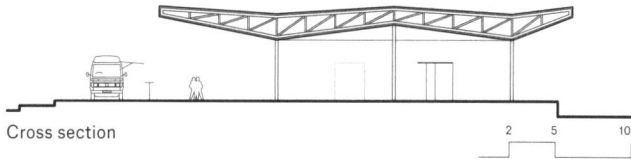

Cross section

Architecture: Coastal Plain 181

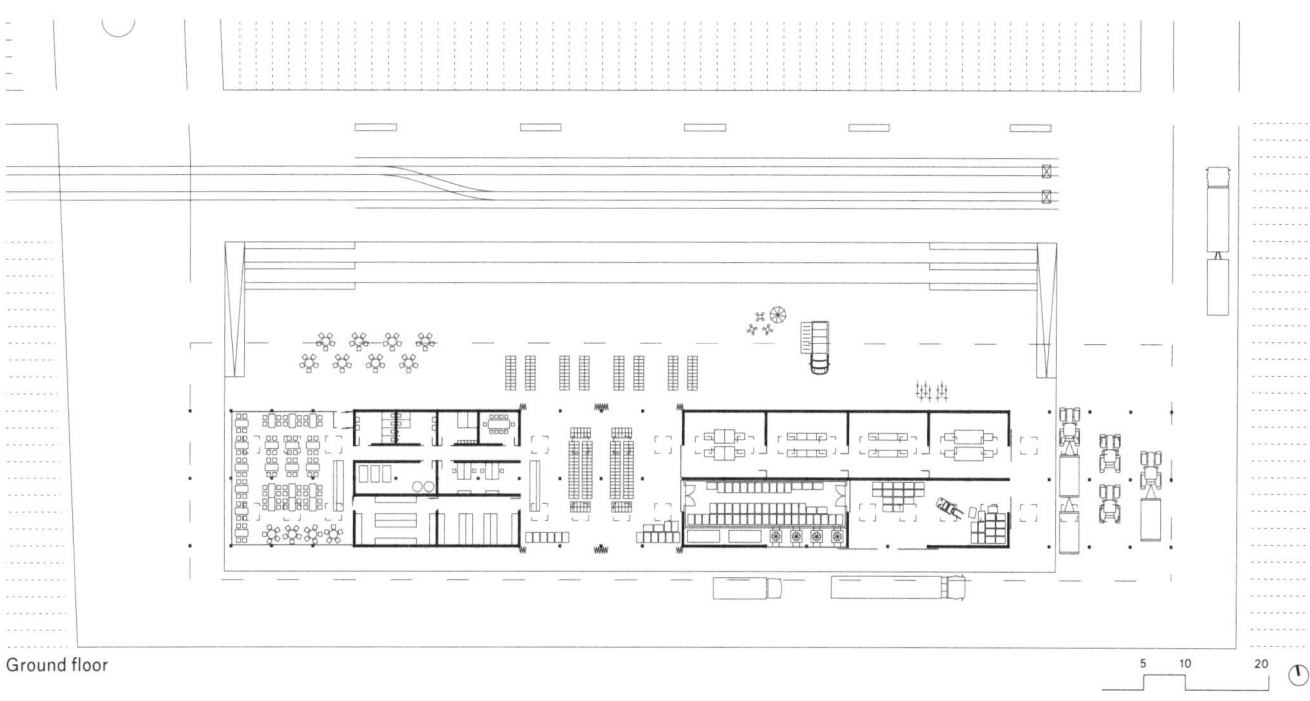
Ground floor

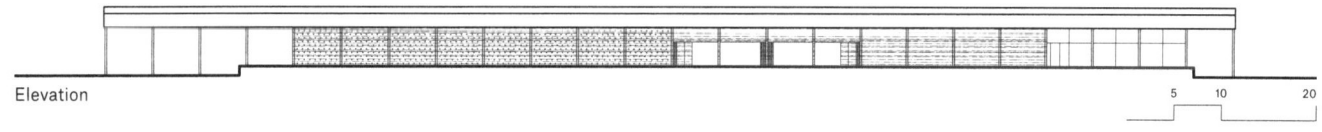
Elevation

# 17  Tel Aviv Hashalom Bridge Station

*Hashalom* in Hebrew means "the peace." This meaning has been the driver of the proposed project. It is the project's aim to give special entrances in order to slow highway traffic and to create a public space protected from the present heavy infrastructures.

The river Ayalon runs north to south and crosses Tel Aviv before flowing into the Mediterranean sea. Highways and railways follow the river bed and create a major cut in the city fabric. To deal with that issue the Master Plan for 2025 foresees a Metropolitan Park on a slab covering all the infrastructures, including the river.

The current Peace Bridge over the Ayalon is planned for cars only. Slow mobility and public space are neglected. The density around the Hashalom Station district is one of the highest in the city. The Tel Aviv–Yaffo Master Plan is projecting the construction of several high-rises all along the main corridor of infrastructures where the station is located. The majority of these new constructions are planned to be office spaces. Thus, the number of commuters is going to increase, necessitating an extension of the station planned by the city.

It is in that specific context of densification and flattening that the new Hashalom Station is reconsidered. The implantation of the future station follows the Master Plan. The main difference of the project is the creation of a rolling slab that generates on the one hand a bridge between the two parts of the new park cut by the Peace Bridge, and on the other hand a roof for the new station. Three arched bridge structures with two different slopes allow both crossing and covering. This primary concrete structure follows the frame of the underground infrastructure.

The project proposes to bring new life to the river by uncovering it around the station and incorporating it into the interior space. Even though the scheme is based on the Metropolitan Park project, it tries to question it by revealing the nature of these infrastructures that compose the urban landscape of the site.

The station can be accessed either from the Peace Bridge, which has been reworked in order to offer entrances protected from traffic, or from the park in the north and south. The aim of the project is to create a continuous ground floor, offering two open halls crossed by the Peace Bridge. The whole building will be open, which reinforces the continuity with the ground of the city. Given the climate, the total opening of the building allows for a continuous ventilation of the building.

The dividing of the roof into three parts generates two different heights, openings for light, and hierarchy in the programs. The two footbridges, at the ends of the project, allow thresholds to be created and an interiority for the station. The central roof is constructed in order to have a generous height for the station program.

The concrete structure is determined by the infrastructure below. The secondary structure is composed of steel beams to which the façade is fixed. The two footbridges are covered by slatted timber that provides shading.

On the lower platform levels, direct natural light comes from the opening above the river side. Like the railways, the river has its own platform that is used as a cycle park, and it guarantees the continuity of the park at that level as well. The roof too is conceived as an extension of the park. The project and the park will intertwine with each other.

— *Alessandra Patarot*

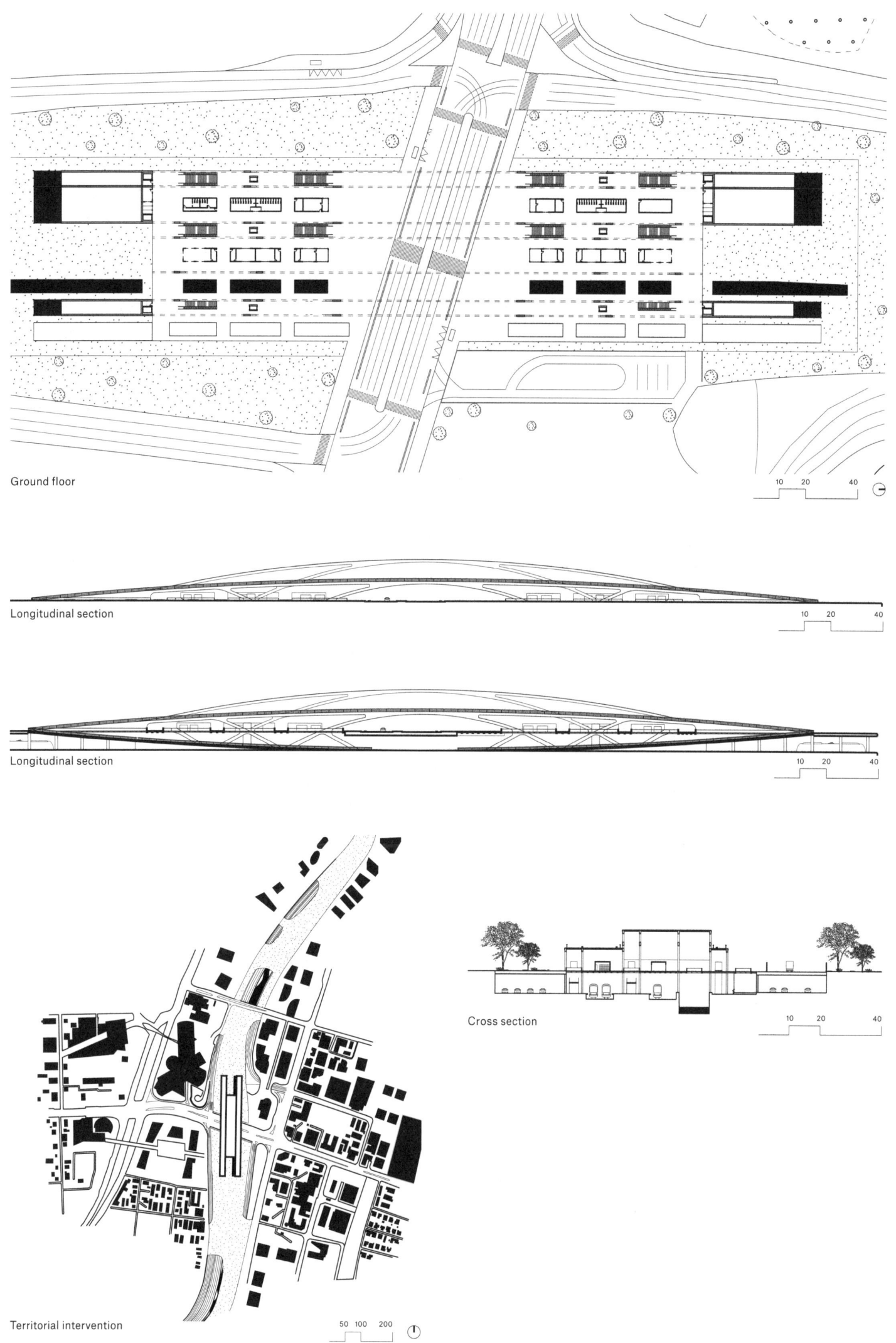

Ground floor

Longitudinal section

Longitudinal section

Cross section

Territorial intervention

Architecture: Coastal Plain 185

Architecture: Coastal Plain 187

# 18 A *Kibbutz* in Tel Aviv

Because the cost of living in the Tel Aviv area is very high, the metropolitan population is moving to new suburban settlements in search of affordable living space. As such, people are attracted to living in *kibbutzim*, collective communities traditionally based on agriculture and that offer good facilities and services for members, such as swimming pools, communal spaces, education for children, and a strong connection to the landscape. This proposed project is about tackling the uncontrolled sprawl by realizing the qualities of a *kibbutz* in the center of Tel Aviv.

The urban *kibbutz* is situated in a buffer zone between the White City (a UNESCO World Heritage Site) and the main highways and high-rises of Tel Aviv. The buffer zone is intended to protect the World Heritage site. It creates a transition with the high-rises and completes missing infrastructure such as playgrounds, swimming pools, offices, and parking. The implementation of this urban *kibbutz* is at a strategic point where in the near future a stop of the new metro line will be a short walking distance away. The building is situated in a home-block, a basic urban unit planned by Patrick Geddes. According to his ideology, the block offers a green area with communal services as a social venue for the neighborhood's residents.

This *kibbutz* is developed according to the ideas of Ron Waldniger, a member of an urban *kibbutz* near Tel Aviv. His community is living in several apartments in different communes. They are currently looking for a unique building that would enhance their communal life experience. The program of the urban *kibbutz* reflects their need to accommodate 60 members. According to the specialization of the community in the education field, the ground floor is dedicated to the kindergarten. It contains six classrooms, a sleeping room, a multi-use room, and a teacher's room. An auditorium will allow members to discuss the future of the *kibbutz*, and hold seminars. A public restaurant and a cafeteria are also shared at the entrance. The heart of the *kibbutz* is an atrium with a ceremonial stair, creating informal spaces where people can meet.

The four upper floors are dedicated to housing and communal spaces. Offices for start-ups are placed along the atrium and provide the *kibbutz* with an additional income source. The architectural expression is defined by an exterior circulation and surrounding balconies, sometimes enlarged to create convivial outside spaces. Planting is used as a buffer to the private sphere.

The apartments are developed according to minimal dwelling standards. The living room with the kitchen is common to each group or family, and additional space is redistributed in shared spaces such as library, playroom, music room, TV room, computer rooms, and workspaces. These rooms can become an extension of the living rooms by using movable walls, allowing residents to make private spaces part of the heart of the *kibbutz*. The rooftop terrace with a swimming pool and a vegetable garden allows members to celebrate events and grow their own vegetables. Like the other communal spaces, the swimming pool and the vegetable garden play a role in the education of the children. Altogether, trees, plants, and the garden create a luxurious landscape.

The structure of the *kibbutz* allows for a flexible plan. All the elements are standardized and prefabricated to a module of 1.6 meter. Four main concrete cores sustain the whole building. Industrial elements allow for a quick construction of the *kibbutz* and a reduction in cost. The building has a passive energy strategy. Taking advantage of its implementation and the breeze coming from the sea, the atrium is used as a wind catcher to cool down the building. The use of recyclable materials leads to a low carbon footprint. The vegetable garden has a multiple role in the insulation, thermal inertia, and rainwater management of the building. Combined with integrated photovoltaics and solar thermal panels, the building is compatible with the green label, the highest green certification standard in Israel.

— *Alois Rosenfeld*

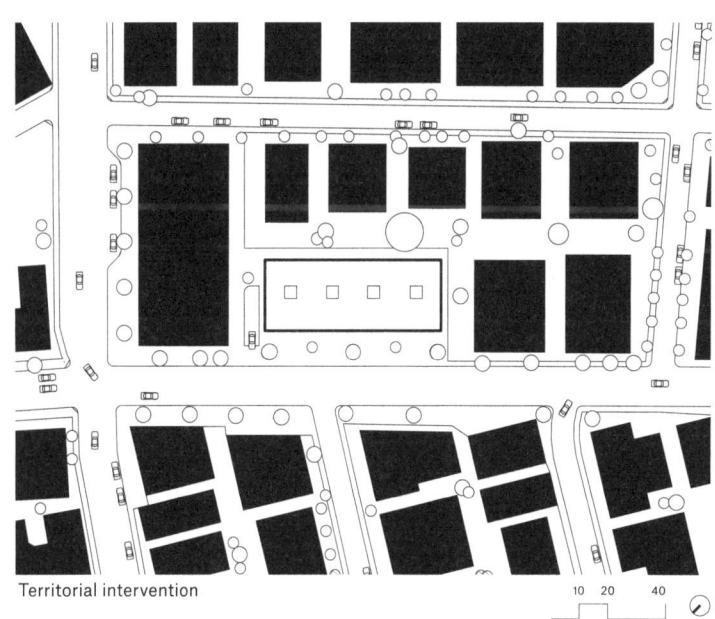

Territorial intervention

10  20  40

190

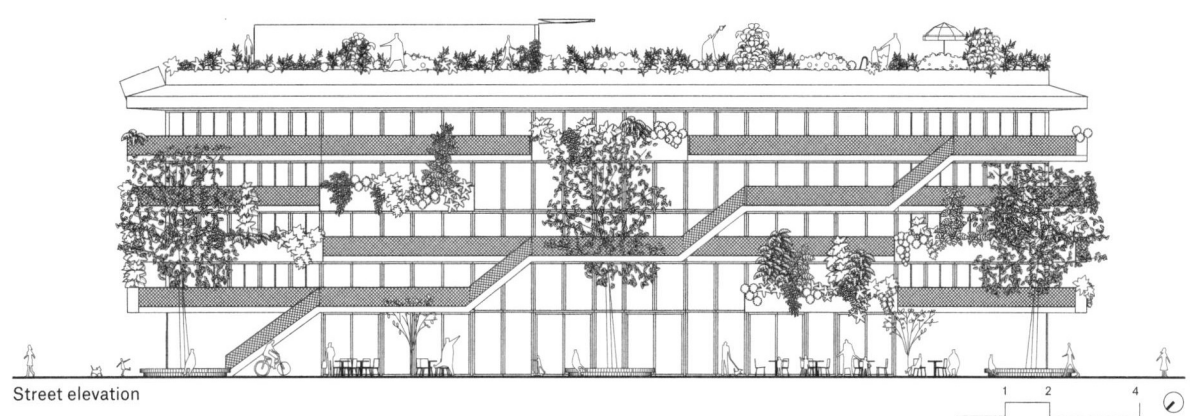
Street elevation

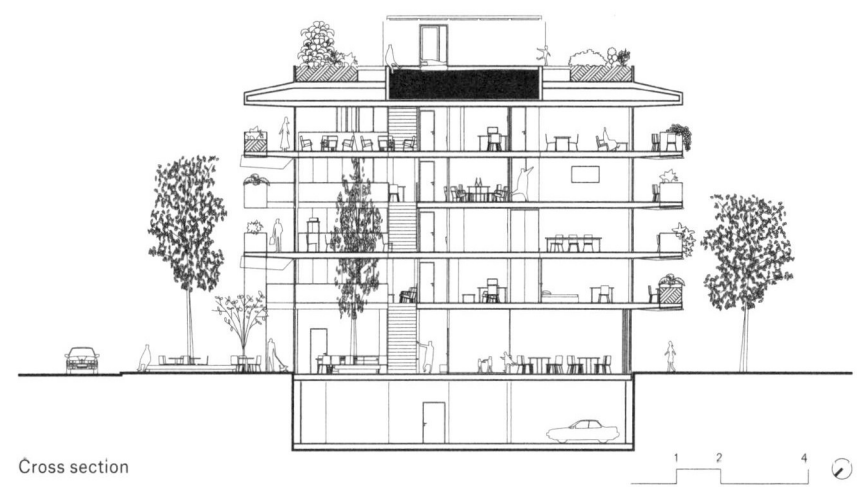
Cross section

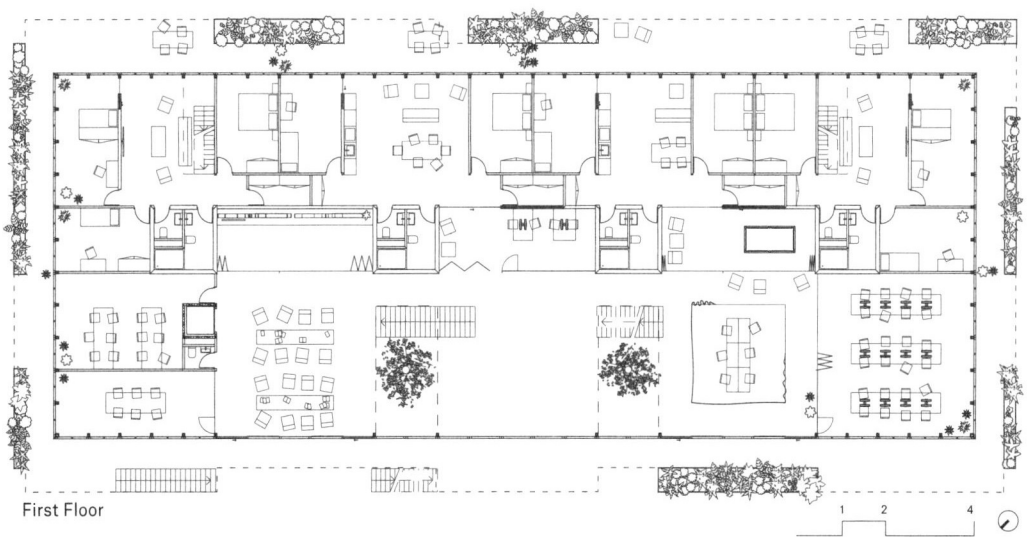
First Floor

Architecture: Coastal Plain 191

# Notes and References

## Teaching and Research in Architecture

1. XIV Entretien, in E.-E. Viollet-le-Duc, *Entretiens sur l'architecture*, Paris, vol. 2, 1872: 173.
2. William Morris, *Hopes And Fears For Art* (Worcestershire: Read Books) 2012 [1882].

## Arcadian Dreams and Agricultural Myths

1. Tiiu Speek, "Environment in Literature: Lawrence Buell's Ecocritical Perspective," in *Place and Location I*, edited by Kaia Lehari and Virve Sarapik (Tallinn: Estonian Academy of Arts, 2000): 160–171.
2. Genesis 2:7.
3. Genesis 3:19.
4. Genesis 2:8.
5. John B. Jackson, "Nearer than Eden," in *The Necessity for Ruins, and Other Topics* (Amherst: University of Massachusetts Press, 1980): 19–35.
6. Jean-Jacques Rousseau and Maurice Cranston, *A Discourse on Inequality* (Harmondsworth and New York: Penguin Classics, 1985): 109.
7. Bárbara M. Costa, "Eugenic Garden City: the Urbanism of Controlled Evolution," in *Kritische Berichte*, vol. 2 (2017): 18–27.
8. In Roman Law, *occupatio* was an original method of acquiring ownership of unowned property (*res nullius*) by occupying with intent to own. Any previously unowned thing becomes the just property of the first occupant able to "capture" it.
9. Hanna Scolnicov, "Meeting One's Death in Arcadia," in *Phenomenology of Life: Meeting the Challenges of the Present-Day World*, edited by Anna-Terese Tyrnieancka (Norwell, MA: Springer, 2005): 254.
10. Lynn White Jr., "The Historical Roots of Our Ecological Crisis," in *Ecocriticism: the essential reader*, edited by Ken Hiltner (London and New York: Routledge, 2015 [1966]): 39–46.
11. White Jr., "Historical Roots": 45.
12. "Humans represent roughly 32 percent of vertebrate biomass. The other 65 percent is creatures we keep to eat. Vertebrate wildlife counts for less than 3 percent." In: Timothy Morton, *Dark Ecology* (New York: Columbia University Press, 2016): 44.
13. Hillary Mayell, "Human 'Footprint' Seen on 83 Percent of Earth's Land," in *National Geographic News*, October 25, 2002, http://news.nationalgeographic.com/news/2002/10/1025_021025_HumanFootprint.html.
14. Will Steffen, Paul J. Crutzen, and John R. McNeill, "The Anthropocene: Are Humans Now Overwhelming the Great Forces of Nature?" in *Ambio*, vol. 36, no. 8 (December 2007): 614–621.
15. Anna Tsing, "A Feminist Approach to the Anthropocene: Earth Stalked by Man," lecture, Barnard College, New York, NY, November 10, 2015.
16. Shlomo Sand, *The Invention of the Land of Israel* (London and New York: Verso, 2012): 67–69.
17. Genesis 15:18.
18. Deuteronomy 8:8.
19. Leviticus 20:24; Exodus 3:8; Deuteronomy 27:3.
20. Timothy J. Mitchell, "Israel, Palestine and the American Wilderness," in *Landscape and Power*, edited by Timothy J. Mitchell (Chicago and London: The University of Chicago Press, 1994): 277.
21. "A land without a people for a people without a land" is a widely cited phrase associated with the movement to establish a Jewish homeland in Palestine during the nineteenth and twentieth centuries. Its origins are traced back to mid-eighteenth century Christian Zionism.
22. Unnamed Zionist leader speaking to kibbutzniks at Ein Harod. Quoted in Ari Shavit, *My Promised Land: The Triumph and Tragedy of Israel* (New York: Spiegel & Grau, 2015): 44.
23. Simon Schama, *Landscape and Memory* (London: Harper Collins, 1995): 5–6.
24. Shlomo Sand, *The Invention of the Jewish People* (London, New York: Verso, 2009): 28.
25. Hannah Arendt, *The Origins of Totalitarianism* (New York: Harcourt Books, 1994 [1966]): 292.
26. Sand, *Land of Israel*: 256–257.
27. Mitchell, "Israel, Palestine and the American Wilderness": 262.
28. Naftali Bennett, "Israeli Minister: The Bible Says West Bank is Ours," interview with Mehdi Hasan, *Up Front*, Al Jazeera, February 24, 2017, audio, 16:34. "If you want to say that our land does not belong to us, I suggest you go change the Bible first. ... That land is ours and no one can occupy his own home."
29. Raphael Ahren, "Jewish Home Minister says PM's peace overtures will go nowhere," in *The Times of Israel*, June 8, 2016, http://www.timesofisrael.com/israeli-minister-remove-palestinians-from-west-bank-area-c-annex-territory/.
30. The Green Line is also known as the pre-1967 border, or 1949 Armistice border. It is the line set drawn in the 1949 Armistice Agreements between Israel and its neighbors Egypt, Jordan, Lebanon, and Syria after the 1948 Arab-Israeli War. It was the official border of Israel from 1949 until the Six Day War in 1967.
31. Amira Hass, "Conforming to Israel's Malignant Occupation" in *Haaretz*, Jan 1, 2017, https://www.haaretz.com/opinion/.premium-1.762478.
32. Emmanuel Levinas, "Heidegger, Gagarin and Us," in *Difficult Freedom: Essays on Judaism* (Baltimore: Johns Hopkins University Press, 1990 [1961]): 231–4.
33. Sarah Jaquette Ray, *The Ecological Other: Environmental Exclusion in American Culture* (Tucson: University of Arizona Press, 2013): 23.
34. Costa, "Eugenic Garden City:" 26.
35. See U.N. Resolution 242 and the Fourth Geneva Convention.
36. It should be noted that no Israeli state funding was used for this studio or publication.

[Fig. 1] Athanasius Kircher, *Arca Noë*, Amsterdam: J. J. Waesberge, 1675: bet. pp. 196/197.
[Fig. 2] Wikimedia.
[Fig. 3] *Ost und West*, Berlin, Jan 1902: 17–18.
[Fig. 4] Wikimedia; Shamir Archive via the PikiWiki—Israel free image collection project.
[Fig. 5] Wikimedia; from Uri Dan, *To the Promised Land*, New York: Doubleday, 1988, via the PikiWiki—Israel free image collection project.
[Fig. 6] Flickr Creative Commons, Copyright Attribution 2.0 Generic (CC BY 2.0).
[Fig. 7] Wikimedia.
[Fig. 8] United Nations Office for the Coordination of Humanitarian Affairs—Occupied Palestinian Territory (UN OCHA OPT).

## Territory: Agriculture as Settlement

- Reichman, S., *From Foothold to Settled Territory. The Jewish Settlement, 1918–1948. A Geographical Interpretation and Documentation*. Jerusalem: Yad Izhak Ben-Zvi Publications, with the assistance of the Ministry of Education and Culture (1979).
- Ruppin, A., *Agricultural Settlement in Israel of the Zionist Organization (1908-1924)*, Dvir Publishing (1925).
- Sharon, A., *Physical Planning in Israel*, Government Press (1951).
- Golan, A. et al., *Settlements Geography of Israel: Spatial Experiments*, Units 7-8, Tel Aviv: Open University (1997).
- *Agricultural and Rural Planning Policy Document in Israel*: Ministry of Agriculture and Rural Development (2015).
- Eliav, M., *Eretz Israel and its Yishuv in the 19th Century, 1777-1917*, Jerusalem: Keter Publishing House (1978).
- Groner E., Orenstein D. et al., *The Effects of Solitary Farms on Surrounding Biodiversity*, Ecology and Environment, 2012, vol. 4 (December 2012): 320–329.

1. Photo: Matanya Sack, 2010.
2. Sack and Reicher.
3. Photo: Kibbutz Shoval archive.
4. Photo: Uri Reicher, 2006.
5. Design: Gabriel and Maxim Shamir. Courtesy of Shamir Brothers Collection
6. The Ministry of Agriculture and Rural Development of Israel.
7. ibid.

[Fig. 1] Sack and Reicher.
[Fig. 2] Sack and Reicher, source: Reichman, S.
[Fig. 3] Sack and Reicher.
[Fig. 4] ibid.

## Territory: A Land of Scarcity

1. Latest Population Statistics for Israel. Press Release. Israel Central Bureau of Statistics. 31 December 2015. Accessed 2 January 2016.
2. "Population, by Religion." *Statistical Abstract of Israel*. Israel Central Bureau of Statistics. 11 September 2012 accessed 5 April 2013.

[Fig. 1] "Population Growth, Israel." World Population Review, accessed September 12, 2017, form http://worldpopulationreview.com/countries/israel-population/.
[Fig. 2] OECD (2017), Fertility rates (indicator). doi: 10.1787/8272fb01-en (Accessed on 12 September 2017).
[Fig. 3] HaMaarag—Israel's national Nature Assessment Program Ministry of Agriculture and Rural Development.
[Fig. 4] Yoav Gal, Efrad Hada, "Land allocation: Agriculture vs. urban development in Israel" Land Use Policy, Article, 2011. https://www.researchgate.net/publication/257098661_Land_allocation_Agriculture_vs_urban_development_in_Israel
[Fig. 5] KKL—Jewish National Fund.
[Fig. 6] GIS Online.
[Fig. 7] Annual rainfall: GIS Online; Rainwater status: Agvriel Weinberger, The Natural water resources between the Mediterranean Sean and the Jordan river, Jerusalem, 2012.
[Fig. 8] Environmental map of Israel, circa 1975 (Central Intelligence Agency).
[Fig. 9] Drylands, UNEP World Conservation Monitoring Centre.
[Fig. 10] GIS Online.

## Territory: The Jordan Rift Valley

1. Comair, G. F., D. C. McKinney, and D. Siegel. 2012. "Hydrology of the Jordan River Basin: Watershed Delineation, Precipitation and Evapotranspiration." Springer Science+Business Media.
2. "Red Sea-Dead Sea Project." 2014. *Fanack Water*, September 24. https://water.fanack.com/specials/red-sea-dead-sea-project/.
3. https://www.flickr.com/photos/georgedement/24207670413/.

[Fig. 1] Reuven Belmaker et al., "Be dating of Neogene halite," Science direct: 420.
[Fig. 2] "Origins of the Dead Sea, Part IV: Lake Lisan – The Jordan Valley Under Water," Naturalis Historia, September 17, 2014.
[Fig. 3] Jreisat, Kamal, and Tawfiq Yazjeen. 2014. "A Seismic Junction." In Atlas of Jordan: History, Territories and Society, edited by Myriam Ababsa: 47-59. Contemporain Publications. Beyrouth: Presses de l'Ifpo. http://books.openedition.org/ifpo/4861.
[Fig. 4] Burdon, 1959. Conception: F. Aldersons Design: F. and E. Aldersons, Ifpo, 2010.
[Fig. 5] GIS Online.
[Fig. 6] "Red Sea-Dead Sea Project." 2014. Fanack Water, September 24, 2014.
[Fig. 7] Al-Mooji, Yusuf, Eileen Hofstetter, and Andreas Renck. 2013. "Chapter 6, Jordan River Basin, Inventory of Shared Water Resources in Western Asia." https://waterinventory.org/surface_water/jordan-river-basin.
[Fig. 8] Land Use Israel: Survey of Israel; Land Use West Bank: Palestinian Hydrology Group. 2016. "West Bank Land-Use, Hydrology," 2010; Land Use Jordan: Ababsa, Myriam. 2014. "Jordan's Land Cover. A Land of Contrasts." In *Atlas of Jordan : History, Territories and Society*: 40–41. Contemporain Publications. Beyrouth: Presses de l'Ifpo.
[Fig. 9] Hotel locations on the Dead Sea, n/a.
[Fig. 10] Hayat, Tilda, Omri Romano, and Lena Ostrovsky. 2013. "Tourism in Israel 2000-2012." http://www.cbs.gov.il/statistical/touris2013e.pdf.
[Fig. 11] ibid.
[Fig. 12] ibid.
[Fig. 13] IWWI + ESCWA.
[Fig. 14] ibid.
[Fig. 15] Al-Mooji, Yusuf, Eileen Hofstetter, and Andreas Renck. 2013. "Chapter 6, Jordan River Basin, Inventory of Shared Water Resources in Western Asia." https://waterinventory.org/surface_water/jordan-river-basin.
[Fig. 16] ibid.
[Fig. 17] Dead Sea Research Center, Tel Aviv University, *Bathymetric Chart of the Dead Sea*, dnd.

*[Fig. 18]* Yechieli, Yoseph, Meir Abelson, Amos Bein, Onn Crouvi, and Vladimir Shtivelman. 2017. "Sinkhole 'swarms' along the Dead Sea Coast: Reflection of Disturbance of Lake and Adjacent Groundwater Systems," *GSA Bulletin*, Vol. 129: 3–4, March.
*[Fig. 19]* laba, contour line based on a withdraw of 1 meter per year.
*[Fig. 20]* 2016: François Molle et al. "Irrigation in the Jordan Valley: Are water pricing policies overly optimistic?," Agriculture Water Management, (2008): 427–438. 2050: laba projection.
*[Fig. 21]* ibid.
*[Fig. 22]* ibid.
*[Fig. 23]* GIS Online.
*[Fig. 24]* laba, student constitution.
*[Fig. 25]* U.S. Central Intelligence Agency. "West Bank Land-Use," n.d. https://www.lib.utexas.edu/maps/gazastrip.html.
*[Fig. 26]* Existing sites: GIS Online; vision: laba projection.

## Territory: The Negev Desert

1. Isaac A Meir, "Climatic sub-regions and design contextualism," *Building and Environment*, Vol. 24, (1989): 247.
2. Glassner, Martin, "The Bedouin of Southern Sinai under Israeli Administration." Geographical Review, (1974): 64.
3. Frantzman, Seth J., and Ruth Kark, "Bedouin Settlement in Late Ottoman and British Mandatory Palestine: Influence on the Cultural and Environmental Landscape, 1870–1948, *New Middle Eastern Studies*, 1 (2011).
4. Elizabeth Nassar, "The Naqab (Negev) Under the Microscope: Roots, Reality, Destiny," Badil Ressource Center, (2006).
5. ShlomoSwirski and Yael Hasson, *Invisible Citizens: Israel Government Policy Toward The Negev Bedouin*; (Ben-Gurion University of the Negev: Center for Bedouin Studies & Development, 2006): 11–13.
6. "A Bedouin welcome—Israel Travel, Ynetnews". Ynetnews.com. 1995-06-20. Accessed 2011-10-09. https://www.ynetnews.com/articles/0,7340,L-3420595,00.html.
7. Le P. Antonin Jaussen, Coutumes des Arabes au pays de Moab (Paris: Librairie Victor Lecoffre, 1908): 479.
8. Photo: Ilan Molcho.
9. David Ben-Gurion "Importance of the Negev" (in Hebrew), (17 January 1955). Archived from the original on 23 February 2007.
10. "The Renewed State of Israel" (October 6, 1963), accessed from "Inspired by Ben Gurion," Haluza Sustainable city in the desert, 2017.
11. "About | Arava." Central & Northern Arava-Tamar R&D, Accessed February 21, 2017.
12. Antonio Marquina, *Environmental Challenges in the Mediterranean 2000–2050*, Vol. 37 (Earth and Environmental sciences): 132.
13. "The Test of Creativity and Israel's Capacity for Science and Research," accessed from "Inspired by Ben Gurion," Haluza Sustainable city in the desert, 2017.
14. "Statistical Abstract of Israel," 2001
15. Portnov B.A., Safriel U.N. (2004) Prospective Desertification Trends in the Negev—Implications for Urban and Regional Development. In: Marquina A. (eds) Environmental Challenges in the Mediterranean 2000–2050. NATO Science Series (Series IV: Earth and Environmental Sciences), vol 37. Springer, Dordrecht.
16. Raphael Semiat, Emily Frangenberg, "Israel's Chemicals Industry: From the Desert to the Dead Sea," CEP Magazine, 2015.
17. M. Ragheb, "Uranium ressources in Phosphate rocks," 2017.
18. "Informations on Industrial Sites," Israel Ministry of Economy and Industry.
19. Image source: Israel Ministry of Economy and Industry, Informations on Industrial Sites, *Noam Industrial Park*.
20. ibid.
21. "Company Sites: Dudaim," Negev Ecology, 2017.
22. Tal, Alon, *Pollution in a Promised Land: An Environmental History of Israel*. (University of California Press, 2002).
23. Images source: "Company Sites: Dudaim," Negev Ecology, 2017.
24. Naqab Desert Socio-Environmental Timeline Bustan, 2006 Archived April 21, 2008, at the Wayback Machine.
25. Avil Perevolotsky, "Conservation, reclamation and grazing in the northern Negev: Contradictory or complementary concepts," Pastoral development Network, Series 38: 1–6.
26. Alon Tal, *Pollution in a Promised Land: An Environmental History of Israel* (University of California Press, 2002): 77.
27. Léopold Lambert, "Palestine, Make the desert bloom, Manufacturing the Israeli territory/narrative," The Funambulist, Paris, April 7, 2015.
28. Pollution in a Promised Land: An Environmental History of Israel By Alon Tal: 79.
29. Shoshana Gabbay, "Israel Environment & Nature: Nature Conservation," Jewish Virtual Library.
30. Eyal Weizman, Fazal Sheikh, *The Conflict Shoreline: Colonization as Climate Change in the Negev* (Steidl, 2015).
31. "National Parks Overview," Jewish Virtual Library, 2008.
32. ibid.
33. "Without boundaries: Palestinian Bedouin under attack by Israel," Palestinian Grassroots Anti-Apartheid Wall campaign, January 25, 2017.
34. Alistair Lyon, "Israel to build desert mega-bases, freeing up land in Tel Aviv," Reuters, March 18, 2013.
35. A. Pe'er, Hamodia, "Cabinet Approves Transfer Of IDF Bases to Negev," Hamodia, January 4 2015. http://hamodia.com/2015/01/04/cabinet-approves-transfer-idf-bases-negev/.
36. Tierney Smith, "UNCCD : World Leaders must set ambitious desertification goals at Rio+20," Climate Home, April 23, 2012.
37. Image source: David Shankbone, *Liman irrigation system*, 2009.
38. Courtesy of Wadi Attir, image by Michael Ben Eli.
*[Fig. 1]* "Drylands," Millennium Ecosystem Assessment.
*[Fig. 2]* GIS Online.
*[Fig. 3]* GIS Online.
*[Fig. 4]* Isaac A. Meir, "Climatic Sub-Regions and Design Contextualism, Vol. 24 (1989): 245–251.
*[Fig. 5]* GIS Online and "List of localities, in Alphabetical order" (PDF). Israel Central Bureau of Statistics. Accessed 16 October 2016, http://www.cbs.gov.il/ishuvim/reshimalefishem.pdf.
*[Fig. 6]* laba.
*[Fig. 7]* laba.
*[Fig. 8]* GIS Online.
*[Fig. 9]* KKL—Jewish National Fund.
*[Fig. 10]* GIS Online.
*[Fig. 11]* GIS Online.
*[Fig. 12]* GIS Online.
*[Fig. 13]* ICBS (1998) Agricultural Survey. Israel Central Bureau of Statistics, Jerusalem.
*[Fig. 14]* NASA/Goddard Space Flight Center, Whole world—Land and Oceans, 2010.
*[Fig. 15]* Lieutenant Commander Scott Bennie, "The Perils of Energy Independence," Proceedings Magazine, 2015 retrieve from https://www.usni.org/magazines/proceedings/2015-10/perils-energy-independence
*[Fig. 16]* Israel Export Institute.
*[Fig. 17]* GIS Online.
*[Fig. 18]* GIS Online, Central Bureau of Statistics + NOP 35—Integrated National Outline Plan of Construction, Development and Preservation; Administration of Planning; Ministry of Finance.
*[Fig. 19]* National Fire and Rescue Authority.
*[Fig. 20]* GIS Online + National Fire and Rescue Authority.
*[Fig. 21]* GIS Online.
*[Fig. 22]* GIS Online.
*[Fig. 23]* GIS Online.
*[Fig. 24]* Yossi Leshem & Yoram Yom-Tov, Routes of migrating soaring birds: 50.

## Territory: The Coastal Plain

1. Evans, Matt. 2011. "Population Dispersal Policy and the 1990s Immigration Wave." *Israel Studies*, Indiana University Press, Vol. 16, No. 1, Spring: 104–28.
2. Sharon, Arieh. "The Sharon Plan." Arieh Sharon Archive. Accessed April 11, 2017, http://www.ariehsharon.org/Archive/Physical-Planning-in-Israel/Outline-of-National-Plan/i-BzJgqX7.
3. As defined by the CBS, Central Bureau of statistics, in "Localities, population and density per sq. km., by metropolitan area and selected localities," In accordance with the boundaries of metropolitan areas as they were updated 2013.
4. 45.6 percent, based on CBS, 2015.
5. Razin, Eran, and Igal Charney. 2015. "Metropolitan Dynamics in Israel: An Emerging 'metropolitan Island State'?" *Urban Geography* 36, no. 8, November 17: 1131–48. doi:10.1080/02723638.2015.1096117.
6. "2016 Cost of Living Ranking." 2016. *Cost of Living Ranking*, n.d. https://www.imercer.com/content/mobility/cost-of-living-city-rankings.html#.
7. Heinelt, Hubert and Razin, Eran. 2011. *Metropolitan Governance: Different Paths in Contrasting Contexts: Germany and Israel*. Frankfurt am Main. Campus Verlag.
8. Alka Levi-Basson, *exemplary development town Migdal HaEmek*, 1999.
9. December 2016.
10. The World Bank, OBRD IDA. "Population, Total (2015)," n/d. http://data.worldbank.org/indicator/SP.POP.TOTL?locations=IL.
11. United Nations, Department of Economic and Social Affairs, Population Division. 2015. "World Population Prospects; The 2015 Revision, Key Findings and Advance Tables." https://esa.un.org/unpd/wpp/publications/files/key_findings_wpp_2015.pdf.
12. NOP 35, n/a, 2005.
13. http://www.un.org/esa/agenda21/natlinfo/countr/israel/land.pdf.
14. NOP 35, 2005.
15. laba: student constitution.
16. Calculations by laba students, based on official statistics, Central Bureau of Statistics, Israel.
*[Fig. 1]* JamesDay at English Wikipedia, transferred from en.wikipedia to Commons using CommonsHelper. https://commons.wikimedia.org/wiki/File:Map_of_Jewish_settlements_in_Palestine_in_1947.png.
*[Fig. 2]* The Sharon Plan: First National Master Plan, n/a.
*[Fig. 3]* GIS Online.
*[Fig. 4]* GIS Online.
*[Fig. 5]* Percentage of population by size of settlement, n/a.
*[Fig. 6]* Deconcentration in a context of population growth and ideological change: The Tel-Aviv and Beer-Sheva metropolitan areas, *Metropolitan Areas in Israel*, 2003.
*[Fig. 7]* Noam Gruber, Taub Center for Social Policy Studies in Israel.
*[Fig. 8]* ibid.
*[Fig. 9]* Central Bureau of Statistics.
*[Fig. 10]* Taub Center. "Taub Center for Social Policy Studies in Israel." Accessed June 19, 2017, http://taubcenter.org.il/mission-vision-2/.
*[Fig. 11]* Noam Gruber, Taub Center for Social Policy Studies in Israel, Data: Bank of Israel (2012).
*[Fig. 12]* Population growth development and projection of four major Israeli cities, n/a.
*[Fig. 13]* GIS Online.
*[Fig. 14]* ibid.
*[Fig. 15]* Moti Kaplan, National Outline Plan for Forests and Afforestation NOP22 Policy Document, 2011, http://www.kkl.org.il/files/forests/tma/TAMA22_eng.pdf.
*[Fig. 16]* GIS Online.
*[Fig. 17]* laba projection.
*[Fig. 18]* ibid.
*[Fig. 19]* ibid.
*[Fig. 20]* ibid.
*[Fig. 21]* ibid.
*[Fig. 22]* GIS Online.

## Participants

Studio Director
Harry Gugger

laba Team
Augustin Clément
Bárbara Maçães Costa
Juliette Fong
Salomé Gutscher
Stefan Hörner
Karolina Slawecka
Charlotte Truwant

laba Students
Stéphanie Amstutz
Xavier Barreca
Arnaud Baudouin
Marlon Biétry
Victoria Bodevin
Félix Chase
Marie-Pauline Cryonnet
Tania Depallens
Martin Handley
Jonas Inhelder
Yann Junod
Juliette Lucarain
Maïlys Marty
Quentin Menu
Florian Papp
Alessandra Patarot
Laure Péquignot
Anton Rosenberg
Alois Rosenfeld
Nicola Schürch
Laura Stoll
Sophie Würzer

## Acknowledgments

We would like to thank the lecturers mentioned below, as well as the reviewers Marc Angelil, Christoph Girot, Martin Fröhlich, Götz Menzel, Alexandre Theriot, Christine Binswanger, Laurent Stalder, Jean Paul Jaccaud and Deborah Saunt for their collaboration throughout the laba studio 2016/17 "Industrial Arcadia: Israel."

The workshop "Territorial Agriculture" in Haifa was organized in collaboration with LandBasics, Faculty of Architecture and Town Planning of the Technion. We cordially thank Matanya Sack and her students for their invaluable help in organizing the symposium. We also extend our gratitude to the symposium lecturers.

We would like to express our sincere thanks to all organizations, experts, and friends who have supported us, specifically to the State Secretariat for Education, Research and Innovation, and the School of Architecture and Environmental Engineering ENAC EPFL, which provided substantial funding for this publication.

Lectures at the Symposium "Landbasics, Territorial Agriculture," December 2016, Haifa, Technion
— Iris Aravot, Technion
— Matanya Sack, Technion
— Harry Gugger, EPFL
— Ruti Frum Aricha, Ministry of Agriculture and Rural Development
— Moti Kaplan, Kaplan Planners
— Ran Haklai, The Hebrew University of Jerusalem
— Maayan Kitron, Arava R&D
— Nurit Lissovsky, Technion
— Naomi Angel, Technion

Lectures at laba
— Prof. Christian Bréthaut, University of Geneva
— Ben Gitai, Gitai Architects
— Prof. Ita Heinze-Greenberg, ETHZ
— Harry Gugger, EPFL
— Pierre Loeb, New Israel Fund
— Anna Minta, Katholische Privatuniversität Linz
— Matanya Sack, Technion
— Charlotte Truwant, EPFL

Student Assistants
Yann Junod
Sophie Würzer

## Imprint

Editors
Harry Gugger
Bárbara Maçães Costa
Salomé Gutscher
Stefan Hörner
Charlotte Truwant

Copy Editor
Siân Gibby

Editorial Concept and Graphic Design
© Helen Ebert, Zurich
www.helen-ebert.eu

Typefaces
Atlas Grotesk, Berthold Baskerville

Project Photography
© Eik Frenzel
www.dreierfrenzel.com

Field Photography
© laba staff and students

Lithography, Printing and Binding
DZA Druckerei zu Altenburg GmbH, Germany

Every reasonable attempt has been made by the authors, editors, and publishers to identify owners of copyrights. Errors or omissions will be corrected in subsequent editions.

This work is subject to copyright. All rights are reserved, whether the whole or part of the material is concerned, specifically the rights of translation, reprinting, re-use of illustrations, recitation, broadcasting, reproduction on microfilms or in any other ways, and storage in databases. For any kind of use, permission of the copyright owner must be obtained.

© 2017 Laboratoire Bâle (laba)
Institut d'Architecture Faculté ENAC
École Polytechnique Fédérale de Lausanne
and Park Books, Zurich

EPFL ENAC IA laba
Ackermannshof
St. Johanns-Vorstadt 19–21
4056 Basel
http://laba.epfl.ch

Park Books
Niederdorfstrasse 54
8001 Zurich
Switzerland
www.park-books.com

Park Books is being supported by the Swiss Federal Office of Culture with a general subsidy for the years 2016–2020.

ISBN 978-3-03860-087-9

PARK BOOKS